The Music Export Business

The Music Export Business examines the workings of the fast-changing world of music industry exports. The music industry is in a state of flux, resulting from changes in technology, markets, government policies and most recently the COVID-19 pandemic.

In analysing the ability of organisations to access international markets from inception, this book assesses global trends in music industry business models, including streaming and national export policies. The book deploys author interviews with industry insiders including musicians, managers, record labels and government stakeholders, using case studies to highlight cultural and economic value creation in a global value chain.

Providing research-based insights into "export readiness" in the global music industry, this book reassesses the "born global" phenomenon, providing a unique and valuable resource for scholars and reflective practitioners interested in the evolving relationship between music industries, national economies, government policies and cultural identity.

Stephen Chen is Professor of International Management at Newcastle University, UK. Previously he held academic positions in the UK (at Manchester Business School and City University), USA (at UCLA) and Australia (at the Australian National University, Macquarie University and the University of Newcastle).

Associate Professor **Shane Homan** teaches media and cultural studies at Monash University, Melbourne.

Tracy Redhead is a composer, researcher, producer and lecturer of Electronic Music and Sound Design at the University of Western Australia.

Richard Vella is a composer and academic. From 2007 to 2019, Vella was Professorial Chair of Music at the University of Newcastle Conservatorium of Music.

Routledge Research in the Creative and Cultural Industries
Series Editor: Ruth Rentschler

This series brings together book-length original research in cultural and creative industries from a range of perspectives. Charting developments in contemporary cultural and creative industries thinking around the world, the series aims to shape the research agenda to reflect the expanding significance of the creative sector in a globalised world.

Racial and Ethnic Diversity in the Performing Arts Workforce
Tobie S. Stein

Understanding Audience Engagement in the Contemporary Arts
Stephanie E. Pitts and Sarah M. Price

Access, Diversity, Equity and Inclusion in Cultural Organizations
Insights from the Careers of Executive Opera Managers of Color in the US
Antonio C. Cuyler

Digital Transformation in the Cultural and Creative Industries
Production, Consumption and Entrepreneurship in the Digital and Sharing Economy
Edited by Marta Massi, Marilena Vecco and Yi Lin

Researching Arts Markets
Past, Present and Tools for the Future
Edited by Elisabetta Lazzaro, Nathalie Moureau and Adriana Turpin

Strategic Cultural Centre Management
Tomas Järvinen

The Music Export Business
Born Global
Stephen Chen, Shane Homan, Tracy Redhead and Richard Vella

For more information about this series, please visit: https://www.routledge.com/Routledge-Research-in-the-Creative-and-Cultural-Industries/book-series/RRCCI

The Music Export Business

Born Global

Stephen Chen, Shane Homan, Tracy Redhead and Richard Vella

Routledge
Taylor & Francis Group
LONDON AND NEW YORK

First published 2021
by Routledge
2 Park Square, Milton Park, Abingdon, Oxon OX14 4RN

and by Routledge
52 Vanderbilt Avenue, New York, NY 10017

Routledge is an imprint of the Taylor & Francis Group, an informa business

British Library Cataloguing-in-Publication Data
A catalogue record for this book is available from the British Library

Library of Congress Cataloging-in-Publication Data
A catalog record has been requested for this book

ISBN: 978-0-367-42705-4 (hbk)
ISBN: 978-0-367-74463-2 (pbk)
ISBN: 978-1-003-00280-2 (ebk)

Typeset in Times New Roman
by Deanta Global Publishing Services, Chennai, India

Contents

Figures

Foreword

At the time of writing, the pilot edition of Global Music Match was launched, a project born entirely as a consequence of the impacts of COVID-19 on the music industry across the world. Ninety-six artists from 14 countries came together in a world first, to introduce each other to their respective fan bases via the use of social media. Whilst the project gave participating artists a much-needed platform to connect and collaborate internationally, and simultaneously develop new skills to navigate the digital environment, it's entirely due to the concept and existence of the music export sector that such an ambitious programme could have ever been created during these times.

As countries closed their borders and the live music industry ground to a halt overnight, the need for export schemes to work together was never more apparent. For many years, while our key goals and objectives were for our own artists and professionals to garner international success, we have long acknowledged that there was a lot more to be gained when we put aside those competitive agendas and worked together. Over the last decade, music industry bodies have united to provide market education and export networking opportunities for music professionals around the world at international showcase events, such as SXSW, The Great Escape, AMERICANAFEST and Folk Alliance International, under the banner of Country Connections. We understood that whilst attendance at these international music market events was a significant driver in securing career-defining opportunities for the showcasing artists, it was also the direct relationships being facilitated by the combined efforts of the export bodies that were making a tangible difference.

The role of a national export initiative is one that, until now, has been significantly under-researched, which highlights the importance and timeliness of *The Music Export Business*. Multiple chapters establish the fact that all music export initiatives exist at the coalface of their country's music export strategies, even if their structure, governance, funding and resources are different. They play a substantial role in the health, prosperity and global success of their respective nations' economic and cultural standing. Published in May 2017, Sound Diplomacy's Global Music Export Pledge introduced the benefits of music export to governments around the world. It identified that there is no formal definition of what an export office is. Many forms and variants exist, but the core values are the same.

They represent nations, regions, artist collectives, cities and trade associations and have created an ecosystem based around showcase festivals that foster trade, artistic development and business.

The Music Export Business builds significantly on this notion. It intrinsically outlines how a nation can build its capacity for export and economic return, with a focus on music technology, artist development, entrepreneurship, export readiness and music policy. Having worked with the four co-authors previously on the Australian Research Council (ARC) Linkage project, The Economic and Cultural Value of Australian Music Exports, it is apparent that the unique set of academic specialty, professional and personal perspectives they each bring to the analysis has combined effortlessly to provide a comprehensive and important investigation of contemporary export activity and a framework for the continued growth of this vital sector. This is especially true amidst the evolving digital landscape, which in a post-COVID world will be more important than ever for the export of music.

Millie Millgate, Executive Producer,
Sounds Australia

Acknowledgements

The authors thank all managers and artists interviewed and industry participants who responded to the surveys; AMPAL and ARIA for providing information on the Australian music publishing and music recording industry sectors; NESTA for providing advice on the data collection and Professor Phil Graham for providing feedback on the research. The project team also thanks the Australian Research Council (ARC) and our linkage grant partners: The Australasian Performing Rights Association (APRA AMCOS), the Australia Council for the Arts and Sounds Australia for their funding and collaboration in the research.

Thank you to the international music market events for allowing us permission to observe and attend: Music Matters, Singapore; Primavera, Spain; Folk Alliance, US; Canadian Music Week (CMW), Canada; Americanafest, US; CMJ, US; MIDEM, France; Reeperbahn, Germany; A2IM, US; Showcase Scotland, UK; Liverpool Sound, UK; The Great Escape, UK; WOMEX, Spain; and SXSW, US.

We also thank the researchers who assisted in desktop search and translation work on various national infrastructures at Monash: Declan Martin, José Morais and Jess Carroll.

1 Introduction

Music exports and cultural policy

Music is an important and celebrated cultural form, part of the entertainment and creative industries. The "cultural turn" (Ray and Sayer, 1994) has taken many forms in the past three decades, with various implications for cultural and creative industries, governments and consumers as "the economy is increasingly culturally inflected and … culture is more and more economically inflected" (Lash and Urry, 1994, p. 64). This book traces the rise of music exports within contemporary popular music contexts,[1] and the subsequent emergence of particular industry and state policies seeking commercial advantage and improved cultural trade balances. It derives from an Australian Research Council (ARC) Linkage project, *The Economic and Cultural Value of Australian Music Exports*, led by the University of Newcastle (Australia) in partnership with Monash University, APRA AMCOS, the Australia Council for the Arts and Sounds Australia. The project comprised three overlapping stages to:

- Map and assess the economic and cultural contribution of the Australian music export sector;
- Document the strategies and practices of Australian artists, managers and industry as entrepreneurs, including surveys and interviews of selected managers and artists; and
- Broadly assess the entrepreneurial modes of nations, including analysis of international export organisations and models and comparative case studies of international music export offices and schemes.

Beyond its emphasis upon Australian contexts, we were also interested in examining how the music export sector was faring in relation to a number of global debates about the popular music industries that range across the technological, cultural, governmental and industrial. Like other creative industries (such as books, gaming, fashion, film and television), the popular music industries have not been immune to rapid change that has forced re-assessments of production, consumption and regulatory practices.

This book, then, engages in debates about how industries and nations organise "culture", and specifically, changing relationships between economics and culture. The history of related debates about cultural/creative economies and cultural policy is worth briefly reflecting upon here, especially the broader shift from arts to cultural policy, and what this implied for activities on the ground. While arts policy from the 1950s to the 1970s in most western nations constituted funding of (and access to) "elite" and "heritage" arts, the 1980s wrought decisive shifts to forms of entrepreneurialism designed to ensure the "creative industries" contributed to an economic nationalism:

> Culture creates wealth ... Culture employs ... Culture adds value, it makes an essential contribution to innovation, marketing and design. It is a badge of our industry. The level of our creativity substantially determines our ability to adapt to new economic imperatives. It is a valuable export in itself and an essential accompaniment to the export of other commodities. It attracts tourists and students. It is essential to our economic success.
>
> (Commonwealth of Australia, 1994, np)

The subsequent marketisation of both arts and cultural practices and products was "a growing recognition of the place of creativity—and the 'creative' in place—as a key driver of economic growth in the new economy, with its associated appetite for content and lifestyle goods" (Luckman, 2015, p. 351). The much-discussed emergence of "Britpop" is a useful example of the intersection of nation, culture and economy in the UK. The 1990s sub-genre refers to a particular moment of British international chart success (driven by bands such as Oasis, Blur and Pulp) that also came to stand for recycled discourses of Britishness. In this instance, individual band ambitions and broader national creative industries policy became hard to separate in terms of marketing and national identities (see Harris, 2004). "Creative Britain"/"Cool Britannia" embodied New Labour thinking on the need to connect individual entrepreneurialism to national industrial/export goals.

We broadly concur with the United Nations Conference on Trade and Development's thinking (UNCTAD) (2008, p. 15) in arguing that:

- The "creative economy" is an evolving concept based on creative assets potentially generating economic growth and development;
- It can foster income generation, job creation and export earnings while promoting social inclusion, cultural diversity and human development;
- It embraces economic, cultural and social aspects interacting with technology, intellectual property and tourism objectives;
- It is a set of knowledge-based economic activities with a development dimension and cross-cutting linkages at macro and micro levels to the overall economy;
- It is a feasible development option calling for innovative, multidisciplinary policy responses and inter-ministerial action;
- At the heart of the creative economy are the creative industries.

At the same time, UNCTAD's definitions of the "creative industries" and related sub-categories sidestep various complexities. For example, popular music is not only part of the "performing arts", but also encompasses "heritage" aspects. There are also problems (cf. Peck, 2005; Hesmondhalgh, 2013, pp. 172–174) in their incorporation of Richard Florida's boundaries of precisely who can be labelled as "creative"; we take issue with "creative entrepreneurs" being so loosely conceived as to include "creative professionals in business, finance and law … artists or engineers, musicians or computer scientists, writers or entrepreneurs" (Florida, 2002, p. 16). As discussed in the next section, explanations of the creative process no longer hold with artist-centric foci. Indeed, this book examines an increasingly complex network of industry workers where the artist (and the song) is situated at the beginning of interlocking processes of creation and promotion; and where branding and identity construction in some ways are brought more sharply into focus than within fan–artist relationships.

The central 2008 UNCTAD definitions of "creative economy" do retain and acknowledge social and cultural contexts and values that go some way to incorporating the "symbolic" dimensions of industrial and consumption practices (Hesmondhalgh, 2008) (which has led others to use "cultural and creative industries"—CCI—as an all-encompassing term). It is a useful summary of the interdependencies of states and industries that captures the emergence of the creative industries as both national and city assets for wider economic growth.

The "Creative" Artist

The "arrival" of the creative industries provoked a reappraisal of the situation of the "creatives" in large and small creative enterprises. A new "creative class" (Florida, 2002) recognised the individual and social qualities of such work, evident in the growth of technical and higher education courses teaching generic and industry-specific skills (Flew, 2012, pp. 100–101) as attractive career choices. This was complemented by examining wider networks of creativity that privilege practical teamwork and divisions of knowledge and skills. This was important in moving beyond emphases upon stardom and celebrity:

> Creativity in the commercial creative industries is represented through the branding and packaging of individual talent and the personality cult fostered around stars and celebrities. Yet behind the scenes, a more realistic unit of analysis for creative processes and product is the team or partnership … Creative thinking … depends upon a union of contrasting abilities and styles of thinking.
>
> (Bilton, 2007, p. 19)

The different kinds of personal (and non-economic) investments in creative work for creators mark these industries differently to the rest of the economy in terms of risk (Caves, 2000). The "'nobody knows' characteristic that encapsulates the radical uncertainty regarding the likely market success of a cultural product"

(Throsby, 2015, p. 61) equally applies to the music industries where a relatively small cache of superstars subsidises artist failures.

This has obvious consequences for the individual musician/artist in production contexts, especially when viewed through contemporary notions of entrepreneurship. The glamour associated with song-writing, performing and related media tasks is mitigated by the sometimes hidden costs of entrepreneurial labour: Unpaid labour (undertaken within discourses of "I love being an artist"), long hours, unreliable/seasonal wages (e.g. McRobbie, 2005; Hesmondhalgh and Baker, 2011) and other risks associated with self-employment or contracted employment (Neilsen and Rossiter, 2005).

Reporting from 2015, an Australia Council study of Australian artists across a range of creative fields reinforces the realities for working in the music industries. Contrasting different survey periods, the mean creative income for musicians in 1986–1987 was $22,200; by 2015 it was $15,600 (Throsby and Peteskaya, 2017, p. 177). While the study encompassed all music work (including classical and art musics), the income figures reflect anecdotal evidence within the popular music industries, where (for example) live performance wages at pubs have remained static for a quarter of a century (e.g. Newton and Coyle-Hayward, 2018). In relation to the multiple tasks artists are now expected to perform (who do not have access to professional teamwork), 77% of musicians in the survey reported that they were responsible for the promotion of their work (Throsby and Peteskaya, 2017, p. 229). Asked about the most important factor inhibiting their professional development, the highest responses for musicians were "lack of economic return" (28%) and "lack of time to do creative work due to other pressures and responsibilities" (24%) (ibid., p. 197).

A United Nations report reflects the global nature of personal careers and returns, entwining issues of structural frameworks and individual agency:

> The music industry faces a difficult paradox: while more and more music is being consumed worldwide, particularly by youth, the earnings received by songwriters, producers and performers have been declining. This situation reflects two key issues: (a) the lacunae in the current regimes of IPRs, and (b) the need for songwriters and the singers [sic] to retain greater control over their music and make better use of all ICT tools for accessing global markets.
>
> (UNCTAD, 2010, p. 143)

Mindful of these domestic contexts, we look in particular at the circumstances of Australian artists strategising to maintain national/regional careers and an international presence. In the first decades of rock and roll and pop, few Australian artists (Rolf Harris, The Seekers, Olivia Newton-John) managed to gain visibility in overseas markets. The subsequent international successes of acts such as INXS and Midnight Oil into the 1980s coincided with—and reinforced—emerging strands of interest and support from national governments about the potential for popular music to forge some forms of consistent cultural and economic returns. Beyond attempting to make their mark in key markets that were foundational to these genres, Australian managers and artists have been acutely aware of the added financial and time burdens in seeking European, Asian or North American success. Music economies of similar or smaller size, such as New Zealand and Canada, have long realised the limitations of domestic markets to career longevity; as discussed in Chapter 7, a 2016 Canadian report revealed that six out of ten music companies regarded export activities as crucial for long-term survival: "It's not just domestic deals – it's global deals or nothing" (Canadian Independent Music Association's Stuart Johnston cited in O'Kane, 2016).

This raises a much larger set of career questions for artists, including moral and economic control of their work in overseas contexts; the sets of expertise to be acquired to minimise the "nobody knows" characteristics of creative work, magnified in relation to new markets; and the extent of time and effort to be expended on international markets. In the following sections, we briefly introduce further contexts, macro and micro, influencing artist and company decisions to export, and the changing ways in which international audiences might be sought.

Music-Media Technologies

The pace and extent of change wrought by technological shifts within the music (and cultural) industries over the past two decades have been profound. This has seen a shift from music as product to music as a "service" (Tschmuck, 2003) that offers consumers new contexts of consumption (Wikstrom, 2013). Indeed, "mobile telephony-driven music streaming … looks set to be the most important development, on a par with the introduction of the phonograph, vinyl records and the CD [in] producing new dynamics of personalisation and mobility" (Hesmondhalgh and Meier, 2018, p. 1562), with music primarily used as a cultural form to lead consumers to new digital technologies, with music consumption a secondary consideration (ibid., pp. 1566–1568). This has been accompanied by the presence of new global companies (such as Amazon, Google, Apple, Spotify, Live Nation) that are significant for their distributional power, which is increasingly translated into influence across related sectors, including music publishing, live performance and recording. The new (unequal) shifts in power were forcefully put by one of *The Guardian*'s music writers:

> [Spotify] is still a thing of wonder, easily among the most miraculous manifestations of digital ingenuity … [but] you have quite a charge sheet: exploitation, the turning of music into wallpaper, and the slicing and dicing of great art according to the crassest of considerations … why do artists still blithely put their art into such unreliable care?
>
> (Harris, 2018)

In relation, the rights of artists—and consumers—remain contested as nations attend to significant lags in intellectual property law and governance of the digital aggregators, and as industries confront ever-increasing sources of song revenues and exploitation. While digital streaming revenues have corrected the precipitous decline in artist and company incomes experienced since the 1990s, the inverted business model for most artists (except the "superstars") remains, placing greater dependence upon touring and merchandise revenue (rather than recording income). The decreased prospect (unlike in the "golden age" for recording artists from the 1950s to the end of the 1980s) of artists with national recognition achieving durable careers requires them to increasingly look to international markets for economic viability.

How and where to locate (and maintain) audiences was an explicit concern for the musicians, artist managers and export managers we interviewed. At the same time, complaints about jet lag and doing business in different time zones are now accompanied by acknowledgements of the possibilities of the digital platform era. Songwriters and performers are confronting both the threats and opportunities presented by constantly evolving digital networks of production, consumption and networking. Increasingly complex digital technologies have various obvious implications for the music industries, including opportunities for "co-evolution between the streaming and live music industries" (Naveed et al., 2017, p. 1).

As with other forms of mainstream media/entertainment, the music industries are part of a new era where both producers and consumers are confronted by an "infoglut" (Andrejevic, 2013, pp. 1–19) with an attendant increasing "'datafication' of listening" (Prey, 2016, p. 32). In the broader historical shift from media scarcity to media abundance, the music sector is required to pay much greater attention to data management as a core rationale for success. David Hellburg, Head of Digital for Warner Music Sweden, argues that:

> The huge amount of data that we have access to now is really, really interesting. It allows us to make smarter choices when it comes to marketing and even in terms of how we want to portray an artist, or what type of content we want to release. But the most exciting part is probably the fact that we don't know what the next big thing in music will be. Things change so fast, which forces us to always be on top of our game, trying new things and making educated decisions based on the outcome – that's really something I love.
>
> (Hellburg cited in IFPI, 2018, p. 39)

"Datafication" represents new opportunities for artists, managers and recording labels to better plan for emerging export opportunities, especially in tracking and analysing new potential territories. However, it also requires industries and firms to be equipped with the means and knowledge to manage and exploit the precise information on offer across markets and platforms.

Certainly, the internet now "enables the development of niche markets that make specialised and esoteric cultural goods available to consumers all over the world, thus increasing cultural diversity" (Towse, 2009, p. 400). In the contexts of export, this entails advantages and threats in relation to ideas of the "creative" career discussed earlier. Many of our interviewees spoke to the potential of access to instant sales data, and forging (hopefully) long-term relationships with international fans in ways that can transform older ways of "doing" export. At the same time, artists, managers and industry bodies have raised the problems for export offices in enabling strong international profiles amongst very crowded markets and social media platforms, the related need to work with the "right" online curators/platforms and being able to respond to quickly emerging interest from audience bases. It seems, too, that digital track records of domestic/overseas success will be increasingly used in evaluating requests for market assistance.

Music exports and trade in creative goods/services

Earlier identifications of the creative industries as a success story in international trade (Flew, 2012, pp. 125–132) are borne out by recent statistics, with the global market for creative goods "more than doubling in size from $208 billion in 2002 to $509 billion in 2015" (UNCTAD, 2018, p. 10). The list of leading western creative exporters has remained relatively stable, with the United States, France, Italy, United Kingdom, Germany, Switzerland, Netherlands, Poland, Belgium and Japan comprising the top ten exporters (ibid., p. 9). The report noted the "exceptional" performance of China with annual growth rates in the creative sector of 14% (ibid., pp. 10–11). Large discrepancies remain between "developed" and "developing" countries in export performance (and results are skewed due to both China's "exceptional" performance and its definition within the report as a "developing" export nation) (ibid., p. 20). Among the usual factors determining trade volumes (the price of goods, types of productivity, etc), "cultural differences" (comprising wider cultural histories of engagement and influence) should be considered, although in the case of music, digital streaming and copyright mechanisms increasingly complicate trading patterns (Takara, 2018).

While cultural exports can constitute goods (e.g. songs, television programs, films) and services (e.g. library, copyright, licensing, promotional and other distribution activities), a significant proportion of music exports exist within rights: The bundle of royalty payments derived from performance, composition, synchronisation of live and recorded works allowing various parties the rights to exploit particular works. This shift is captured in 2016 data where the decline of recorded music (by 27%) was matched by what UNESCO labelled the "dematerialisation" of cultural goods, and the move "into the realm of cultural services, often sold as web-based subscriptions".

Figure 1.1 is useful for our later examination of music export nation case studies. While the United States might enjoy significant exporter status across audiovisual goods (film, music, games), the table is a reminder of the substantial amount of creative goods it imports. Four of the nations on the top ten list include our music export case studies—France, Australia, Canada and the UK—who are mainly deficit countries. While the US is seeking to address its creative goods deficit through intellectual property reform, primarily through the reformation of free trade agreements eliminating cultural protectionisms (e.g. Rimmer, 2006; Gagne, 2016), countries such as the UK and Canada have shown consistent interest in developing export programmes and policies to improve creative trade balances. Specific data on music (nor the performing arts) is not presented in the UNCTAD

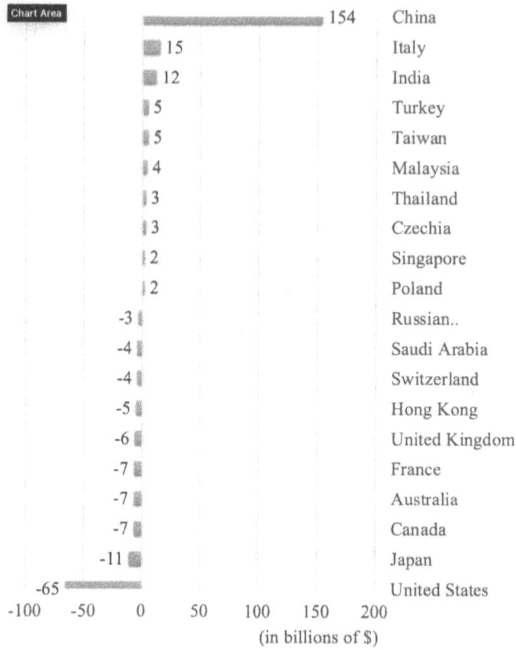

Figure 1.1 Creative goods top ten trade surplus and deficit countries in 2015 (in billions of $). Source: UNCTAD, 2018, p. 25.

2018 report; an earlier *Creative Economy Report* (UNCTAD, 2010, p. 143), which emphasised the "missing links" of key national data (that can incorporate performance and copyright data and intra-firm transactions), perhaps explains this absence in the 2018 findings.

Collectively, Europe remains a dominant creative industries exporter: From 2012 to 2017, the European Union's cultural trade surplus rose from €6.3b to 8.6b, increasing at a slightly faster rate than imports (European Commission, 2019, p. 106). Music exports are included in two categories: "Recorded media" (€7.3m) and "musical instruments"[2] (€2.2m) of an estimated €28.076m within the cultural goods export sector (European Commission, 2019, p. 115). An earlier UNCTAD report in 2008 valued music exports at almost $15b, with Europe accounting for 75% of activity (UNCTAD, 2008, p. 5). Since statistics have come to be reliably collated, there has been a pattern of western dominance, complicated by "the fact that major exporters are also major importers" (Towse, 2009, p. 413).

The global frameworks organising cultural trade—such as the General Agreement on Tariffs and Trade (GATT), the World Trade Organization (WTO) and the Multilateral Agreement on Investment within the Organization for Economic Cooperation and Development (OECD)—raise complex issues in measuring value. Given its symbolic qualities, carrying with it other embodiments of national identity and place-bound innovation, the cultural export has been the subject of fierce debate against the usual arguments for free movement of goods and services. Music has been central to "cultural exception" arguments made by some nations seeking protection for the local cultural product (film, television, music, radio industries). Here, "culture is the misfit, a hindrance to the achievement of an otherwise perfect uniformity in the world trading system" (Throsby, 2000, p. 133). This has led to nations constructing mechanisms (primarily local content quotas governing radio airplay, television and film content) to ensure a level of local visibility/audibility, working with funding structures designed to boost local production. Those interested in a "pure" free market see the "dangers accompanying promotion of a culture of dependency and deviations from profit-maximizing behaviour among local producers" (Doyle, 2011, p. 279).

The history of economic arguments about cultural protectionism versus open cultural markets in part rests on distinctions made between the benefits for consumers or industries:

> If trade is voluntary, the argument for economic liberalization is persuasive, but what is the right amount? Economists often support free trade based on the first welfare theorem, but that argument is inapplicable because of the cost conditions and informational problems faced by the cultural industries. There is no scarcity of applicable models, each with different policy implications that could be applied, but economists cannot effectively distinguish empirically among them. As a result, the case for openness rests on a time-tested theme – open borders counter the adverse effects of concentrated production at home, provide alternative interpretations of events and possibilities, increase choice for consumers, and stimulate business, professional and artistic creativity and performance – rather than on a particular model of imperfect competition.
>
> (Acheson, 2011, p. 227)

This is apparent through the contradictions of global cultural trade frameworks in practice, with cultural exceptions at odds with liberalisation. More importantly, the "case law … has demonstrated that the measures available to protectionist Members do not appear to be convinced … that cultural goods and services are to be considered not only in terms of economic goals but non-economic goals" (Schere, 2017, p. 573). This had led some member states to see UNESCO agencies as a more viable source for resolution than the WTO (ibid., p. 574). Others regard trading blocs such as the EU operating through historical codes of conduct, with cultural policy buttressed by "soft law instruments" containing "non-enforceable recommendations and incentives" (Dewey, 2010, p. 115). It is appropriate, then, to turn to the mix of "instruments" (laws, regulations, policies and frameworks) that are evident at national levels in shaping music export activity.

National Structures, Global Frameworks

In one of the first examinations of how nations deal with popular music in policy terms, Cloonan (2007) articulates a gradual shift from "benign" to "promotional" policies in the United Kingdom. For Britain, a series of business/industry initiatives was favoured over the "soft" instruments of (for example) content quotas and tax breaks. While the UK music sector had succeeded in achieving support, both governments and industries had found agreement in pursuing copyright reform and business support, while ignoring the cultural possibilities for policy, and the different policy agendas amongst very different bodies and practices (Cloonan, 2007, pp. 141–144). Cloonan was prescient in noting potential problems for the United Kingdom in dealing with the European Union, and with recently devolved states such as Scotland (ibid.).

House of Commons reports documenting trade and investment policies from 2010 to 2012 are instructive in the ways in which Feargal Sharkey, then CEO of UK Music, articulated the value of music in terms of broader economic value, and export value in particular:

> in certain places it is still, to quote one rather senior economist of my acquaintance, "Oh, the creative industries; that's that fluffy stuff." Well, in the case of the music industry, it is fluffy stuff that actually generates quite a lot of revenue and taxable income for UK plc …
>
> In terms of the music industry, it is true: we are internationally quite successful. However, as an industry we published a strategy outline paper for the industry almost 12 months ago and made our ambition very clear in that. We want to be number one: we want to become the number one exporter of music in the world. We are positioned to do that. To give you some specifics, PRS for Music at the minute are currently forecasting potentially 40% growth within their sector over the next five years. So we are incredibly fortunate to be blessed with all of these things. It falls back on the quality of British talent and the records and the music they create, and thank God, we have a long and fine pedigree and history of producing some globally recognised, remarkable talent.
>
> (House of Commons, 2011, pp. 57, 59)

Beyond reaffirming current arrangements, Sharkey took the opportunity to support further funding for United Kingdom Trade and Investment (UKTI, their chief export partner in government) and SMEs; and backed the idea of "IP attachés" to protect British copyright interests in key markets (ibid.). All music industry representatives to the Business, Innovation and Skills Committee stressed the need to address existing larger markets (such as the United States) as much as the lure of emerging markets in Asia and Latin America.

In New Zealand contexts, Scott (2013, p. 144) has charted "the contours of the incipient 'after neo-liberal promotional state' … a state that would partner, enable and facilitate popular music-makers for existing institutions". The goals were similar to those of the UK identified by Cloonan, with popular music policy "mobilised to address job creation and social inclusion (especially for young people), domestic industry construction, the generation of export opportunities and the fostering of sentiments of national identity" (ibid.). Scott is deeply critical of the underlying rationale for such policies, regarding them as part of a wider turn to neo-liberal governance with an emphasis on individual mobility that should be self-actualised to engage in market solutions.

The examination of the music export sector is also relevant to recurring debates about local, national and global influences and determinations in locating cultural, economic and regulatory power across various forms of music exchanges. Company (and related technological) innovation remains concentrated within western centres of power (the US, Germany, Europe). The ubiquity of the larger western platform companies—Alphabet (Google, YouTube), Apple, Amazon, Spotify, Microsoft, Facebook—has recently been challenged by eastern companies such as Tencent, Alibaba and Baidu, who are either territorial rivals, or have engaged in strategic mergers. They share a common desire to be truly transnational, which poses renewed questions for nation-states and their treatment of music-media corporations. First, what are the short- and long-term consequences in how music-media firms are linked/backed by deeper structures of capitalism? For governments, audiences and musicians, when are the companies' claims to "competition" valid, and when are they masquerading as monopoly power? In relation, how to reconcile the nation-state's self-interested workings of the local, regional and cultural identity with the utopian display of pure, unfettered digital markets?

Given the number of contexts in which popular music has led new configurations of digital culture, media and financial flows, "Power as enabling and constraining is a theme that scholars of popular music often allude to, and deploy plausibly in arguments" (Negus, 2019, p. 12). In this book, we adopt a cautious "theoretical optimism" (ibid., p. 11) as to how digital flows might assist artists in the production and maintenance of their careers. At the same time, how nation-states are to deal with a rapid succession of digital music technologies is an enormously complicated question in relation to globalisation discourses. The digital cultural economy may well be at "a moment at which the Global North uses culture as a selling point for deindustrialized societies, and the Global South does so for never-industrialized ones" (Durrer et al., 2017, p. 3). Copyright is a case in point, where nations at the periphery are told to adopt the intellectual property mechanisms of established music nations (see, e.g. IFPI, 2019). The many problems related to live gig ticketing practices (Behr and Cloonan, 2020; Waterson, 2018) also present a powerful case study of transnationalism with interrelated problems: Companies with global footprints wilfully ignoring national/regional consumer laws; the same companies increasingly interwoven deeply into the ownership of venue, recording and promotional structures; and as a new site of struggle between artist, audience and company rights.

Assessing the complex contexts of European cultural policy, Littoz-Monnet (2007, pp. 23–29) discerns three policy models:

- *Liberal*: At "arm's length", "coupled with low levels of state financial involvement";
- *Dirigiste*: "Strong public intervention"; often marked by public subsidies where appropriate;

- *Federal*: "Subsidiarity governs", with municipal/regional governance empowered in cultural affairs/policy.

This model is useful in tracing export policy shifts. In our case study nations (explored in Chapter 6), governments can be seen to have moved from relatively low levels of involvement in export activity to rising levels of subsidy through a range of schemes for internal growth and outward promotion. In some cases, this has been matched by growing networks of assistance at state/regional levels, funnelling upward into national programmes. Yet exports remain one of the few areas within popular music policy where naked appeals to rampant commercialism can hold sway. We explore the ways in which the state and industries have agreed that significant commercial returns can be achieved. Increasing forms of culture–business symbiosis have occurred for two central reasons. Firstly, both industries and governments have sought a better understanding of the sector through increased reportage of economic performance, and how and where exports can better fit within local ecosystems. Secondly, in relation, national industries have been convincing in broader arguments to states that increased export funding is an investment in future returns, rather than a continuance of older subsidy models. In UK contexts, its Music Export Growth Scheme is "not a cultural fund, we're not an arts fund, we are a business fund" (Chris Tamms cited in Malt, 2017), also evident in the comments of Feargal Sharkey cited above. In Chapters 5 and 6, we examine the ways in which nations are deploying mixtures of *dirigiste* and *federal* policies that are as much about broadening the knowledge base of industrial expertise as direct promotional work.

We also need to recognise particular national histories and circumstances of policy models. Within western nations, for example, the US remains an outlier in terms of a coordinated creative and cultural industries policy as recognised by European countries. While retaining a forceful presence in intellectual property and cultural trade frameworks, "the bulk of policy initiatives are highly localised and sub-national in focus, as seen with the rise of the creative cities movement" (Flew, 2012, p. 33). In contrast, "Asian approaches … strongly emphasise the role of national socio-cultural and political circumstances, but still identify opportunities for export growth and successful branding of global-city regions … and the dominance of ICT sectors in driving economic growth" (ibid.). Other key regions—South America, South Africa, the Caribbean—have focused on "cultural heritage maintenance, poverty alleviation and provision of basic infrastructure" (ibid., p. 34). De Beukelaer and Spence (2018, p. 21) flag important discursive tropes in evaluating different national/regional approaches where "developing" music economies such as Africa's have "potential", with the implication that it has never been realised. The authors caution that "cultural economy" considerations too often minimise or erase public/private tensions, and wider issues of diversity, ownership, sustainability and inclusion.

In some respects, De Beukelaer and Spence's work provides an update of Malm and Wallis's (1992) examinations of national/regional frameworks. In focusing upon "smaller" nations' music and media policies, Malm and Wallis were equally interested in how media technologies and localised ideas of culture played out within rapidly changing global platforms (Malm and Wallis, 1992, pp. 3–4). Their work is also a stubborn call to examine the workings of the nation-state that retain the ability to shape the broadcasting, live performance and educational contexts of music-making. As Cloonan (1999, p. 204) has noted:

> the desire to express allegiance to domestic products and artists is not necessarily a reactionary one. To admit that some forms of popular music need Nation-State assistance can be to defy the market rather than to promote xenophobia.

We find Freedman's (2008, pp. 13–14) distinctions between *policy* (goals and intentions), *regulation* (operational instruments and agencies) and *governance* (institutions and instruments shaping industry systems) to be useful. While Freedman's model was developed in the context of the media industries, it can equally be applied in properly accounting for the full range of activities, responsibilities and actors in complex supra-national frameworks evident in the music industries. This book also investigates how popular music might be a rich area to reflect changes in the types of policy produced, not only to confront digital cultures and economies, but in how the *national* is portrayed and configured within such global frameworks. This includes asking (again) much older questions about relationships between cultural practices and industries and the nation-state: Should the public purse support the cultural/creative industries (and if so, by how much); what are the correct relationships to be had between industries and government; and how to locate the "public interest" in increasing marriages between the cultural/creative industries and public sectors? In the contexts of our national case studies, arts/culture budgets have been subjected to renewed pressures where "value for money" discourses are always implicit within media and government, accompanied by calls for clear measurement of the results of public culture funding.

Partly in response, it is thus no accident that many nations have rebranded their arts/culture ministries as "creative" (e.g. Creative Scotland; Creative New Zealand; Creative Ireland). This not only signifies that "creativity" (no matter how differently it might be defined in each national context) lies at the heart of public funding, but that the nation-state itself is engaging in more innovative arrangements about how "the creatives" might be unleashed. In relation to considerations of national systems of entrepreneurship, we suggest that *entrepreneurial nation* might be useful to describe the range of ways in which nation-states are engaging with other actors and sectors to achieve cultural and economic returns. In relation, combinations of "political entrepreneurs" (either politicians or public servants) can provide:

> innovative approaches [that] encourages entrepreneurship/business and where the goals are growth, employment and the common good … to open up windows of opportunity in new sets of formal and informal institutions.
>
> (Silander, 2016, p. 18)

In later chapters, we examine some of the ways that the music export field comes to be simultaneously defined as cultural and entrepreneurial; and the increasing willingness of governments and industries to re-define where entrepreneurship is located and supported.

Music Exports and Soft Power

It is not surprising that governments see cultural exports as important components of a wider *cultural diplomacy*, "said to take place when formal diplomats, serving national governments, try to shape and channel this natural flow [of organic cultural relations] to advance national interests" (Arndt, 2006, p. xviii). Thus distinctions need to be made between governmental and cultural spaces where a simpler sharing or exchange of cultural products/performances is in evidence (often captured by vague appeals to *cultural relations*; see Ang et al., 2015), and where other national interests and ambitions (economic and discursive) come into view. Joseph Nye's much-cited "soft power" (1990, pp. 166–168) is clearer in delineating the use of culture to promote a set of national values on foreign shores, where not only international standing is to be achieved, but hopefully the adoption of national values by other nations and regions. Historically, US cinema provided an exceptional vehicle for economic dominance of a cultural market that also acted out the "US way of life" on the screen for international audiences (Miller, 2005). US culture was state-funded to achieve a range of political aims during the Cold War across various international spaces and cultural forms (e.g. Shaw, 2016). Jazz was used in the 1950s to connote popular culture with US discourses of freedom via international tours of well-known musicians such as Louis Armstrong and Dizzy Gillespie that ignored the myriad ways that "freedom" was curtailed for black musicians at home (Schneider, 2010, pp. 104–105). Debate continues about just how successful the deployment of popular culture for culturally diplomatic ends can be, given the wide availability of counter-narratives across social media and the growth of alternative media/cultural production that can actively negate various nationalist aims and narratives. This points to the need for further examination of how soft power operates in practice, especially how audiences are "reading" particular meanings (Ang et al., 2015, pp. 374–375).

Yet music exports are regarded as a means of cultural diplomacy in aid of economic objectives, seeking competitive advantages that will boost cultural trade ledgers. Departmental reports across different case study nations in our project revealed how national governments retain a belief in music as a vital source of soft power, even if it simply collapses into national branding exercises. For example, Japan's "pop-culture diplomacy" of the early 2000s, driven by "Cool Japan" branding, was a "one-way encouragement of foreigners to deepen their appreciation of Japan" (Iwabuchi, 2015, p. 429). While J-pop might be more about the localisation of global pop genres (Lancashire, 2015), it has also proved to be part of wider cultural industries strategies and successes (Allison, 2008; Tsutomu, 2008).

We have noted earlier in this chapter the UK music industries' representations to government in arguing for the greater involvement of the state to reap greater economic returns. This has been accompanied by recognition that the government can similarly harness the creative industries for soft power ambitions. A 2013 report, *Influence and Attraction: Culture and the Race for Soft Power in the 21st Century*, is interesting in these respects. Commissioned by the British Council, the Demos think tank authors provide some advice which runs against some of the usual economic concerns and "short-term transactional and instrumental thinking" (British Council, 2013, p. 34). It states the importance of culture in potentially erasing the usual transnational power relations, "where the economically and politically weak can have an equal status – where Bob Dylan and Bob Marley could meet in a way that the US and Jamaica could not" (ibid., p. 32). Traditional media structures (such as the BBC) and new digital networks remain important forums for two-way understanding through the dissemination of popular culture. In noting the rise of formal cultural exchange infrastructure (national institutes, cultural centres, foundations and offices) in other countries, the report also sees the reduction of cultural budgets (post-Global Financial Crisis) as an opportunity for governments to effect a more "hands-off" approach, where the facilitation of more autonomous cultural bodies can perversely produce greater results (ibid., pp. 31–35).

The *Influence and Attraction* report also reaffirmed a sense of the UK as "a modern day cultural superpower" (ibid., p. 2). This is in part attributed to the powerful ways in which British popular culture circulates to denote national attributes (*Wallace and Gromit* television; Bond films), evidenced in the Britpop example discussed earlier. We also need to acknowledge that "… just as the unique music of particular localities … has proved impossible to distinguish, so distinctive national styles are similarly marked by strategic essentialism, marketing and local boosterism" (Connell and Gibson, 2003, p. 124). This implicates the music export in wider ambitions to provide an international stage for the local music product, that in turn invokes a sense of national identity. While not the primary focus, we will examine the extent to which artists believe they are representative of their nations (and industries).

Methodology

The Australian Research Council project comprised four overlapping methods, involving combinations of surveys, interviews, observations and/or policy analysis:

(i) ***Australian music industry data***

Online Australian music industry surveys were distributed to Australian musicians, publishers, recording labels, booking agents and related sector workers. Two surveys were conducted with the assistance of partner investigators, Sounds Australia and APRA AMCOS. Survey questions related to different industrial activities (manager, artist, booker, etc.), the frequency and nature of both domestic and international work, types of (public, private) assistance and funding and annual revenue streams for different activities. Enquiries about revenue streams proved difficult for many participants, who were wary of revealing incomes (despite assurances from industry bodies that individual responses would not be highlighted, and that all data adhered to university guidelines of confidentiality). The first survey (November 2016–June 2017) targeted Australian industry participants (including musicians, singers, songwriters, composers, DJs, music managers, music publishers, record labels, record producers and booking agents). Participants were identified through email invitations to Sounds Australia contacts, and national radio and press releases. The relatively low response (127 completed surveys) prompted a second survey (March–October 2018) targeting music publishers and recording labels that produced a further 22 responses. An additional survey of major booking agents in the United Kingdom and the United States, to obtain information on the revenues of Australian acts they had booked in the last three years, garnered a further eight responses.

Additional data were gained from central industry and government sources to complement the surveys, including the Department of Jobs and Small Business, the Australasian Performing Right Association – Australasian Mechanical Copyright Owners' Society (APRA AMCOS), the Australian Independent Record Labels Association (AIR), the Australian Recording Industry Association Limited (ARIA) and the Australasian Music Publishers' Association Limited (AMPAL).

(ii) ***Export Data Collection***

Sounds Australia survey: The team gained access to a set of surveys undertaken by Sounds Australia between 2009 and 2016, cataloguing artist, manager and industry experiences where Sounds Australia had a presence at an international event. Questions related to combined forms of financial assistance and outcomes (opportunities, deals made). This constituted 58 surveys (2009–2016) and 701 participants, which were compiled and analysed. The insights from these surveys informed the design of the final Export Strategies survey to investigate the impact of exporting opportunities over time.

An **Export Strategies survey** was conducted in 2018 of 405 artists and artist managers who had completed the above Sounds Australia survey, to identify the impact and strategies that may have resulted from selected international music market events. Questions related to possible opportunities relating to export activities; income streams; financial investments; and non-tangible investment activities such as promotions, publicity and network-building.[3] Artists and managers were also interviewed, with 15 interviews completed between 2015 and 2018, focusing on themes of export readiness, export strategies and their experience of international industry events.[4]

(iii) ***Policy data/analysis***

In 2016, a project database was created of government, industry and academic literature relating to music exports, and the role of culture in national/global trade. For non-English-speaking nations, research assistants with relevant language skills were hired for key translations of core policy and industry documents (France, South Korea). From 2016, project members attended core music export events within and outside of Australia, including music trade fairs (for example, MIDEM), and core music showcase and festival events designed (at least in part) to present acts to new audiences and markets (for example, SXSW, The Great Escape, Primavera). National export managers and key workers charged with promotional activities at these events were observed, and in many cases, interviews were conducted with them on-site. In addition, team members observed Sounds Australia information sessions for aspiring exporters in Melbourne and Sydney. A total of 66 export administrator interviews were conducted from 2016 to 2018, including export office administrators, governmental department workers and heads and export event administrators and workers. Questions related to their roles in policies and strategies, national branding strategies, local funding infrastructure and music export activities in relation to wider local industrial ecosystems.

In consultation with partner investigators APRA AMCOS and the Australia Council, seven nations were selected for further investigation as countries with active music export schemes/offices: France, South Korea, Canada, United Kingdom, Sweden, Finland and Norway. These nations were chosen as good examples of export policy innovation, as longstanding music export countries or as examples of both. Beyond these case studies, Australia's music export office, Sounds Australia, was examined as a separate entity through access to our funding partners' data. This level of access meant that Australian contexts are inevitably more detailed than the other case study nations, where the project team has relied upon interviews and public industry and government documents for assessment. In some cases (South Korea), the relative lack of access to key government and industry figures has been a barrier to a more comprehensive analysis.

(iv) ***Observation/analysis***

As we will discuss later in the book, international circuits of trade fairs, industry conferences and promotional festivals retain considerable influence in music export activity. Such gatherings provide "settings in which people from diverse organizations and with diverse purposes assemble periodically, or on a one-time basis, to announce new products, develop industry standards, construct social networks, recognize accomplishments, share and interpret information, and transact business" (Lampel and Meyer, 2008, p. 1026). Beyond the advantages of like-minded professionals catching up, they also offer "occasions for information exchange and collective sense-making" (ibid., p. 1027). Export music event organisers, then, are part of broader creative industries' efforts in "seeking economic gains [that] are consequently deeply entwined with their need to react to and anticipate field developments, and to position themselves as intermediaries between potential audiences and broader field developments" (Schlusser et al., 2014, p. 418). These "festivals, fairs, and conferences build on the social networks present in a field (Maskell et al., 2006), but the selection of particular audiences contributes to the forming or redesigning of these networks" (ibid., p. 419). In their 2014 study of German popular music industry events (including Reeperbahn), Schüßler, Dobusch and Wessel found a considerable need for events to offer different platforms than their rivals (with some separating commerce from other activities); intense competition for hosting events, related to local boosterism; different understandings of industrial connections; and continual validation of the "new" ("disrupted fields") (Schüßler et al., 2014, p. 419).

This broader understanding—that a music trade fair is not simply representative of the field, but also comes to actively construct it—is useful in this project. Project members attended various global export gatherings, including South by Southwest, The Great Escape, MIDEM and A2IM. In addition to interviews with national export office staff, we also observed the array of presentations, national stand displays and interactions with delegates, performances and related business meetings (brief and protracted) central to these events. We acted as "observer[s] as participant" (Brewer, 2000, p. 84): We made those we came in contact with aware of our research intentions as we participated as audience members (checking out industry and national stands, attending conference presentations, collecting materials offered in relation to export presentations). Beyond finding other potential interviewees (with key industry workers providing introductions to other industry sectors and figures), we were more interested in observing how both seasoned participants and newcomers made sense of the intense milieu which was a recurring feature of such events, including the networking choices and decisions made. This global circuit was also useful in assessing the "social" and "symbolic" frames (Moeran, 2011, pp. 86–87) of interaction, particularly attempts to interpret how each nation regarded other representations and strategies; and the degree of collaboration between seasoned industry workers. In later chapters, we provide occasional snapshots, drawing on contemporaneous notes of the project team at different industry events.

Research limitations

Our research has focused upon those directly involved with different export offices and schemes across different national contexts. However, we acknowledge that there are many ways that artists and artist managers approach exporting their goods and services. For our purposes, we primarily engaged with those who became involved with and through international music market events; how artists and managers fare outside existing export circuits awaits further study. In keeping with the primary focus of our case study nations, popular music was the central context of activities for exporters. While international marketing events such as Classical:NEXT and Jazzahead have become prominent in their own right, jazz, classical and experimental genres were not a primary concern here. The artists and managers surveyed and interviewed also regarded themselves as professional or semi-professional. While the project focused on the different career stages of musicians, we did not investigate the contexts of amateurs, hobbyists and formal or informal music education-related activities. In relation, the wider tentacles of an export ecosystem—software and instruments, music books, the music (higher education) sector, online resources and inbound tourism, for example—are not examined in this study.

While there were exceptions, we encountered a persistent problem in attempting to provide a decent picture of the Australian music industry in general, and its export activities in particular. Despite reassurances from our industry partners that the project surveys were designed to assist the industry (in providing an export focus for the first time to governments and industry sectors), survey participants were loath to provide economic data relating to their annual incomes. Many participants completed the first two stages of surveys—with questions about types of music activity, locations and so on—while leaving the income data section blank. While this is not surprising, we clearly did not ease participants' concerns about the ways in which the data were to be (anonymously) deployed.

At the same time, we found general enthusiasm among the various industry workers and administrators about the project. Before and after interviews, we often received "it's about time" comments from interviewees who believed passionately that the export sector was under-researched. This certainly assisted us in obtaining interviews, and for the most part, industry and government interviewees were generous in sharing their experiences and data. On occasion, this provoked repetition of industry or government positions with little deviation from the party line. For some, the interviews were possibly regarded as a "rhetorical strategy" (Hesmondhalgh and Baker, 2011, p. 16). For others, it was an opportunity to reflect more broadly on domestic relationships to other international experiences. As researchers, there was implicit (and sometimes explicit) pressure to "deliver a good narrative" about exports that reflected the same local concerns across different national contexts in relation to funding, opportunities and the overall viability of popular music as a cultural and public good.

Conclusion: "Born Global"?

While we explore the ways in which popular music export activities have become more complex, the basic processes and thinking have not changed since the arrival of rock and roll in the 1950s: A music act seeks aesthetic and commercial approval of their music "product", where hopefully wider recording, performance and genre traditions allow the artist to be "read" by another territorial audience. The music export sector represents a good example of similarly "reading" globalisation, discursively and in practice. The much longer debates about the possible homogenisation of culture (e.g. Tomlinson, 1995) have lessened, perhaps, in the 2000s to more practical questions about *how* and *where* the cultural industries can become part of much larger cultural structures. Across film, television, fashion, sport and music, the "nation is not enough": The cultural industries must increasingly seek markets beyond their borders. For the Swedish government, not only should SMEs seek to export, but we are told that "'born global'" industries "such as IT, computer gaming, music, design and trade, start-up enterprises are global from the very beginning" (Government Offices of Sweden, 2015, p. 15).

In this sense, the term "born global" requires some unpacking, where it might entail a series of industrial processes (preparing and executing merchandise, performance and promotional activities for export), a general (industrial) "structure of feeling" about desires or acknowledgement of wider consumption/production circuits of exchange or as a warning to cultural industries ("you *must* be born global to survive"). The term first appeared in a report to describe small and medium-sized Australian enterprises in the manufacturing industry that operate globally in a short time after their creation (generally within six years) (Rennie, 1993). Others have referred to "firms establishing international revenue streams after two to three years" or "firms specifically created to go international by design" (Skene, 2017).

In transferring the "born global" concept to the music industries, we are concurrently investigating many current understandings about contemporary practices, not the least that older pyramid career structures (gradual transitions from local to national to international success) are less relevant in an era of instant streaming success, and where national borders are also less relevant in constructing regional and global audiences. In relation, the range of social and digital media platforms holds the promise of more immediate (and potentially deeper) connections between audiences and artists beyond their immediate national borders. The implications do not simply rest with individual careers or even national markets; they reveal an enormous capacity for not simply producing local inflections of

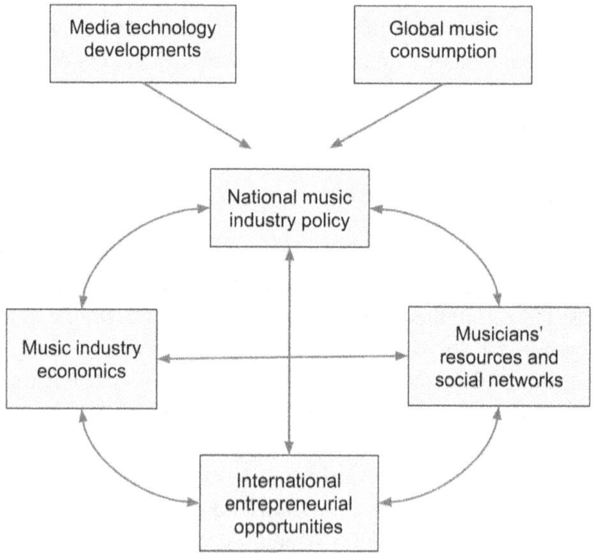

Figure 1.2 Music export framework.

global genres, but artists from the "outside" actively leading and reshaping them. Rather than dissolving into cliché ("we are all born global now"), in this book we wish to interrogate the extent to which the entrepreneurial instinct has changed for aspiring artists, and the consequences for how the music export is organised, promoted and coded across a range of industrial and governmental contexts.

In relation to the mixture of cultural policy, creativity, media technologies, trade and "nation" themes, this book offers the following central questions as pertinent to understanding the contemporary music export:

- What are the economic and cultural contributions of the music export sector?;
- What are the export strategies and practices of artists, managers and related industry workers?; and
- What are the entrepreneurial modes of national export activity, including national music export offices and schemes?

Throughout this book, Australian contexts and practices are prominent in discussing these questions. We also examine the same activities in those countries notable for music export activity, amidst the rise in the allocation of resources by industries and governments to capture increased exposure and revenues. In Chapter 2, we examine the global scope of music exports, the impact of different music-media technologies upon the sector and the flows of artists and songs across different territories. In Chapter 3, we look more closely at the structures and mechanisms artists, managers and labels must confront, and the meanings of being "export ready". Negotiating a range of key players and gatekeepers is significant, and in Chapter 4 we investigate the global circuits of presentation and promotion, and the implications for understanding contemporary networking practices. Chapter 5 examines the emergence of Australian government and industry efforts to export, and the contemporary operations of Sounds Australia as the nation's export scheme. In Chapter 6, we look at international practices through examination of national export schemes/offices in Norway, Finland, Sweden, France, the United Kingdom and Canada. In Chapter 7, we conclude with key observations about contemporary music export practices by revisiting understandings of "born global", the significance of ongoing technological change and the potential impacts of COVID-19 for future markets.

Notes

1 We broadly define contemporary popular music as the forms and genres of music-making that are most accessible to, meaningful to and enjoyed by large numbers of people.
2 The inclusion of musical instruments (for their ability to "enable artistic expression") (European Commission 2019, p. 120) is unusual.
3 We did not examine industry workers and artists who chose not to be involved in export events facilitated or supported by Sounds Australia.
4 The 12 managers who responded oversee a range of artists at different career levels (Emerging, Breakthrough, Established and Epic). In terms of career stages, the 12 managed 2 Epic, 3 Established, 2 Breakthrough and 5 Emerging artists. Two managers were female; ten were male. Seven were based in Australia, while five had international offices (see Chapter 3 for definitions of these artist stages/categories).

References

Acheson, K. (2011). Globalization. In R. Towse (ed.) *Handbook of Cultural Economics*. Cheltenham: Edward Elgar, pp. 220–228.

Allison, A. (2008). The attractions of the J-wave for American youth. In Y. Watanabe & D.L. McConnell (eds.) *Soft Power Superpowers: Cultural and National Assets of Japan and the United States*. Abingdon: Routledge, pp. 99–110.

Andrejevic, M. (2013). *Infoglut: How Too Much Information Is Changing the Way We Think and Know*. Abingdon: Routledge.

Ang, I., Isar, Y.R. & Mar, P. (2015). Cultural diplomacy: beyond the national interest? *International Journal of Cultural Policy* vol. 21, no. 4, pp. 365–381.

Arndt, R. (2006). *The First Resort of Kings: American Cultural Diplomacy in the Twentieth Century*. Washington: Potomac Books.

Behr, A. & Cloonan, M. (2020). Going spare? Concert tickets, touting and cultural value. *International Journal of Cultural Policy* vol. 26, no. 1, pp. 95–108.

Bilton, C. (2007). *Management and Creativity: From Creative Industries to Creative Management*. Oxford: Blackwell.

Brewer, J.D. (2000). *Ethnography*. Buckingham: Open University Press.

British Council (2013). *Influence and Attraction: Culture and the Race for Soft Power in the 21st Century*. London: Demos/British Council.

Caves, R. (2000). *Creative Industries: Contracts between Art and Commerce*. Cambridge: Harvard University Press.

Cloonan, M. (1999). Pop and the nation-state: towards a theorisation. *Popular Music* vol. 18, no. 2, pp. 193–207.

Cloonan, M. (2007). *Popular Music and the State in the UK: Culture, Trade or Industry?* Aldershot: Ashgate.

Commonwealth of Australia (1994). *Creative Nation: Commonwealth Cultural Policy*. Canberra: Department of Communication and the Arts.

Connell, J. & Gibson, C. (2003). *Sound Tracks: Popular Music, Identity and Place*. London: Routledge.

De Beukaeler, C. & Spence, K.-M. (2018). *Global Cultural Economy*. Abingdon: Routledge.

Dewey, P. (2010). Power in European cultural policy. In J.P. Singh (ed.) *International Cultural Policies and Power*. Basingstoke: Palgrave Macmillan, pp. 113–126.

Doyle, G. (2011). Media economics and regulation. In Towse, R. (ed.) *A Handbook of Cultural Economics*. Cheltenham: Edward Elgar, pp. 273–281.

Durrer, V., Miller, T. & O'Brien, D. (2017). Towards global cultural policy studies. In V. Durrer, T. Miller & D. O'Brien (eds.) *The Routledge Handbook of Global Cultural Policy*. Abingdon: Routledge, pp. 1–16.

European Commission (2019). *Culture Statistics 2019 Edition*. Luxembourg: European Union. https://ec.europa.eu/eurostat/statistics-explained/index.php?title=Culture_statistics

Florida, R. (2002). *The Rise of the Creative Class and How It's Transforming Work, Leisure, Community and Everyday Life*. New York: Basic Books.

Flew, T. (2012). *The Creative Industries: Culture and Policy*. London: SAGE.

Freedman, D. (2008). *The Politics of Media Policy*. Cambridge: Polity Press.

Gagne, G. (2016). *The Trade and Culture Debate: Evidence from US Trade Agreements*. Lanham: Lexington Books.

Government Offices of Sweden (2015). *Sweden's Export Strategy*. Stockholm: Ministry for Foreign Affairs.

Harris, J. (2004). *Britpop! Cool Britannia and the Spectacular Demise of English Rock.* London: Da Capo Press.

Harris, J. (2018). My problem with Spotify - even though I'm a subscriber. *The Guardian*, 29 January. https://www.theguardian.com/commentisfree/2018/jan/29/spotify-subscriber-playlists-finances-low-pay-music-fans

Hesmondhalgh, D. (2008). The cultural and creative industries. In T. Bennett & J. Frow (eds.) *The SAGE Handbook of Cultural Analysis*. Los Angeles: SAGE, pp. 522–569.

Hesmondhalgh, D. (2013). *The Creative Industries*, Third Edition. Los Angeles: SAGE.

Hesmondhalgh, D. & Baker, S. (2011). *Creative Labour: Media Work in Three Cultural Industries*. London: Routledge.

Hesmondhalgh, D. & Meier, L.M. (2018). What the digitalisation of music tells us about capitalism, culture and the power of the information technology sector. *Information, Communication & Society* vol. 21, no. 11, pp. 1555–1570.

House of Commons (2011). *Rebalancing the Economy: Trade and Investment, Seventh Report of Session 2010–2012*, Volume II. London: Business, Innovation and Skills Committee.

IFPI (2018). *Global Music Report 2018: Annual State of the Industry*. London: International Federation of Phonographic Industries.

IFPI (2019). *Global Music Report 2019: State of the Industry*. London: International Federation of Phonographic Industries.

Iwabuchi, K. (2015). Pop-culture diplomacy in Japan: soft power, nation branding and the question of 'international cultural exchange'. *International Journal of Cultural Policy* vol. 2, no. 4, pp. 419–432.

Lampel, J. & Meyer, A.D. (2008). Guest editors' introduction: field-configuring events as structuring mechanisms: how conferences, ceremonies, and trade shows constitute new technologies, industries, and markets. *Journal of Management* vol. 45, no. 6, pp. 1025–1035.

Lancashire, T. (2015). J-pop's elusive "J": is Japanese popular music Japanese? *Perfect Beat* vol. 9, no. 1, pp. 38–59.

Lash, S. & Urry, J. (1994). *Economies of Signs and Space*. London: SAGE.

Luckman, S. (2015). Cultural policy and creative industries. In V. Durrer, T. Miller & D. O'Brien (eds.) *The Routledge Handbook of Global Cultural Policy*. Abingdon: Routledge, pp. 341–354.

Malm, K. & Wallis, R. (1992). *Media Policy and Music Activity*. London: Routledge.

Malt, A. (2017). CMU@TGE 2017: facilitating export – UK export initiatives. *CMU (Complete Music Update)*. 26 May. https://completemusicupdate.com/article/cmutge-2017-facilitating-export-uk-export-initiatives/

Maskell, P., Bathelt H. & Malmberg, A. (2006). Building global knowledge pipelines: the role of temporary clusters. *European Planning Studies* vol. 14, no. 8, pp. 997–1013.

McRobbie, A. (2005). Clubs to companies. In J. Hartley (ed.) *Creative Industries*. Malden, MA: Blackwell, pp. 375–390.

Miller, T. (2005). *Global Hollywood 2*. London: BFI Publishing.

Morean, B. (2011). Trade fairs, markets and fields: framing imagined as real communities. *Historical Social Research – Historische Sozialforschung* vol. 36, no. 3, pp. 79–98.

Naveed, K, Watanabe, C. & Neittaanmäki, P. (2017). Co-evolution between streaming and live music leads a way to the sustainable growth of the music industry – Lessons from the US experience. *Technology in Society* vol. 50, pp. 1–19.

Negus, K. (2019). Nation-states, transnational corporations and cosmopolitans in the global popular music economy. *Global Media and China* vol. XX, pp. 1–16.

Neilsen, B. & Rossiter, N. (2005). From precarity to precariousness and back again: labour, life and unstable networks. *Fibreculture Journal*, Issue 5, online, September.

Newton, D. & Coyle-Hayward, R. (2018). *Melbourne Live Music Census 2017 Report*. Melbourne: Music Victoria.

Nye, J.S. (1990). Soft power. *Foreign Policy* vol. 80, pp. 153–171.

O'Kane, J. (2016). Exporting necessary for survival: Canadian musicians. *The Globe and Mail*, 28 November. https://www.theglobeandmail.com/report-on-business/international-business/exporting-necessary-for-survival-canadian-musicians/article33066352/

Peck, J. (2005). Struggling with the creative class. *International Journal of Urban and Regional Research* vol. 29, no. 4, pp. 740–770.

Prey, R. (2016). Musica analytica: the datafication of listening. In R. Nowak & A. Whelan (eds.) *Networked Music Cultures*. London: Palgrave Macmillan, pp. 31–48.

Ray, L. & Sayer, A. (eds.) (1994). *Culture and Economy After the Cultural Turn*. London: SAGE.

Rennie, M.W. (1993). Born global. *McKinsey Quarterly* vol. 4, no. 45, pp. 45–52.

Rimmer, M. (2006). Robbery under arms: copyright law and the Australia-United States free trade agreement. *First Monday* vol. 11, no. 3, pp. 31–85.

Schere, L. (2017). The culture war: look at the cultural exception principle in international trade law. *Fordham International Law Journal* vol. 40, no. 2, pp. 561–582.

Schneider, C.P. (2010). Cultural diplomacy: the humanizing factor. In J.P. Singh (ed.) *International Cultural Policies and Power*. Basingstoke: Palgrave Macmillan, pp. 101–112.

Schussler, E., Dobusch, L. & Wessel, L. (2014). Backstage: organizing events as proto-institutional work in the popular music industry. *Schmalenbach Business Review* vol. 66, pp. 415–437.

Scott, M. (2013). *Making New Zealand's Pop Renaissance: State, Markets, Musicians*. Aldershot: Ashgate.

Shaw, T. (2016). Cinema and the cold war: an international perspective. In G. Kassimeris & J. Buckley (eds.) *The Ashgate Research Companion to Modern Warfare*. London: Routledge, pp. 365–382.

Silander, D. (2016). The political entrepreneur. In C. Karlsson, C. Silander & D. Silander (eds.) *Political Entrepreneurship: Regional Growth and Entrepreneurial Diversity in Sweden*. Cheltenham: Edward Elgar, pp. 7–19.

Skene, D. (2017). Born global firms – a growing feature of Australia's internationally active business community. *Australian Trade and Investment Commission*, 19 December. https://www.austrade.gov.au/News/Economic-analysis/born-global-firms-a-growing-feature-of-australias-internationally-active-business-community

Takara, Y. (2018). Do cultural differences affect the trade of cultural goods? A study in trade of music. *Journal of Cultural Economics* vol. 42, no. 3, pp. 393–417.

Throsby, D. (2000). *Economics and Culture*. Sydney: Allen & Unwin.

Throsby, D. (2015). The cultural industries as a sector of the economy. In K. Oakley & J. O'Connor (eds.) *The Routledge Companion to the Cultural Industries*. Abingdon: Routledge, pp. 56–69.

Throsby, D. & Peteskaya, K. (2017). *Making Art Work*. Strawberry Hills: Australia Council for the Arts.

Tomlinson, J. (1995). Homogenisation and globalisation. *History of European Ideas* vol. 20, no. 4–6, pp. 891–897.

Towse, R. (2009). *A Textbook of Cultural Economics*. Cambridge: Cambridge University Press.

Tschmuck, P. (2003). How creative are the creative industries? A case of the music industry. *Journal of Arts Management, Law, and Society* vol. 33, no. 2, pp. 127–141.

Tsutomu, S. (2008). Japan's creative industries: culture as a source of soft power in the industrial sector. In Y. Watanabe & D.L. McConnell (eds.) *Soft Power Superpowers: Cultural and National Assets of Japan and the United States*. Abingdon: Routledge, pp. 128–153.

UNCTAD (2008). *Creative Economy Report 2008 The Challenge of Assessing the Creative Economy: Towards Informed Policy-Making*. Geneva: United Nations.

UNCTAD (2010). *Creative Economy Report 2010*. Geneva: United Nations.

UNCTAD (2018). *Creative Economy Outlook: Trends in International Trade in Creative Industries 2002–2015*. Geneva & New York: United Nations.

UNESCO (2016). *The Globalization of Cultural Trade: A Shift in Consumption–International Flows of Cultural Goods and Services 2004–2013*. Geneva: UNESCO Institute for Statistics.

Waterson, M. (2018). *Ticketing As If Consumers Mattered*. The Warwick Economics Research Paper Series (TWERPS) 1177. University of Warwick: Department of Economics.

Wikstrom, P. (2013). *The Music Industry: Music in the Cloud*. Cambridge: Polity Press.

2 The economics of music exports

Introduction

This chapter analyses the economic distribution of global music exports and the implications of new developments in music technology for the career choices of artists and government music policy. First, we examine the scale and scope of global music exports; global music flows between countries and the distribution of export income within the industry. Then we examine the impact of new technologies on existing industry structures, business models and artists' careers in the music industry and possible implications for government music export policies.

Exports are defined as goods or services produced in one country and sold to a customer in another country, and although economists differ on whether trade deficits (where the value of imports exceeds the value of exports) are necessarily bad, export figures are commonly used in assessing the economic strength of a country. A trade surplus is beneficial in increasing a country's foreign currency reserves and in creating employment for local workers in the exporting industries as well as supporting industries that provide goods and services to the exporting industries. Hence, export figures are often quoted by economists and policy-makers as an indicator of the comparative advantage of a country and its industries relative to other countries. This has been accompanied by a greater emphasis on economic analysis in cultural policy generally in many countries (Throsby, 2010).

The music industry has been similarly affected by the need to demonstrate economic value. This is despite the music industry's relatively small size compared to other industries in most countries. (In the US, the world's largest music market, it represents less than 0.1% of GDP and 0.2% of employment. Globally music consumption was only 0.06% of world GDP in 2017.) However, as Krueger (2019) has pointed out, the music industry's importance is greater than might be suggested judging purely by its economic value. As one of the main creative industries in a country, like the film and book publishing industries, the strength of the music industry exports of a country is often seen as a key indicator of the importance of the national culture on a global stage.

The popular music industry is also interesting from an economic perspective for several reasons. We can do no better than repeat the comments made by Connolly and Krueger (2006) in explaining the importance of studying the economics of the popular music industry. Firstly, popular music is an important cultural industry in its own right, which sheds light upon global and national culture. Secondly, because non-traditional economic concerns such as emotion play a significant role in the industry, the industry can provide new insights into the role of these factors in economics. Thirdly, as a "superstar" industry in which the financial rewards are heavily skewed towards a few individuals, the popular music industry provides a testing ground for some important economic theories, for example, about the relationship between financial rewards and creativity. Fourthly, as the music industry and associated media industries have been profoundly affected by several technological changes (such as radio, TV, records, cassette tapes, CDs, MP3 players and the Internet), which continue to this day, the music industry provides a unique setting to understand how rapid technological change affects an industry. Finally, the popular music industry is, by definition, very familiar to the general public and, consequently, it provides interesting examples that many people can relate to.

With respect to music exports, there is also an increased interest owing to the growth in sales of recorded music globally in developing countries, and the increase in music streaming services which promise increased global markets. According to the IFPI (2019), the global recorded music market grew by 9.7% in 2018, the fourth consecutive year of growth, fuelled mainly by rises in streaming revenues, which grew by 34.0%, more than offsetting a 10.1% decline in physical revenue and a 21.2% decline in download revenue. The growth has been strongest in developing countries, with Latin American markets showing an increase of 16.8% while markets in Asia and Australasia grew by 11.7%. Similarly, according to a report by consulting firm PricewaterhouseCoopers (PwC), the live music market was expected to show a compound annual growth rate (CAGR) of 3.33% from $21.256bn in 2018 to $25.036bn in 2023 (Chapple, 2019). There are, therefore, significant differences between markets for music worldwide. As will be explained in more detail later, although the markets for much music are global there are significant differences in local markets and an elaborate system of interconnected institutions has developed to collect and distribute income to artists and other players in the industry at global and national levels.

International music trade flows

Three main groups of industry participants can be identified in the music industry in each country: Artists (songwriters and performers), publishers and record labels, who are connected to each other in a series of contractual relationships. Although contracts are generally agreed between artists, publishers and record labels within their own country, increasingly cross-border deals are occurring, as shown in Figure 2.1, leading to a complex network of deals between parties in different countries. These complex relationships within and between countries lead to quite heterogeneous economic effects in music markets worldwide. The distribution of revenues in the global music industry varies significantly along three dimensions as shown in Figure 2.2 between countries, industry groups and

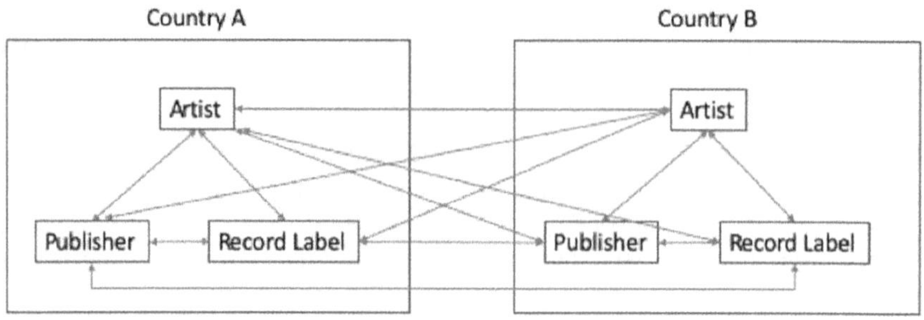

Figure 2.1 Income flows between industry actors and across countries.

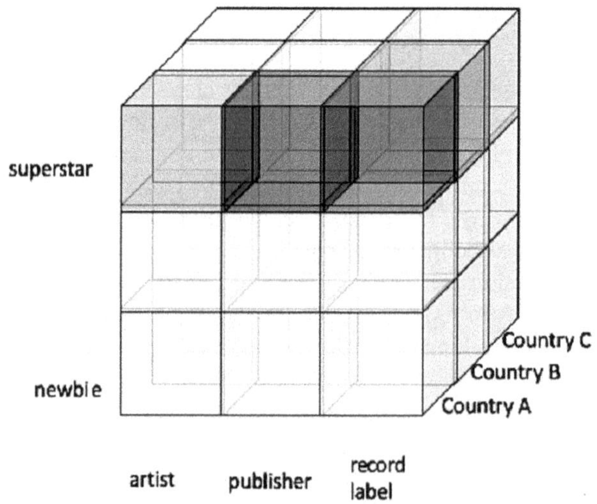

Figure 2.2 Division of music industry exports.

artists. The factors that affect the division of export income at each level are discussed in more detail below.

How large are global music exports?

The first question that we consider is how large are global music exports? The answer is not straightforward, as defining the global music industry is tricky. Most industrial classifications used by statistical agencies were designed to capture more traditional parts of the economy such as manufacturing. Music is often grouped with the visual and performing arts, making it difficult to identify a figure for music-only exports. In response, national music export agencies which are charged with increasing music exports have had to develop their own definitions of the industry.

For example, UK Music has developed a definition consisting of a core industry and a wider industry beyond. The inner core is defined by its relationship to the commercial assets of the UK music industry:

- Commercial asset 1: A musical composition and/or lyrics (the notes on a page);
- Commercial asset 2: A (master) recording of a musical composition;
- Commercial asset 3: A live musical performance;
- Commercial asset 4: An artist him- or herself (as a brand, reputation or image) (UK Music, 2017).

Thus, UK Music (2019) includes the following groups in its definition of the music industry:

- Musicians, composers, songwriters and lyricists, who create and perform the songs;
- Live music promoters and venues, who promote and provide the venues to listen to live music;
- Record companies, who record and distribute music;
- Music publishers, who publish the music written by composers, songwriters and lyricists;
- Music producers, recording studios and staff, who provide services to support musicians, record companies and others in recording music;
- Music representatives, such as collecting societies who act on behalf of the music industry;
- Music retail, including retail of musical instruments, physical music and digital music.

On the other hand, Music Finland's (2019) definition of music exports also includes sales of audio equipment and computer software. This difference in industry definitions makes it difficult to directly compare export figures across countries.

The second issue with examining music exports is defining what exports mean in the music industry. "Exports" in economics refer to the value of goods and services produced by a country in a given period and which are sold abroad, where products refer to tangible items that can be consumed and services refer to tasks provided by individuals or organisations. Traditionally, most countries have only collected trade statistics on exports of goods, for example, commodities, manufactured components and finished goods, partly owing to the difficulty in collecting statistics on services. The definition of goods includes recorded music in the form of records and CDs. However, as noted in Chapter 1 and discussed further in this chapter, as music listening has increasingly moved towards digital streaming and downloads provided by music service providers in recent years, these sales of physical goods have become less important, and increasingly much more music is being traded as a service, such as the provision of streaming or download services, which is not reflected in the figures for tangible goods. A distinction between services and goods exports is that many services that are "exported" never cross any physical boundaries. For example, a local live music event is considered as engaging in export when foreign visitors pay to attend the event even though the event is held locally, and a local musician may be engaging in export without leaving the country when a listener in another country pays to listen to a song on the Internet. Such payments are difficult for government trade agencies to track, making the collection of national and international trade statistics on music difficult.

In addition to differences in defining the scope of the industry, different methods have been used to estimate the economic value of the industry. The simplest and most common method is to take the total value of international sales or income earned by music industry participants overseas. However, this neglects the inputs required to produce the exports. A more nuanced approach that might be taken is to estimate the total contribution of the music industry to the country's gross domestic product (GDP). The GDP of a country provides a measure of the monetary value of the goods and services that country produces in a specific year and is often used by economists as a measure of the strength of the economy.

Three methods are commonly used to calculate the GDP of an economy (OECD, 2009):

(1) In the expenditure approach, a country's GDP is measured by the total expenditures that occur in a country, i.e. consumer spending plus business investment and government spending as well as its net exports (i.e. exports minus imports);
(2) With the income approach, the GDP of a country is calculated as its national income plus its indirect business taxes and depreciation, as well as its net foreign factor income (the difference between the aggregate amount that a country's citizens and companies earn abroad);
(3) A problem with both the expenditure and income approaches is avoiding double-counting the value of intermediate goods (goods and services that are used in producing other goods and services). Therefore, an alternative approach that is sometimes used is to estimate the value-added (the difference between the cost of inputs to production and the price of output for each good and service). The value-added in different sectors of the industry is summed to arrive at the total gross value added (GVA). This is the approach that has been taken by UK Music (2017).

An alternative approach has been used by the Live Music Office (2015) in Australia in estimating the value of live music to the Australian economy. Costs include the direct costs (such as costs borne by individuals in the support of live music consumption and associated activities), and indirect costs, such as the opportunity cost from investing resources in live music (i.e. the cost of foregoing alternative uses of the resources). Benefits include "changes in the states of physical, human, social and symbolic capital in individuals, firms and communities" (p. 39). Interestingly, the Live Music Office report (2015) also includes the concept of non-use value or the benefits that individuals may obtain even if they do not use a service such as:

1. Option value—reservation of the right to use the resource at some time in the future;
2. Bequest value—maintenance of a resource for future generations;
3. Existence value—the satisfaction people receive from knowing that something exists; and
4. Altruistic value—appreciation of the right of others to use the resource.

The costs and benefits-based approach will generally provide a larger figure than the conventional GDP-based approaches, but the problem in the music export context is how to determine the export component (e.g. the increase in physical, human, social or symbolic capital that results from a music export).

In addition to differences in the methodology used to estimate the value of music exports, another issue is the lack of comprehensive statistics on the music industry. As other researchers (e.g. Krueger, 2019) have noted, comprehensive financial data for the global music industry do not exist, including data on music exports, and much information (such as information on contractual arrangements) is private and only rarely disclosed. There are, therefore, few reliable studies of the size of music exports in a country for the reasons above. The most comprehensive study to date is that conducted by UK Music, which estimated the value of the UK music industry (defined as above) to be £4.4bn in 2017 and the total exports to be worth £2.5bn (UK Music, 2018). A smaller study conducted in Australia by the authors estimated the total value of exports of the three main groups in the industry (artists, publishers and record labels) to be $195m (Australia Council, 2019). This also closely matches the figure of $250m for Australian film industry exports (Screen Australia, 2016). Comparing the exports of just the three main groups of artists, publishers and record labels in Australia and in the UK, this equates to approximately 0.06% of total exports (USD 232 billion) in Australia compared with 0.36% of total exports (USD 752 billion) in the UK. This reflects the much larger value of exports from Australia from industries such as mining and agriculture as well as the stronger export power of UK musicians. (It should also be noted that the figure for Australian exports may be an underestimate as some Australian artists who have become international superstars have adopted foreign nationalities and so their earnings will be included in the export earnings for their adopted country. Notable examples include Kylie Minogue and Olivia Newton-John.)

Where is export income generated?

A second question in analysing global music exports is: Where is the income generated globally? Numerous empirical studies have been conducted to examine patterns of international trade in cultural products. Studies generally find that international media products, on the whole, tend to flow from developed countries to developing countries. Consistent with these findings, research in the recording industry shows that the global music market is dominated by the developed countries, including the USA, Germany, the UK, the Netherlands, France and Japan (Alexander, 1994; Bishop, 2005). Moon et al.'s (2010) study, based on a study of tangible music goods (e.g. records, CD, magnetic tape and other recorded media for sound) in 124 different countries, confirmed the imbalance of international music trade between a core group of countries (the USA and European countries including Germany, the UK and the Netherlands) and other countries.

Various reasons have been advanced for this unequal trade flow between countries, including the differing sizes of consumer markets and production as well as trade barriers. For example, Wildman (1995) argues that the USA's dominance may be due to the relatively large size of its media markets and more favourable policies towards commercialisation. In terms of the international music trade, countries with relatively large and wealthy domestic markets for music products have an advantage in exporting their music goods. This seems to be confirmed by our analysis of statistics on music production and consumption by country. Obtaining reliable statistics on numbers of artists and recordings by country is difficult, but *Discogs*, a website which claims to be the most comprehensive crowdsourced database of recorded music, shows the ranking of countries seen in Figure 2.3. With some notable exceptions such as China and Brazil, which are highly ranked consumer markets but not so highly ranked in terms of music production, this ranking closely matches the "top 10 music markets globally" according to the IFPI (Figure 2.4), suggesting that countries which are the largest music producers are also the largest consumers.

However, most studies have concluded that in addition to economic factors, other factors (e.g. cultural, religious, linguistic and geographical) are important in explaining and predicting international media trade patterns (Verboord and Brandellero, 2018) . This might explain why Japan, China and Brazil have large consumer markets but are not large producers, while the Netherlands has a small consumer market but is a large producer. Culture, or more precisely, language, also seems to play a role; Australia and Canada, which are both English-speaking nations, have relatively large markets (eighth and ninth largest) despite having relatively small populations. This confirms economic studies of trade that have found that the linguistic distance between countries affects bilateral trade (Hutchinson, 2005) and that linguistic barriers affect trade (Lohmann, 2011). Language is particularly important in the case of music where the international advantages of using English in songs has been a noticeable, and sometimes controversial feature, as can be seen in the number of songs in English in the Eurovision Song Contest by non-English speaking countries (Wolther, 2012) and the examples of artists from non-English speaking countries who have achieved international stardom only after singing in English, for example, the Swedish group, ABBA. There are some indications, however, that the dominance of English language in popular music is diminishing in some emerging markets (Furness, 2019). For example, Latin American markets, where most songs are in Spanish, have shown the greatest growth, with an average growth rate of 17.7% in 2017, assisted by the growth

Rank	Country	Number of releases
1	United States	55,466
2	United Kingdom	34,265
3	Germany	24,414
4	Unknown	18,673
5	Europe	13,372
6	Netherlands	11,745
7	France	11,157
8	Italy	10,300
9	Russia	9,727
10	Japan	9,530
11	Spain	6,577
12	Canada	5,905
13	Sweden	4,658
14	Australia	4,494
15	Poland	3,472
16	Belgium	3,321
17	Finland	2,666
18	Greece	2,418
19	Ukraine	2,213
20	Brazil	2,093

Figure 2.3 Ranking of countries according to number of music releases in 2018. Source: Discogs.

Ranking	Market	Retail value US $ (millions)	Physical	Digital	Performance Rights	Synchronization
1	United States	5,916.1	15%	75%	7%	3%
2	Japan	2,727.5	72%	21%	5%	1%
3	Germany	1,323.1	43%	36%	20%	1%
4	United Kingdom	1,310.7	30%	50%	18%	2%
5	France	925.1	36%	34%	27%	3%
6	South Korea	494.4	37%	59%	4%	0%
7	Canada	437.2	21%	65%	14%	1%
8	Australia	412.9	19%	68%	11%	2%
9	Brazil	295.8	5%	60%	34%	0%
10	China	292.3	3%	90%	7%	0%
11	Netherlands	269.5	22%	50%	27%	0%
12	Italy	247.9	39%	36%	22%	3%
13	Spain	205.8	26%	49%	24%	2%
14	Sweden	199.5	10%	72%	17%	1%
15	Norway	139.0	9%	71%	19%	1%
16	Denmark	137.9	7%	56%	36%	1%
17	Switzerland	137.8	27%	52%	21%	0%
18	Mexico	137.0	15%	79%	4%	1%
19	India	130.7	7%	78%	9%	6%
20	Argentina	130.0	8%	31%	60%	1%
	Global total	17,270	n/a	n/a	n/a	n/a

Figure 2.4 Major music markets by retail sales, 2018. Source: IFPI, 2019, p. 13.

in music streaming services, which have grown by 48.9% and brought Latin American music to the attention of a wider global audience (MIDEM, 2019).

Apart from South Korea, which has achieved great export success with K-pop (Kelley, 2019), Asian countries have been less successful internationally. In Asia, the local markets are still dominated by local artists singing in the local language. In Japan, it is estimated that over 90% of all live and recording revenues come from domestic acts (Soundcharts, 2019a). One reason for the low penetration of foreign artists may be the huge popularity of karaoke bars which generate a substantial part of the music publishing business in Japan and where most songs are sung in Japanese as most Japanese still do not feel comfortable singing in foreign languages (Soundcharts, 2019a). Another possible factor is the strong reliance of musicians on fan clubs, which tend to favour local artists and where only Korean K-pop bands singing in Japanese appear to have made much impact. In China, NetEase, a major Chinese website which aims to provide a streaming platform for local and international artists in China, estimates that 30% of all activities on the platform is linked to foreign artists (Soundcharts, 2019b). However, in the live music sector, only 11.4% of revenues in 2017 came from international acts. In India, international acts accounted for only 20% of all music consumption in the country in 2018, and music consumption is strongly linked to soundtracks of Bollywood films, sung in the local language, which are estimated to account for 80% of all recorded music income in India (Soundcharts, 2019c).

How is export income distributed within the industry?

A third important question to consider is how export income is distributed within the industry, including remuneration to creators of music. As one Australian music industry interviewee commented,

> We can all be exporting until the cows come home and supporting things locally, but if creators' rights are curtailed there's no way to monetise any of that.
>
> (Interview 23, 2018)

In most countries, the music industry consists of the following industry groups: Composers and performers, music publishers, recording industry, concert promoters and collecting societies. These groups are connected to each other in a complicated web of institutionalised relationships which date back hundreds of years.

As Kretschmer (2000) shows, the intellectual property rights system for the music industry has roots dating back to the 1500s when intellectual property regimes were first developed in Europe to protect the rights of authors and composers. However, within Anglo-Saxon legal traditions, the Act of Anne (1709) is generally regarded as the origin of modern copyright legislation. Music was not protected under the Act of Anne, as it was considered unnecessary since most musical works would not remain in fashion that long; the most important source of income for composers in that period derived from commissions and performances of new compositions. As it was difficult for composers or publishers to know when and where a certain tune had been played and so claim royalties, it was not until the mid-19th century, with the foundation of the "Agence Central" in France (which later became the *Societe des auteurs, compositeurs et editeurs de musique* (SACEM)), that it became possible for composers and publishers to monitor the usage of their music and to recover royalties. Since then the SACEM model has become the international model for collecting music royalties.

Three types of rights can generally be attached to a musical work: Reproduction, distribution and performance rights (Citi GPS, 2018). Reproduction rights refer to rights to reproduce the work or prepare derivative work. Originally this referred to the right to reproduce sheet music, but nowadays, mechanical rights, i.e. the rights to reproduce music by mechanical means, are more significant economically. Mechanical rights became necessary following the development of mechanical music-playing devices in the 19th century. Up until that time, music had always been performed live. With the development of mechanical music-playing devices such as pianolas and gramophones, copyright needed to be extended to cover music reproduction by mechanical means (Kretschmer, 2000). Today mechanical rights have been extended to cover any physical medium such as vinyl or CDs as well as music that is downloaded or used in an interactive streaming service (e.g. Spotify, Apple).

Following the introduction of mechanical rights, performance rights were introduced in the UK in the *Dramatic Copyright Act* of 1833, enabling opera librettists and composers to claim a performing right for the public performance of their work in theatres, and were extended in the *Literary Copyright Act* of 1842 to non-dramatic musical works (Sevill, 1999). In other countries, similar Acts have been passed to compensate songwriters and composers. Contemporary performing rights cover musical performances via radio and television broadcasts or the Internet (including interactive Internet services such as Spotify, and non-interactive Internet services such as Pandora). With the advent of recorded music, performance rights also include the rights related to the public performance of master recordings (often called phonographic or neighbouring rights). A growing subtype of performance rights is synchronisation (synch) rights when music is used in a film, TV show or a commercial. Synchronisation requires two licences, for the phonographic (performance on the master recording) and the performance rights (composer's royalty.)

Distribution rights authorise a copyright holder to distribute copies or recordings of a copyrighted work to the public. When music was recorded mainly on physical media such as vinyl records, distribution rights referred to the rights to distribute those recordings, and many specialist music distribution companies existed to provide a service to distribute a record label's products to retailers. With the decline in physical record sales, these companies have largely been replaced by digital distribution companies (also known as digital aggregators) such as CD Baby, Tune Core and LANDR that distribute artists' music to digital music providers such as Spotify, Apple Music and Amazon.

Although the three rights for music exist in most countries, there are different models for royalty collection in different countries. As it is difficult for individual artists to monitor the usage of their work and collect payments from users, collection societies have developed to manage the licensing to third parties and payments to artists. This makes it easier for artists and/or the copyright owners to license their work. It also makes it easier for those third parties to obtain a licence to use copyright material (Arts Law Center Australia, 2011). In some countries, mechanical and performing rights are administered jointly by the same collecting society, for example, SACEM (France), SABAM (Belgium), GEMA (Germany), JASRAC (Japan) and APRA-AMCOS (Australia). In other countries, different rights are collected by different societies. For example, in the UK, mechanical rights used to be collected by the Mechanical-Copyright Protection Society (MCPS) and performing rights used to be collected by the Performing Right Society (PRS), but they have now been merged to form PRS for Music, while Phonographic Performance Limited (PPL) licenses radio stations, TV broadcasters and digital media services to play recorded music in the UK. In Australia the Phonographic Performance Company of Australia (PPCA) collects royalties for the performance on a sound recording and music video. In the US, ASCAP, BMI and SESAC collect royalties for performing rights, Harry Fox Agency (HFA) collects royalties for mechanical rights, AARC collects royalties for home recording, rental and lending rights, while Sound Exchange collects royalties for online distribution rights. Each collecting society is responsible for collecting the royalties for its members in its home country and collects international royalties for its members through reciprocal agreements with other collecting societies. Thus, an artist can collect worldwide royalties through several different ways, through their local collection societies, local labels and publishers, and foreign sub-offices of their labels, publishers, sub-publishers and licensees.

There is limited information on how export revenues are distributed between the different industry groups in most countries. The most comprehensive study to date is the study by UK Music (2019). For comparison, we estimated the income distribution in the Australian music industry. This was not as comprehensive as the UK Music study as we were unable to survey all groups in the industry, but based on the combination of estimates provided by APRA AMCOS, AMPAL, ARIA, AIR and data from our surveys of Australian music industry participants, we estimated that 61% of Australian music exports in 2018 was earned by artists, 20% by music publishers and 19% by record labels. Figure 2.5 shows a simplified diagram of the key income flows between different individuals and organisations in the Australian music industry.

In comparison, according to UK Music (2017), the breakdown of music exports in the United Kingdom by the same subsectors is 47% artists, 32% publishers and 21% record labels. Although the figures differ between the countries, generally it appears that most export income is earned by artists as a whole, followed by publishers and record labels. However, it should be noted that this does not consider the number of people in each group. While artists as a whole earn the greatest share of export income, it is shared among a large number of artists, whereas

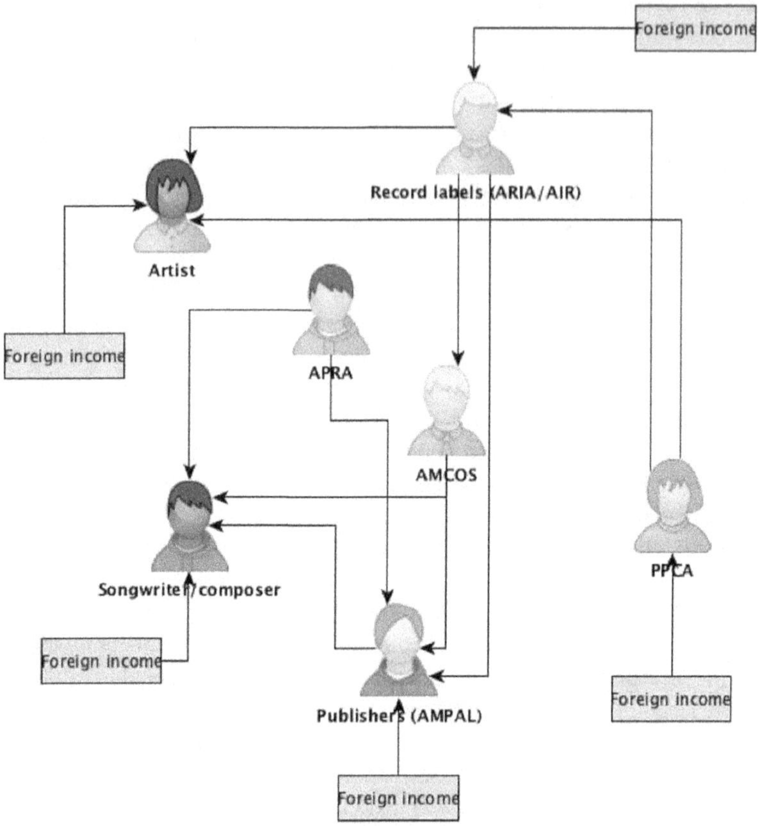

Figure 2.5 Foreign income flows in the Australian music industry.

publisher income is shared among a relatively small number of publishers in each country (Figure 2.6).

The above estimates for exports per artist in each country vary considerably according to the estimate of the number of artists used, highlighting again the difficulty in identifying the number of artists and the difficulty in comparing across countries given the different definitions of who is considered an artist. For example, Throsby and Petetskaya (2017) adjust the official employment figures for artists in the Australian Census based on their survey that accounts for artists who work professionally as artists but did not list music as their main job in the census. Similarly, UK Music (2014) relies on information from sources such as accountants to augment the official employment statistics from the Office of National Statistics based on the United Kingdom Census. However, it appears that in both Australia and in the UK, publishers earn the most individually, followed by record labels and artists, reflecting the small number of publishers relative to record labels and artists.

Australia

	Number of artists, publishers or record labels	Value of Exports	Exports per artist, publisher or record label (AUD)
Artists	7,100 (Dept. of Jobs and Small Businesses estimate)	$119m	$27,408
	15,400 (Throsby and Petetskaya, 2017)	$119m	$12,636
Publishers	59	$38m	$644,000
Record labels	175	$37.5m	$214,286

United Kingdom

	Number of artists, publishers or record labels	Value of Exports	Exports per artist, publisher or record label (GBP)
Artists	50,000 (ONS estimate)	£926m	£18,500
	89,800 (UK Music estimate)	£926m	£10,300
Publishers	200	£519m	£2,600,000
Record labels	800+	£332m	£420,000

Figure 2.6 Exports per artist/publisher/record label in Australia and the United Kingdom, 2016–2017. Source: Compiled from Australian Music Survey and UK Music Report.

How is export income distributed among artists?

As well as considering how export revenues are distributed among groups in the industry, another question which needs to be considered is how export income is distributed among artists. There is scant information available on export income of musicians. However, based on our survey of musicians in Australia, 25 out of the 63 (that is, 40%) artists in our survey reported foreign income or expenses. This closely matches the 39% figure reported by Throsby and Petetskaya (2017, p. 59) of musicians who had a foreign engagement in the previous five years. A comparison of income shows that exporters have a significantly greater average domestic income compared with non-exporters (A$28,545 vs. A$15,147), and exporters on average have a higher total profit (from both domestic and foreign sources)—approximately twice as much (A$10,710 vs. A$5,315).

However, it should be noted that simply taking average incomes may be misleading, as income distribution among artists is highly skewed, with a few artists earning significantly greater amounts than the rest. Krueger (2005, p. 15) found that the top 5% of revenue generators earned 62% of concert revenue in 1982; and this figure increased to 84% in 2003. Similar skewed distributions have been observed in other creative industries such as film (Rosen, 1981) and patent royalties (Scherer et al., 2000), suggesting that this is a general pattern for creative industries. To quote Menger (2015, p. 148):

> creativity has the flavour of a scarce ability much sought after: people well endowed with it come to be rewarded with earnings and prestige disproportionately higher than what the presumable underlying distribution of skills and abilities would command among the workforce concerned.

Krueger (2005) also hypothesised that the increasing skew in concert incomes is because of lower returns from recorded music. In the past, when greater concert attendance translated into greater artists' record sales, artists had an incentive to price their tickets below the profit-maximising price for concerts alone in order to gain more record sales. Now that new technology allows many potential customers to listen to recorded music without purchasing a recording, concerts are being priced more like single-market monopoly products, allowing successful artists to charge much higher prices to attend concerts. These findings seem to confirm the advice of the late David Bowie to musicians that "Music itself is going to become like running water or electricity … You'd better be prepared for doing a lot of touring because that's really the only unique situation that's going to be left" (quoted by Pareles, 2002).

Figures on live music performances globally are difficult to obtain but we found in our survey of Australian musicians that despite the increase in digital music sales, live music and streaming are the two most important income streams in the music industry. Despite the increase in digital music sales, live music still makes the largest contribution to the total foreign income of artists, accounting for approximately 49% of total foreign income. This is compared to 37% from song-writing and performance royalties and 17% from other sources such as merchandising and sponsorship. The Citi GPS (2018, p. 63) report on the music industry in the United States reported similar findings. Of the four major income sources of artists (concerts, music publishing, music platforms and music sales), concerts contributed most to the growth in artists' income since 2002. Similarly, Krueger and Zhen (2018) report that musicians in the US earn most of their income from performing at live events.

The skew also appears to be greater when export earnings are considered. To further investigate the distribution of export revenues, we fitted a Pareto distribution to the royalty data of Australian artists following De Vany (2006). [A Pareto distribution is characterised by thick tails (on one or both sides) and is often used in order to examine income distributions (Wold and Whittle, 1957).] Both the domestic and foreign royalty income distributions (Figures 2.7 and 2.8 respectively) follow a Pareto distribution in which most people earn relatively little and a few people earn the majority of income in the industry. An analysis of domestic earnings from royalties indicates that 10% of artists contribute approximately 90% of total domestic earnings from royalties. The results are highly consistent with those of Pitt (2010) who found a similar pattern in music royalty distribution in the US. However, our analysis of international earnings from royalties shows that the skew is even greater in international royalty earnings, where approximately 10% of artists earn approximately 97% of the total international royalty earnings. This would be consistent with the view that the most successful artists are able to earn disproportionately greater international incomes.

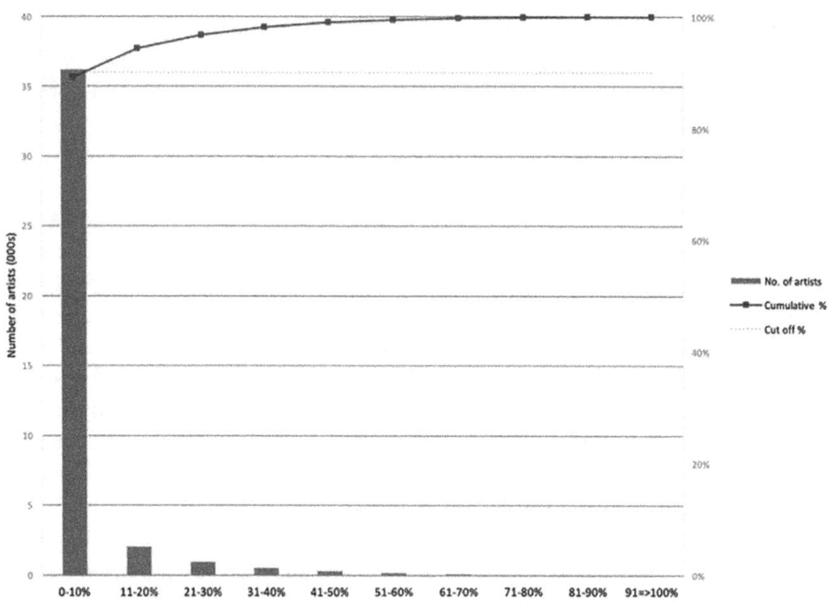

Figure 2.7 Distribution of domestic royalties. Source: Authors' analysis based on aggregate figures supplied by APRA AMCOS.

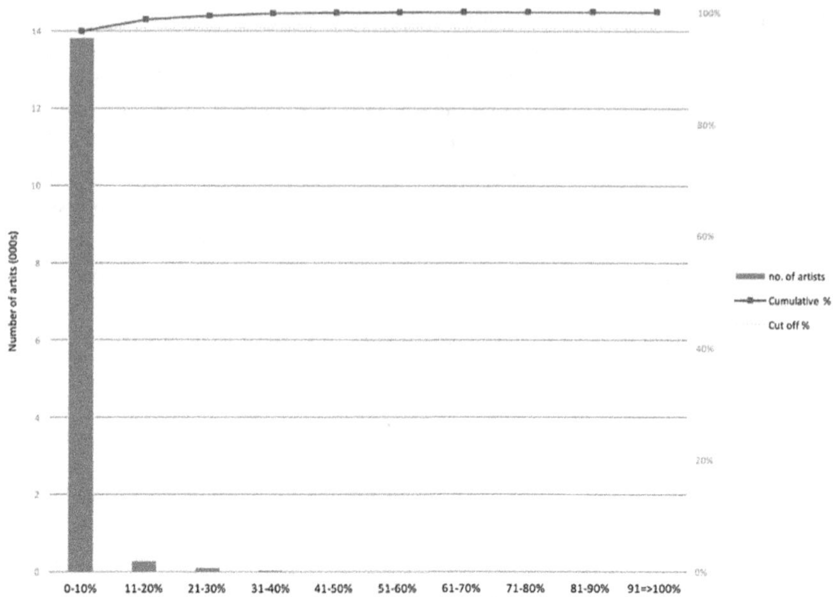

Figure 2.8 Distribution of international royalties. Source: Authors' analysis based on aggregate figures supplied by APRA AMCOS.

This "superstar" phenomenon in music (and other creative industries) where some performers earn a disproportionate share of the income can be explained by a combination of non-substitutability of goods, economies of scale and bandwagon effects (Krueger, 2005). *Substitutability* in economics refers to the ability of two or more goods to be substituted for one another. In other words, if one good is not available, the willingness of a consumer to purchase another good which provides a similar benefit is measured. Krueger (2019) argues that in the case of music, substitutability is generally low since consumers have strong preferences for a particular performer which may not be satisfied by other performers. This leads to a near-monopolistic position in those markets, which enables superstars to command high prices for their performances as they cannot be substituted by other performers. The second factor identified by Krueger is *economies of scale*, i.e. economies that are generated owing to the scale of a particular activity. For example, the costs of production of a particular good or service may be lowered through a greater volume of production. In the case of superstar performers, the large number of their followers might enable them to spread the costs of distributing their song over a larger number of people, enabling them to reach a large number of people at a relatively low cost. The third factor is the *bandwagon effect*. In economics, this refers to a phenomenon whereby the rate of consumption of a product or service increases the more that it has already been bought or adopted by others (Leibenstein, 1950). In the case of music superstars, a bandwagon effect may be observed where the rate of increase in popularity of a performer or song increases with the number of listeners as more people are attracted to songs that other people listen to, regardless of the inherent merits of the song. Such bandwagon effects may be accentuated in global markets by global social network platforms such as Facebook and Twitter, which enable listeners to connect with other listeners worldwide. Xu and Fu (2014) found a global bandwagon effect in Hollywood movies where movies that had been successful at the box office in the US were more likely to be adopted in other countries.

Labour markets for musicians

The superstar effect also has some interesting effects in labour markets for musicians. Firstly, it results in what Frank and Cook (2010) call "winner-take-all" in labour markets, in which a few artists will capture most of the market while the rest struggle to make a living. This seems to be confirmed by data on the jobs and incomes of most musicians. At the lower end of the income scale, several studies have found that artists come out at the top of the list of occupations whose practitioners hold multiple jobs (Menger, 2015, p. 151). Throsby and Zednik (2011) found that the labour market profiles of many artists are characterised by multiple job-holding. They identify three types of jobs that artists engage in, corresponding to three separate labour markets: The market for their creative work (including time spent on all preparation, practice, rehearsal, research related to their creative work, etc.), the market for arts-related work that is not part of their core creative output but that uses their artistic skills in areas such as teaching in their art form and the non-arts labour market (such as working as a taxi driver or a waiter in a restaurant). Throsby (1994) argued that the labour markets for artists do not conform to conventional theories and suggested the following artist-specific model. If the alternative consists of spending time in artistic or non-artistic jobs, when relative wages increase for non-artistic jobs, individuals spend less time on the latter activity, since they have obtained the level of earnings that they need in order to pursue what they consider as their main job.

Our study also highlighted another feature of jobs in the music industry. Fifty percent of Australian musicians in our survey reported having more than one music-related role in the industry, with some holding four or five roles in the music industry, for example, an artist who is also a manager, a record producer and a publisher (Figure 2.9). Although based on a relatively small sample size of 60, our survey suggests that holding multiple roles appears to be associated with high export incomes. The two individuals with the highest foreign incomes (above A$20,000 p.a.) also held multiple roles in the industry. Which one leads to the other is unclear.

Barriers to foreign market entry for artists

Some indication of the challenges for artists in competing in international markets can be gleaned from international music charts. Two of the best known are

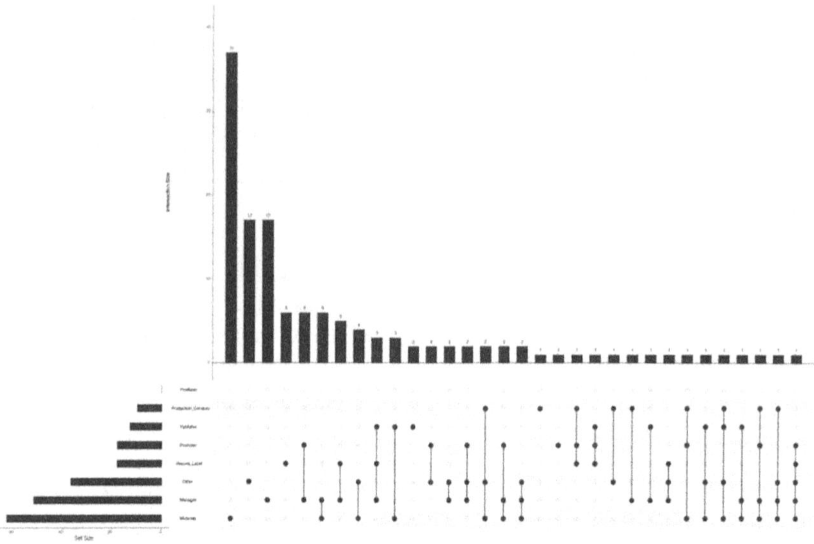

Figure 2.9 Music roles held by artists. Source: Australian Music Industry Exports Survey.

	2018	2017	2016	2015	2014	2013	2012	2011	2010	2009
US	81	77	91	85	89	93	90	93	96	99
UK	8	10	3	6	3	2	4	2		
Canada	8	6	2	2		2	2	2		1
Australia	1		1	1	3		1		1	1
Barbados				1	1	1	1	1	1	
Other	3	5								
France		2	1	1			1	1	1	
Sweden			1	1	3					
Spain					1			1	1	
Denmark			1	1						
Ireland		1		1						
South Korea						1	1			
Norway						1				

Figure 2.10 Appearances in United States Billboard Top 100 Songs by country of lead artist 2009–2018. Source: Compiled from Billboards Charts.

the *Billboard* Top 100 and the Official UK Top 100 charts. *Billboard* magazine monitors the relative popularity of songs and albums in the United States and elsewhere on a weekly and yearly basis. The charts can be ranked according to sales, streams or airplay, and for main song charts such as the Hot 100, all three pools of data are used. The Official UK Top 100 chart is a similar chart compiled by the Official Charts Company, based on official sales of downloads, CD, vinyl, audio and video streams in the UK. Figures 2.10 and 2.11 show the appearances by

	2018	2017	2016	2015	2014	2013	2012	2011	2010	2009
US	44	37	51	54	47	51	55	72	54	42
UK	39	42	29	27	29	36	32	25	40	50
Canada	5	6	7	5	5		3		2	2
Sweden		3	2	4	3	5	1			1
Australia	5	1	1	2	4		1	1	2	
France	1	1	4	1	3	1	2	2		1
Barbados			1	1	1	1	2		1	2
Netherlands	1	1			3	2				
Germany			1	1	2					1
Norway	1	1	2	1						
Denmark		1	2							
Ireland		1		1	1					
Spain				1	1				1	1
Jamaica		1		1			1			
New Zealand		1			1	1				
Puerto Rico	1	1								
Russia	1	1								
South Korea						1	1			
Austria						1				
Belgium				1						
Colombia		1								
Finland		1								
Israel	1									
Lithuania	1									
Romania							1			

Figure 2.11 Appearances in United Kingdom Music Charts Top 100 by country of artist 2009–2018. Source: Compiled from Officialcharts.

country of the lead artist according to Billboard and the Official Charts Company respectively over the period 2009–2018.

What is immediately noticeable is the greater presence of home country (US) artists in the Billboard Top 100 compared with home country (UK) artists in the UK Official Charts. US artists also feature as frequently or more frequently compared with UK artists in the UK charts. This is consistent with the export figures at the country level showing the dominance of the US in music exports and confirms the strong advantages held by US artists in international music export markets. Also noticeable is the relatively low number of appearances of artists from non-English speaking nations such as France and Germany which have relatively large domestic markets, confirming the importance of language in music exports.

The value of music awards

A unique characteristic of cultural industries is that participants are often highly motivated by intrinsic rewards. For example, recent research has highlighted the value of awards. As Frey and Gallus (2017) have noted, awards provide several benefits for recipients that are not always monetary, for example, a sign of appreciation, recognition, a special relationship to the donor and, most importantly, social status. The best-known awards in the English-speaking music industry are the Grammys and BRIT Awards. The Grammys (a term derived from "gramophone") was introduced in 1959 and was modelled on award ceremonies in other media industries (viz. the Oscars for motion pictures, the Tonys for theatre and the Emmy Awards for television). The BRIT Awards are the equivalent awards for the British Phonographic Industry.

As well as symbolic value, awards can also have economic value. Anand and Watson (2004) found that emerging artists who won Grammy Awards subsequently sold more records. As a result of the intense media exposure, industry-level attention and interlocking of retailers promoting the Grammy Awards, they found that the Best New Artist winners outsell nominees by nearly a million units per year. However, beyond the economic value, rewards also serve to structure the cultural field. For example, winning a Grammy or BRIT Award can be seen as a signal by the industry that the artist is one that is worth investing in, leading in turn to greater consumer access to the works of winning artists.

For comparison, we show the Grammy and BRIT Awards won by Australian artists over the period 2015–2018 (Figures 2.12 and 2.13 respectively). What is immediately noticeable is the much larger number of BRIT Awards to Australian artists compared with Grammy Awards. This might be due to the much larger number of US artists compared with UK artists and so higher competition in the US compared with the UK. However, it is also interesting that the Grammy Awards are all for international artists whereas none of the BRIT Awards is an award that is specifically for international artists, suggesting perhaps differences in the way international artists are viewed in the US vs. the UK. It is also noticeable that all the Australian artists who have won a Grammy or BRIT Award are all artists who have previously established some success domestically in Australia, suggesting that domestic success is a requisite for international success.

Impact of digital streaming and download services

A key driver in the global development of the music industry historically has been technology (Laing, 2009), so it is impossible to discuss current and future developments in the industry without some discussion of the impact of technological changes. Historically, the commercial music industry developed as a way to find commercial opportunities for music as a product and or service, in which technological innovation has always been a key driver. Before the invention of the printing press, musicians earned income either through patronage or by getting paid for performances. With the development of the printing press and copyright, a music publishing industry began to develop. Sheet music along with the popularity of the piano enabled the publishing industry to dominate the music industry until the 20th century. However, arguably the largest technological impact on the music industry was the gramophone in 1877, which enabled musical performances to be recorded and played back. This allowed the voices of singers to be recorded and distributed worldwide, thus enabling the rise of global superstars such as Enrico Caruso and Dame Nellie Melba as well as the rise of global recording companies such as EMI (Gronow and Saunio, 1998).

2018
Best Contemporary Christian Music Performance/Song: The Hillsong Worship – *What A Beautiful Name* (WINNER)
2017
Best Pop Vocal Album: Sia – *This Is Acting*
Best Pop Duo/Group Performance: Sia – *Cheap Thrills (feat. Sean Paul)*
Best Dance Recording: Flume – *Never Be Like You (feat. Kai)*
Best Dance/Electronic Album: Flume – *Skin* (WINNER)
Best Country Solo Performance: Keith Urban – *Blue Ain't Your Color*
Best Country Song: Keith Urban – *Blue Ain't Your Color*
Best Country Album: Keith Urban – *Ripcord*
Best Contemporary Christian Album: Hillsong Young & Free – *Youth Revival [Live]*
2016
Best New Artist: Courtney Barnett
Best Alternate Album: Tame Impala
Best R&B Performance: Hiatus Kaiyote – *Breathing Underwater*
Best Country Solo Performance: Keith Urban
2015
Best New Artist: Iggy Azalea
Record of the Year: *Fancy It* – Iggy Azalea
Best Pop Duo/Group Performance: *Fancy* – Iggy Azalea ft. Charli XCX
Record of the Year: *Chandelier* – Sia
Song of the Year: *Chandelier* – Sia
Best Music Video: *Chandelier* – Sia
Best solo Pop Performance: *Chandelier* – Sia
Best Country Duo: *Raise 'Em Up* – Keith Urban ft. Eric Church
Best Country Solo: *Cop Car* – Keith Urban

Figure 2.12 Grammy nominations of Australian artists 2015–2018. Source: Sounds Australia Annual Reports.

2017
International Female Solo Artist: Sia
International Group: Nick Cave & the Bad Seeds
2016
International Female Solo Artist: Courtney Barnett
International Group: Tame Impala (WINNER)
2015
International Female Solo Artist: Sia
International Group: 5 Seconds of Summer

Figure 2.13 BRIT Award nominations of Australian artists 2015–2017. Source: Sounds Australia Annual Reports.

The global expansion of the industry continued following the development of radio and television technologies in the first half of the 20th century which enabled music to be broadcast worldwide, further widening the reach of recorded music. However, the most significant developments in the industry in more recent years have been due to developments in digital technologies which enable music to be stored and distributed in digital format, beginning with the development of compact discs (CDs) in the 1980s which enabled hi-fi quality audio to be stored on laser-readable disks in digital format, followed by the development of the MP3 standard which enables audio files to be compressed to a small size and played on mobile devices.

The development of the World Wide Web and music file-sharing platforms such as Napster which enabled MP3 files to be shared on the Internet further expanded the digital marketplace for music and revolutionised traditional value chains in the industry (Baym, 2007; Bockstedt et al., 2006). While Napster and similar file-sharing services greatly assisted the global reach of music, from the point of view of the music industry, they had a downside in that they made it easier to share pirated music, thus depriving recording companies and artists of revenues.

In response, various legal music download services entered the market in the early 2000s, the most notable example being Apple's iTunes and, more recently, the development of streaming technology, which has now become the most common means of listening to music. Instead of downloading a copy of the audio file to the listener's computer, to be stored and subsequently played by a media player software, streaming works by downloading small chunks of the audio file in a continuous stream, storing the data in a buffer and then playing each chunk of the music after a slight delay. This provides the owners of the recording more control over the song as the listener does not have a copy of the entire song at any one time.

The increase in digital music has led to a reconfiguration of the traditional music industry value chain (Figure 2.14) in which technology-based companies in music downloads and streaming like Spotify, Apple, YouTube, Google, etc., are emerging as the new dominating force of the music industry. One commentator even went as far as to say they are now the most important players in the industry:

> You'll read a lot in the news about YouTube, Spotify, Apple, Soundcloud, Microsoft, Google, Samsung, Nokia and other tech giants "negotiating with the music industry" over one thing or another. But that's not actually what's happening. Those guys ARE the music industry. They're negotiating with record companies. Where "the music industry" is located has shifted again.
>
> (Dubber, 2014)

Streaming technology has transformed music distribution from a model based on ownership to a model based on access. Whereas in the last century the "ownership

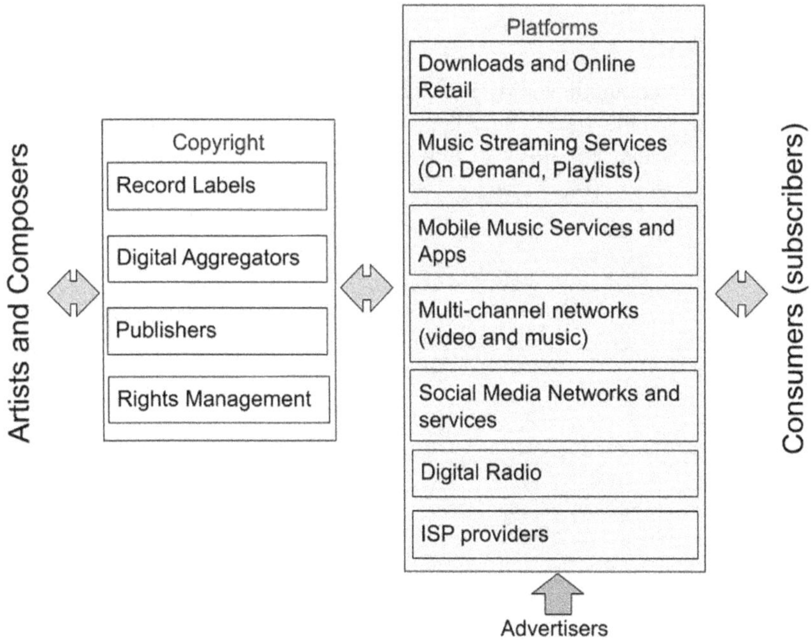

Figure 2.14 The digital music value chain. Source: Adapted from Siemer and Associates 2013.

model" has dominated with the sale of recorded music in formats like CDs, records, sheet music and tape where the user paid for and owned the music, in this century the model has switched to an "access model", where users pay for access to streaming and online subscription-based music services like Spotify, Apple Music and Deezer (Wikström, 2012).

Spotify

Spotify was founded as a start-up in 2006 in Stockholm, Sweden, as a legitimate online music-sharing platform alternative to platforms that offered pirated music. After initial problems convincing record labels to share content, in return for the record labels receiving a 20% stake, Spotify was launched in 2008. A decade later, Spotify went public in April 2018, with a market capitalisation of $26.5 billion after the first day of trading. Spotify is now the world's biggest music streaming platform by the number of subscribers. Spotify is now available in 79 countries. Europe and North America are the largest and second-largest markets for both users and subscribers. However, the fastest growth is occurring in less-established markets. Spotify users from the rest of the world increased by nearly 150%, while growth in Latin America was around 83% in 2016 and 2017 (Figure 2.15). Interestingly, although listeners are widely dispersed, revenues are still highly concentrated, with the US and UK accounting for 48.1% of total revenues (Figure 2.16).

Apple Music

Spotify's main competitor is Apple Music, a music and video streaming service developed by Apple Inc., which launched on 30 June 2015, in 100 countries worldwide. Users select music to stream to their device on-demand, or they can

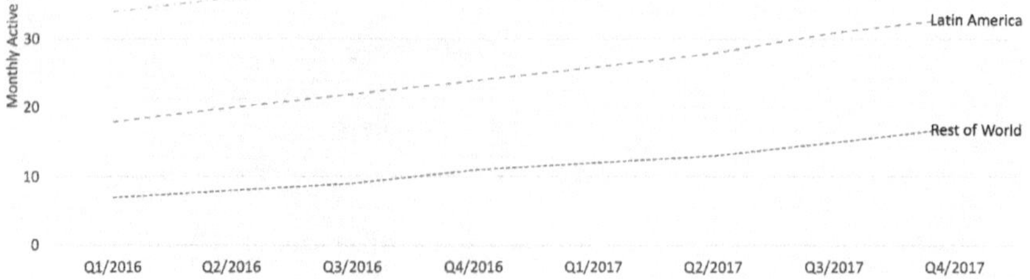

Figure 2.15 Spotify user growth by region, 2016–2017. Source: Business Wire.

Nine months ended September 30, 2019

	€ millions	
United States	1,837	37.4%
United Kingdom	527	10.7%
Luxembourg	2	0.0%
Other	2,542	51.8%
	4,909	

Figure 2.16 Spotify revenues by region, 2019. Source: Spotify.

listen to existing, curated playlists. In 2016, Apple Music introduced video in 2016 and with the support of its parent company, Apple, Apple Music was able to reach 10 million paying subscribers by 2016, just six months after its launch. By July 2018, Apple Music had overtaken Spotify in terms of paying users in the United States, and the worldwide customer base has increased to 60 million as of June 2019.

YouTube

YouTube was launched as a video-sharing service in 2005 and quickly became a source for user-uploaded music videos such that YouTube launched a dedicated music app in October 2015. In May 2018, YouTube Music introduced a separate subscription service (positioned as a more direct competitor to Apple Music and Spotify), offering ad-free and background/audio-only streaming, and downloading for offline playback, for music content on YouTube. The service is available in 69 countries at the time of writing, the top countries for YouTube usage being the USA, Brazil, Russia, Japan and the UK, followed closely by Germany, France, Mexico and Turkey (Figure 2.17). However, as YouTube also offers a free ad-paid service, its reach is much larger and it has become a medium for budding artists to reach a global audience, particularly in Asia (Kist and Verboord, 2018).

Impact on record labels

Streaming has also forced record companies to change their business models. No longer must a label own the master tapes of a work. Instead, labels act like venture capitalists, who provide musicians with financial resources as well as a network of support to record tracks and distribute them to audiences. Digital streaming

Rank	Country	YouTube Users (Millions)
1	United States	167.4
2	Brazil	69.5
3	Russia	47.4
4	Japan	46.8
5	India	21.2
6	United Kingdom	35.6
7	Germany	31.3
8	France	30.3
9	Mexico	29.4
10	Turkey	28.8

Figure 2.17 Number of YouTube users by country. Source: Migiro, 2018.

technologies have also created new competitors to traditional record companies who are increasingly finding themselves in competition with independent labels, managers, artists and streaming services. The WINTEL Worldwide Independent Market Report 2018 found that the global market share of independent labels increased to 40% in 2017 (WINTEL, 2018). In other cases, managers are acting as record labels. As one interviewee commented:

> A lot of managers are actually acting as the labels in a global context. The manager's the one who's actually doing the strategy and using all of the intel in order to plan international global release, sometimes simultaneously.
>
> (Interviewee 18, 2018)

Impact on managers and artists

It is not just record companies' business models that have changed as a result of digital technology. The roles of managers and artists have also changed. In other cases, with access to online fans, networks and new income streams like crowdfunding and Patreon, some artists are choosing to completely bypass the traditional record companies altogether and distribute their music themselves.

Digitisation of music has also changed the traditional approach which involved the development of a local and/or national base only after which export opportunities are sought. For some of the artists and managers, this is still considered a viable strategy. But in a digital environment, accessing international markets from the outset is proving just as viable. Digital streaming and downloads not only provide copyright owners with much more accurate and up-to-date information on global sales but enable new ways to reach the audience. For instance, one manager interviewed during this study discussed how the ability to monitor sales in real-time has enabled more targeted marketing strategies in key export markets.

> We have access in real-time to how strategies are working. Where our markets are. We can, literally, see the time of day that people in Germany are watching … And how old they are and where they are. All that kind of information. Which is wonderful. So, intensive marketing strategies. It comes in handy when you're touring. Got to have your presence. So, in terms of effort in formulating that plan, it's critically important … You can, literally, show people, this is the artist's audience. We really want to help you, have you come in to help us grow it. Even before that, you can detect where that is. You can build a team, using that data. Everything's super transparent … once you've got those, you can use it to plot your tour route. Once you've plotted that tour route, you can use it to market and sell those tickets. Also, your App. So you research within those markets where you know that the audience is. And you can tailor your marketing strategies to be able to have maximum impact. So, it's pretty wild. In terms of tech stuff, I've just done a big session on AI/VR. I kind of wonder how much more that this is going to be the thing. And when we're going to chip into the next lot.
>
> (Interview 8, 2018)

According to our survey of artists and managers, social media is now the most used tool in music exports, closely followed by the use of publicists, streaming and attending trade and showcase events (Figure 2.18).

As a result, increasingly artists and managers are looking at global markets from the outset, including the timing of releases in different formats in different markets.

> Technology, social media, all of those things, they're obviously central to the ecosystem that we operate in … Now we plot global plans for our artists, from the beginning we utilise global strategies to create marketing for even the first song of the first artists, a new artists that we are releasing, it's less geographically bound than it has ever been.
>
> (Interview 6, 2019)

> Streaming has been an even bigger game-changer obviously because the process of how people set up to release music has changed so much. You know, even five to eight years ago the standard process was single, album, single,

Marketing tool used	Importance
Social media	93%
Radio/TV/magazines	58%
Publicists	76%
Streaming	71%
Playlists	56%
Digital analytics	40%
Tastemakers	36%
Trade and showcase events	71%
Blogs/direct marketing	40%
Merchandising	24%
Premium products (for example, apps, etc.)	4%

Figure 2.18 Marketing tools used. Source: Export strategies survey.

> single, album or single, single, maybe one more single, album. And then you go away for two, three years and try and record another opus and, you know, start the process again. Whereas nowadays you can drop a single every second day, you can drop a single, then an album, then an EP, then another album all in one year.
>
> (Interview 1, 2018)

The value of YouTube and Spotify exposure

YouTube offers another route to stardom for performers with no obvious connections to the industry, a notable example being the singer Justin Bieber. After posting a video of himself on YouTube as a teenager, Bieber was discovered by music manager Scooter Braun. Braun secured a record deal for Bieber with RBMG Records in 2008, resulting in an EP recording, *My World,* in late 2009. This was followed by several other hits. Bieber's first studio album, *My World 2.0* in 2010, debuted at number one in several countries. His album *Under the Mistletoe* (2011) debuted at number one on the Billboard 200. His third studio album, *Believe* (2012), generated the single "Boyfriend", which debuted at number one in Canada and the UK and Mexico and number seven in Japan.

The wide global reach of YouTube is reflected in our sample of Australian artists. YouTube searches for Australian artists in the ARIA Top 50 Australian

Artists Singles Chart in the period 2018–2019 were compared using Google Trends. Google Trends does not provide figures on the actual number of searches. However, it does provide figures relative to the number of users in each country. While this does not provide an accurate measure of YouTube music downloads, the comparison indicates the countries where Australian artists generate relatively high interest among YouTube viewers. The top 30 countries are shown in Figure 2.19. When the size of the country (measured by the number of Google searches) is taken into account, some countries increase in importance. For example, Belgium, Ireland, Canada, South Africa, Slovakia, Hungary and Denmark show the highest interest in the top Australian artists relative to other countries, with the exception of Australia. These countries show greater interest than the United States in top Australian artists. It should also be noted that the ranking of countries by YouTube searches varies considerably by artists. For instance, the top three countries searching for AC/DC are Hungary, Slovenia and Slovakia (Figure 2.20). On the other hand, the top three countries for Sia are Albania, Slovakia and France (Figure 2.21). These are also not the same as countries ranked according to the number of Spotify listeners. Figures 2.22 and 2.23 show the top 20 countries for AC/DC and Sia according to Spotify listeners. In both cases, the

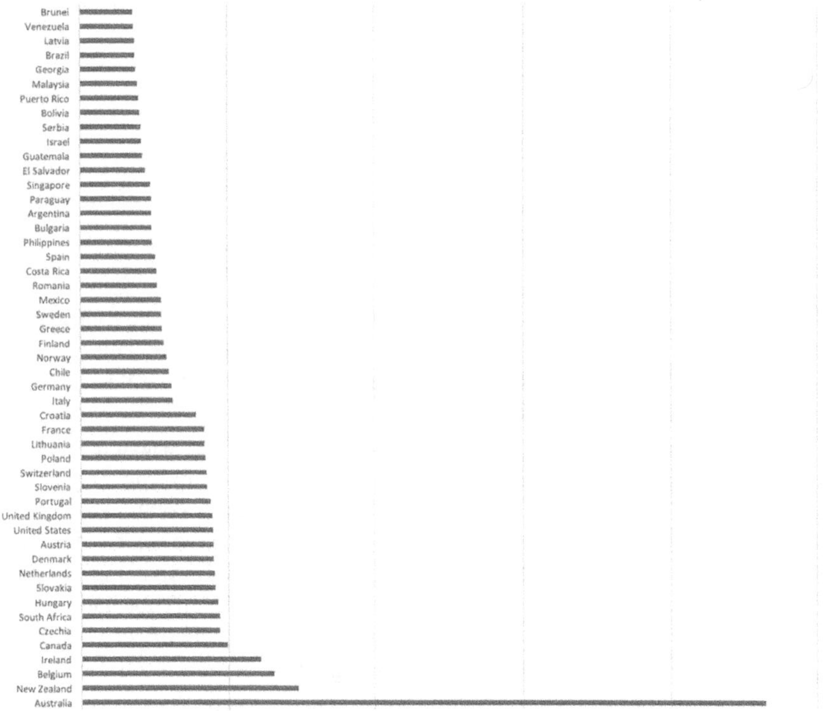

Figure 2.19 Top 30 countries for YouTube searches for ARIA Top 50 artists—18 February 2018–18 February 2019. Source: Google Trends.

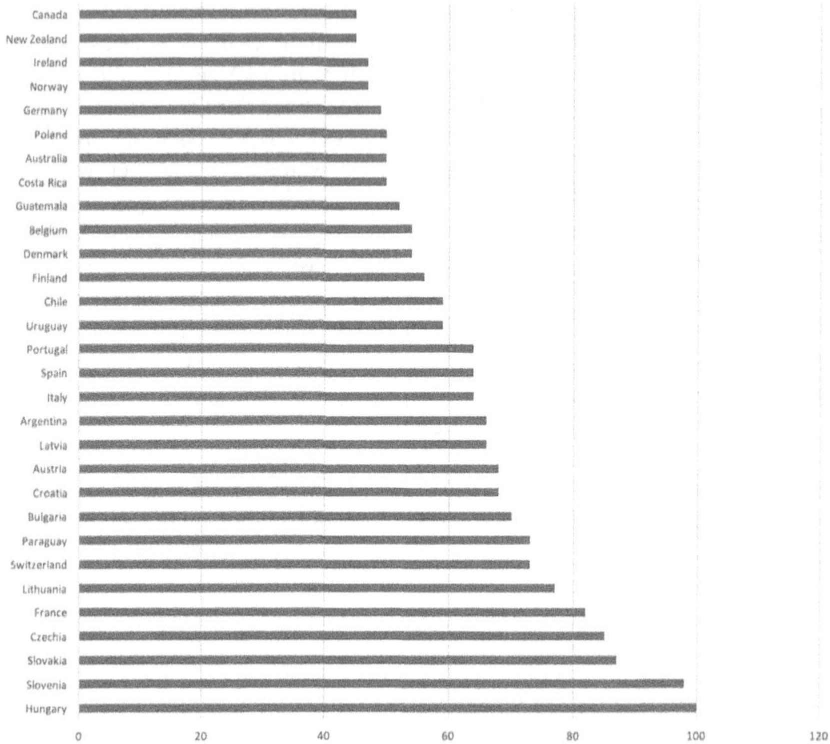

Figure 2.20 Top 30 countries for YouTube searches for AC/DC—18 February 2018–18 February 2019. Source: Google Trends.

United States, Mexico and Brazil show the largest audience figures, followed by Australia in the case of AC/DC and Germany in the case of Sia. This suggests that artists may have a global YouTube presence over and above that which is indicated by Spotify streams, which requires a subscription.

While there appears to be no direct link between YouTube usage and export income, a high level of YouTube views and Spotify streams may be a necessary condition for high percentages of export income. [A necessary condition is a condition in the absence of which the outcome will not occur. These can be identified using necessary conditions analysis (NCA) (Dul, 2016).] As shown in Figures 2.24 and 2.25, the level of export income is zero at low levels of YouTube and Spotify streaming and export income only shows up at higher levels of YouTube and Spotify streaming. In other words, while having a high level of YouTube views and Spotify downloads does not automatically lead to high percentages of export income by musicians, it is necessary to have a sufficiently high level of YouTube views and Spotify downloads in order to be in a position to achieve high percentages of export income.

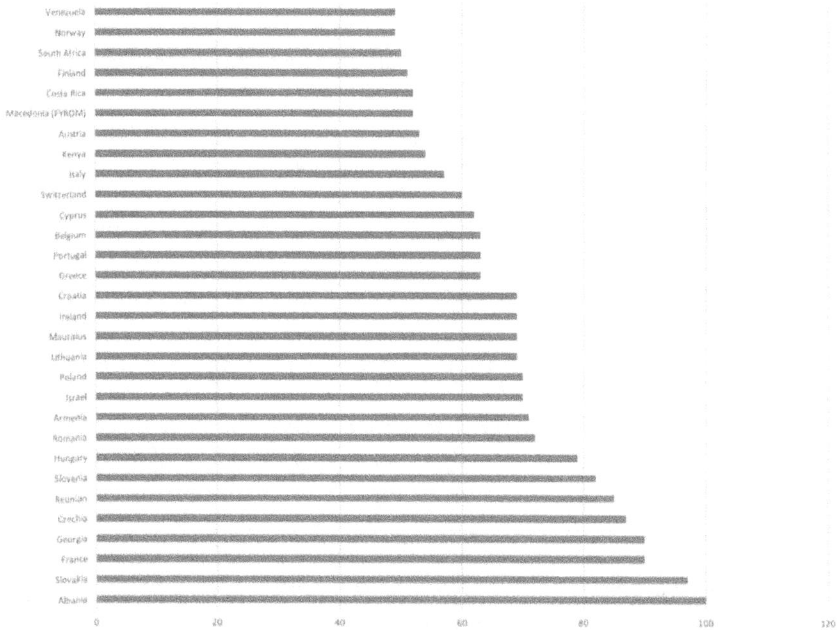

Figure 2.21 Top 30 countries for YouTube searches for Sia—18 February 2018–18 February 2019. Source: Google Trends.

Increasing importance of playlists

Given the global scale of streaming services, curators of playlists on streaming services have become very influential in recent years and have become a target for exporters. As one Australian industry interviewee commented,

> If you're in this territory, we need to ensure that there's an opportunity for Australians to be heard.
>
> (Interview 23, 2018)

> We remind them of the fact they're the ones wanting to form relationships with local artists because they know from their own research and data that you've got to connect to the local community. No-one wants to just hear endless US hip-hop for instance; you've got to tailor to markets.
>
> (Interview 23, 2018)

Impact on other sectors

The growth in music streaming and download services has also had a knock-on effect on suppliers of audio equipment for home studios, which were worth more

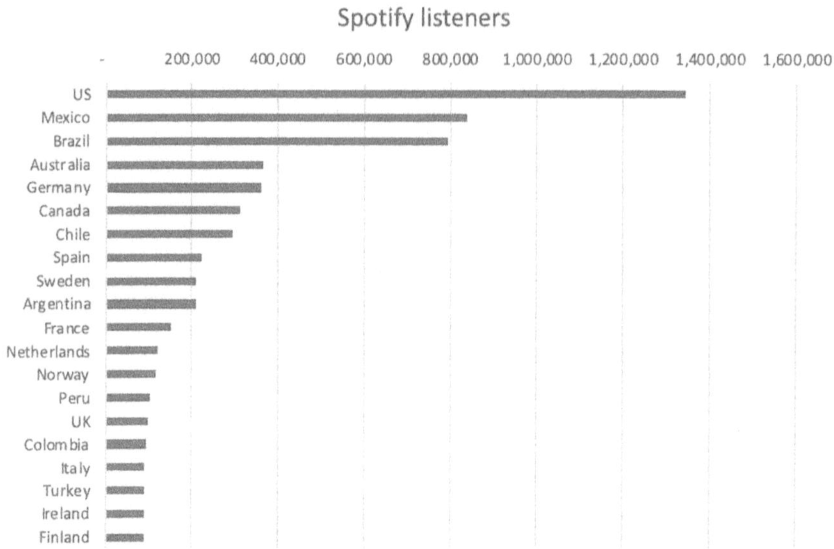

Figure 2.22 Top 20 countries for AC/DC according to Spotify listeners—7 December 2018–6 December 2019. Source: Soundcharts.

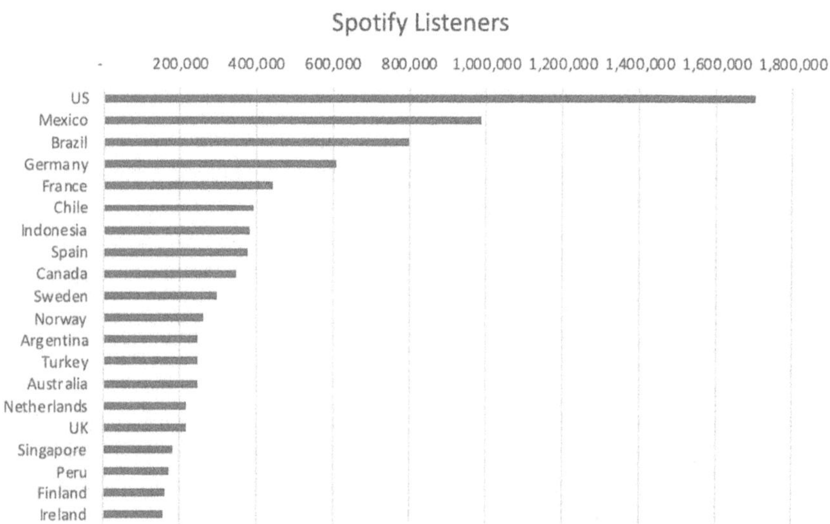

Figure 2.23 Top 20 countries for Sia according to Spotify listeners—7 December 2018–6 December 2019. Source: Soundcharts.

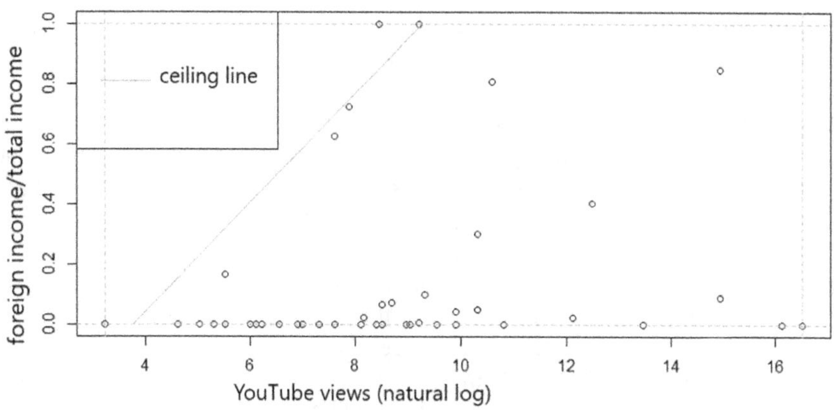

Figure 2.24 Necessary conditions analysis plot of the logarithm of YouTube views against foreign income/total income. Source: Australian Music Industry Exports Survey.

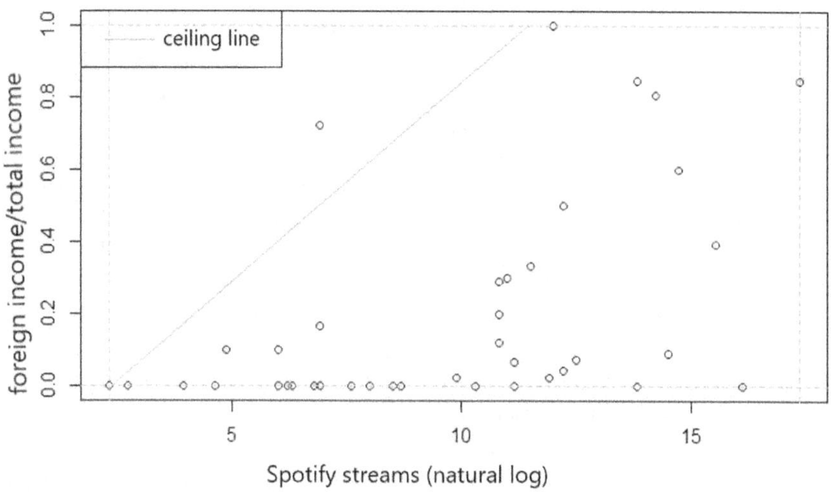

Figure 2.25 Necessary conditions analysis plot of the logarithm of Spotify streams against foreign income/total income. Source: Australian Music Industry Exports Survey.

than $US 1.2 billion in 2018 (Futuresource Consulting, 2019). In Finland, this even exceeds the sales from other music-related sectors. Music Finland estimated that audio equipment companies, as well as start-up companies using music technology, accounted for as much as 54% of Finland's music-related export revenue in 2017 (Music Finland, 2019).

Millennials and emerging markets

What is noticeable in the geographic distribution of all these streaming services is that there are some large markets which do not figure significantly in the top countries according to recorded music sales reported by the IFPI. For example, Russia and Turkey are the 3rd and 9th ranked countries by YouTube usage but do not appear at all among the top 20 countries by record sales. This suggests that digital music and video streaming services are capturing large segments of markets worldwide that are not being captured by traditional recorded music.

One of the reasons for the significant shift to online music is the difference in behavioural characteristics of millennial audiences compared to previous audiences. Balda and Mora (2011) summarise the qualities of millennials to include the following traits: The need for experience, trust, mistrust of organisations, able to multitask with ease, sharing, familiarity with interactive technologies, socially conscious about global issues. Within this context, it is understandable why the rise of the YouTube star phenomenon and their dedicated audiences is seriously challenging the more established approach to music export. As Arnold (2017) writes: "millennials in large part don't watch TV and don't care much what mainstream celebrities have to say about products or services. They trust their social media tribes and peer-to-peer advice the most". This approach can be seen with Australian millennial artists L-FRESH The LION and Troye Sivan, who are bypassing all conventional marketing strategies. Using their own YouTube channels and social media networks to engage with their audiences, they have reached epic stardom independently (see Chapter 4).

The rapid growth of social media usage, particularly among millennials, can also be attributed in no small part to mobile technologies that enable music to be played on mobile devices such as mobile phones. As such mobile devices are more affordable and easily accessible worldwide compared with desktop and laptop computing devices, streaming also increases the potential worldwide audience who can access the song, such as less-developed countries, which are the fastest-growing music markets. This has created new opportunities for new music streaming providers, and in many emerging markets, local streaming services are also increasingly emerging as significant players. An example is the Chinese market, where the music industry is growing at a rapid rate, in the past two years moving from 12th to 7th position in the IFPI global recording rankings, largely on the back of digital streaming (Soundcharts, 2019a). Other examples are Yandex Music and Zvuk in Russia, Gaana and JioSaavn Music in India, Melon in Korea, BoomPlay Music in Africa and Anghami in the Middle East and North Africa. Established streaming services from developed countries such as Spotify, Apple and YouTube Music have also been targeting emerging markets but the different nature of the markets has hindered their uptake while creating opportunities for local players. For example, in China, the market growth has been driven by local streaming platforms such as KuGou, QQ Music, KuWo and NetEase Cloud Music, helped by the banning of global Internet players such as Google and Facebook by the Chinese government (Soundcharts, 2019b). However, the uptake of music streaming differs across countries. In Japan, while physical sales have been declining for the last eight years, streaming has failed to penetrate the Japanese market like it has done in Western markets, owing to a lack of local content on streaming markets and a preference of many Japanese consumers for other platforms such as video-on-demand and physical CDs (Soundcharts, 2019a).

Impact on international royalty collection

In addition to music streaming technology, which is changing the recording and distribution of songs, another digital technology, blockchain, is also potentially likely to affect another part of the industry value chain, i.e. the collection of revenues from music. As noted above, copyright owners and performers receive payments for the playing of recorded and live music overseas through an international system of collecting societies.

With the significant increase in the playing of digital music worldwide, the complexity of the current system has come under increasing scrutiny, and the possibility of simpler and more efficient systems for administering the royalties from digital music has been proposed. According to some music industry commentators, "there has been only a partial implementation of digital technologies in the music industry, creating a tremendously mismatched ecosystem in which we have surface-level, profit-generating elements without the proper digital infrastructure to support them" (Rethink Music, 2015). Pentland, Werner and Bishop (2018) predict that blockchain and AI are the next major technological advances in global networks and that the combination of blockchain and AI technology could offer powerful solutions to many unsolved issues around copyright and rights management by supporting a new infrastructure to support the new digitised and globalised industry.

Royalties can take years to reach the bank accounts of rights holders, sometimes funds are paid to the wrong parties or are tied up as the rightful owner cannot be determined and, when the rights owner eventually receives the funds, he/she may find the amounts substantially reduced owing to the administrative fees charged by the various collecting societies through which the funds need to be channelled (Rethink Music, 2015). A technology which promises to overcome such problems is blockchain technology. Originally developed in 2008 as the technology supporting the digital currency Bitcoin (Nakamoto, 2008), blockchain is a decentralised, peer-to-peer (P2P) network that acts as a distributive ledger which records transactions among parties. All transactions carried out in the network are encrypted and broadcast to the entire network, thus enabling both security and transparency. As the system operates through a decentralised, global network of servers, such a technology, if widely adopted, would obviously greatly simplify the process for rights owners to receive funds from anywhere around the world and eliminate the need for many local performing rights organisations and, according to some commentators, possibly even other intermediaries such as record labels, by enabling rights owners to directly receive payment from consumers (Heap, 2017). However, at the time of writing, existing players in the music industry have shown reluctance to adopt blockchain technology, and the technology faces considerable barriers in gaining widespread adoption (Mire, 2018).

For example, as Baym et al. (2019) discuss, a standardised system for digital music like ISBN in books is required to support the foundation of digital music. Until the music industry can create standardised metadata and a system that can incorporate copyright issues of ownership and contractual requirement, a global database supported by a protocol such as blockchain will not work in practice. Some moves towards this vision have been seen, for example in the "Open Music Initiative for royalty sharing across the music industry" (Pentland et al., 2018). However, there have been many previous attempts to create some kind of centralised universal database (Baym et al., 2019) which have all failed owing to the highly complex labyrinth of micropayments, copyright law, trade agreements, non-disclosure agreements, contracts and royalties, so it remains to be seen if this utopian vision can be realised.

Future developments

The full potential of digitisation has yet to be realised, and more changes can be expected in the music industry. Emerging technologies such as semantic technology, AI, Internet of Things (IoT), wearables and interactive technologies are enabling new experiences in music such as personification and context-based cultural forms. There are many new approaches to how musicians and the industry are designing and producing music products based on these new technologies. New formats are being released and prototyped around collaboration and interaction with audiences using mobile apps, virtual reality albums, 360 videos, gesture-based products, controllers and wearables like brain interface controllers. New start-ups and businesses are rapidly emerging. Examples include machine-learning analytics platforms, audience experience works, and blockchain-enabled "collectables" (Wang, 2020). Based on the examples of previous technologies, how these new technologies develop and are adopted globally will also impact global music consumption and music exports.

Conclusion

This chapter has examined the scale and scope of music exports, how exports in the music industry are distributed at different levels and the key factors determining distribution at each level. As we have discussed, it is difficult to compare industry figures across countries because of a lack of data, compounded by the lack of agreement over the industry definition and difficulties in collecting data. However, the importance of the music industry is greater than might be suggested by export figures alone. Music is often seen as one of the key indicators of a nation's culture and so its cultural value far outweighs its economic value. The balance between the economic and cultural value is, therefore, one of the key issues for many nations in developing a national music export policy.

Despite the rapid technological changes in the industry, changes in the industry structure and institutions such as copyright have lagged behind. In developed countries, although new players such as music streaming services have appeared, they have not completely displaced the role of publishers and record labels. However, in some developing countries, for example, China, the rapid growth of music streaming, combined with political or cultural barriers for foreign companies, has created a new industry and opened up opportunities for new local companies to dominate the market. Therefore, the economic effects of music streaming may vary considerably by country or region.

Despite the claim by some that the technological changes would lead to a "flatter world" (Friedman, 2006), a large imbalance in the global trade of music-related products and services remains. There is also clearly a strong effect of linguistic distance, evident in the bias in the US, UK and Australian markets for artists from English-speaking countries. However, the dominance of English-language songs seems to be diminishing in some fast-growing markets in Latin America and Asia where growth has been mainly driven by local artists singing in the local language. This has implications for artists seeking to exploit these new growth markets. For example, a key decision would be whether or not to release a version of the song in the local language.

Similarly, an imbalance is also evident at the individual level, where our analysis of Australian artists' income shows that export income is highly skewed, with a small number of superstars earning a disproportionately high level of the industry exports, despite the hope by some that new technologies such as the Internet would give new independent artists more power and "level the playing field" (Hracs, 2012; Bernardo and Martin, 2014). This "superstar" effect has previously been observed in domestic markets, but it appears to be even stronger when export income is considered. On the other hand, for non-superstar artists, it is common for artists to hold multiple jobs to support their music careers. To reach the level to be significant superstar exporters, therefore, is not easy and often requires significant personal sacrifices.

It is also evident that although new mobile Internet music streaming services have now taken over physical recording as the main source of revenues in the industry, effects on different parts of the industry value chain are varied. While digital streaming has made physical distribution companies largely obsolete and led to the rise of new players such as Spotify and Apple Music, the often predicted rise of self-publishing by artists at the expense of record labels does not seem have happened, although some reports (WINTEL, 2018) suggest an increase of independent labels at the expense of the major record labels. It is also clear that live music remains a significant source of income for musicians, even in export markets where it might be expected that digital streaming would reduce the "tyranny of distance". What seems to have occurred is that while digital music has become more commonplace, it has become less profitable, increasing the importance of live performance as a source of artists' income. At the same time, global music streaming has opened up new markets for some artists, who have reached large audiences in geographically distant and dispersed markets.

These factors also have implications for music export policy, including how new technologies change existing industry structures and business models in the music industry, how artists balance their multiple roles in their career and government policies for music export. These debates are discussed further in later chapters.

References

Alexander, P.J. (1994). New technology and market structure: evidence from the music recording industry. *Journal of Cultural Economics* vol. 18, no. 2, pp. 113–123.

Arnold, A. (2017). Why YouTube stars influence millennials more than traditional celebrities. *Forbes*. https://www.forbes.com/sites/under30network/2017/06/20/why-youtube-stars-influence-millennials-more-than-traditional-celebrities/#7d338fce48c6.

Arts Law Centre of Australia (2011). Managing your copyright by joining a collecting society. *Arts Law Website*. https://www.artslaw.com.au/images/uploads/Collecting_societies.pdf

Anand, N. & Watson, M.R. (2004). Tournament rituals in the evolution of fields: the case of the grammy awards. *Academy of Management Journal* vol. 47, pp. 59–80.

Balda, J. B., & Mora, F. (2011). Adapting leadership theory and practice for the networked, millennial generation. *Journal of Leadership Studies*, *5*(3), 13–24.

Baym, N.K. (2007). The new shape of online community: the example of Swedish independent music fandom. *First Monday* vol. 12, no. 8, 6 August. https://firstmonday.org/ojs/index.php/fm/article/view/1978

Baym, N.K, Swartz, L. & Alarcon, A. (2019). Convening technologies: blockchain and the music industry. *International Journal of Communications* vol. 13, pp. 402–421.

Bernardo, F. & Martins, L.G. (2014). Disintermediation effects on independent approaches to music business. *International Journal of Music Business Research* vol. 3, no. 2, pp. 7–27.

Bishop, J. (2005). Building international empires of sound: concentrations of power and property in the "Global" music market. *Popular Music and Society* vol. 28, no. 4, pp. 443–471.

Bockstedt, C., Kauffman, R.J. & Riggins, F.J. (2006). The move to artist-led on-line music distribution: a theory-based assessment and prospects for structural changes in the digital music market. *International Journal of Electronic Commerce* vol. 10, no. 3, pp. 7–38.

Chapple, J. (2019). Global live music ticket sales to top $25bn. *IQ*, 23 September. https://iq-mag.net/2019/09/global-live-music-ticket-sales-top-25bn-pwc-outlook-2019/#.X2hgFy8RoUt

Citi GPS (2018). *Putting the Band Together: Remastering the World of Music*. https://www.citivelocity.com/citigps/music-industry/

Connolly, M. & Krueger, A.B. (2006). Rockonomics: the economics of popular music. In V.A. Ginsburg & D. Throsby (eds.) *Handbook of the Economics of Art and Culture*, Volume 1. Amsterdam: Elsevier North-Holland, pp. 667–719.

De Vany, A. (2006). The movies. In V.A. Ginsburg & D. Throsby (eds.) *Handbook of the Economics of Art and Culture*, Volume 1. Amsterdam: Elsevier North-Holland, pp. 615–665.

Dubber, A. (2014). Technology IS the music industry. *MIDEM Blog*, 20 August. http://blog.midem.com/2014/08/andrex-dubber-technology-music-industry/

Dul, J. (2016). Necessary condition analysis (NCA) logic and methodology of "Necessary but Not Sufficient" causality. *Organizational Research Methods* vol. 19, no. 1, pp. 10–52.

Frank, R.H. & Cook, P.J. (2010). *The Winner-Take-All Society: Why the Few at the Top Get So Much More Than the Rest of Us*. New York: Random House.

Frey, B.S. & Gallus, J. (2017). Towards an economics of awards. *Journal of Economic Surveys* vol. 31, no. 1, pp. 190–200.

Friedman, T.L. (2006). *The World Is Flat: The Globalized World in the Twenty-First Century*. London: Penguin.

Furness, H. (2019). English losing crown as unofficial language of pop, as streaming sees Asian and Latin American music climb global chart. *The Telegraph*. https://www.telegraph.co.uk/news/2019/04/02/english-losing-crown-unofficial-language-pop-streaming-sees/

Futuresource Consulting (2019). Home studio and pro studio markets exceed $1.2 billion combined revenue, on track for sustained growth. *audioXpress*, 5 March. https://audioxpress.com/news/home-studio-and-pro-studio-markets-exceed-1-2-billion-in-combined-revenue-on-track-for-sustained-growth

Gronow, P. & Saunio, I. (1998). *An International History of the Recording Industry*. Translated by Christopher Moseley. London: Cassell.

Heap, I. (2017). Blockchain could help musicians make money again. *Harvard Business Review*, 5 June. https://hbr.org/2017/06/blockchain-could-help-musicians-make-money-again

Hracs, B.J. (2012). A creative industry in transition: the rise of digitally driven independent music production. *Growth and Change* vol. 43, no. 3, pp. 442–461.

Hutchinson, W.K. (2005). "Linguistic distance" as a determinant of bilateral trade. *Southern Economic Journal* vol. 72, no. 1, pp. 1–15.

IFPI (2019). *Global Music Report*. https://www.ifpi.org/ifpi-global-music-report-2019/

Kelley, C. (2019). K-Pop is more global than ever, helping South Korea's music market grow into a 'Power Player'. *Forbes*. https://www.forbes.com/sites/caitlinkelley/2019/04/03/kpop-global-bts-blackpink-grow/?sh=2ab5989124e2

Kist, J. & Verboord, M. (2018). The diffusion of music via youtube: comparing asian and European music video charts. In N. Kawashima & H.K. Lee (eds.) *Asian Cultural Flows. Cultural Policies, Creative Industries, and Media Consumers*. Singapore: Springer, pp. 197–214.

Kretschmer, M. (2000). Intellectual property in music: a historical analysis of rhetoric and institutional practices. *Studies in Cultures, Organizations and Societies* vol. 6, no. 2, pp. 197–223.

Krueger, A.B. (2005). The economics of real superstars: the market for rock concerts in the material world. *Journal of Labor Economics* vol. 23, no. 1, pp. 1–30.

Krueger, A.B. (2019). *Rockonomics: What the Music Industry Can Teach Us About Economics (and Our Future)*. London: John Murray.

Krueger, A.B. & Zhen, Y. (2018). Inaugural music industry research association (MIRA) survey of musicians. https://themira.org/mira-survey-of-musicians

Laing, D. (2009). World music and the global music industry. *Popular Music History* vol. 3, no. 3, pp. 213–231.

Leibenstein, H. (1950). Bandwagon, snob, and Veblen effects in the theory of consumers' demand. *Quarterly Journal of Economics* vol. 64, no. 2, pp. 183–207.

Live Music Office (2015). The economic and cultural value of live music in Australia 2014. https://livemusicoffice.com.au/research/#/research/utasresearch/executive-summary/

Lohmann, J. (2011). Do language barriers affect trade? *Economics Letters* vol. 110, no. 2, pp. 159–162.

Menger, P.M. (2015). The market for creative labour. In C. Jones, M. Lorenzen & J. Sapsed (eds.) *The Oxford Handbook of Creative Industries*. New York: Oxford University Press, pp. 148–170.

MIDEM (2019). How Latin American music is redefining the global music market – exclusive white paper. 9 May. https://insights.midem.com/international/latin-american-music-renaissance/

Migiro, G. (2018). Which countries watch the most youtube? https://www.worldatlas.com/articles/which-countries-watch-the-most-YouTube.html

Mire, S. (2018). Blockchain for social media: 11 possible use cases. *Disruptor Daily*. https://www.disruptordaily.com/blockchain-use-cases-social-media/

Moon, S.I., Barnett, G.A. & Lim, Y.S. (2010). The structure of international music flows using network analysis. *New Media & Society* vol. 12, no. 3, pp. 379–399.

Music Finland (2019). Growth in music exports reflects the industry's changing revenue models. 9 September. https://musicfinland.com/en/news/growth-in-music-exports-reflects-the-industrys-changing-revenue-models

Nakamoto, S. (2008). Bitcoin: a peer-to-peer electronic cash system. https://bitcoin.org/bitcoin.pdf

OECD (2009). Gross domestic product: national accounts at a glance. http://www.oecd.org/berlin/44681640.pdf

Pareles, J. (2002). David Bowie, 21st-century entrepreneur. *The New York Times*, 9 June. https://www.nytimes.com/2002/06/09/arts/david-bowie-21st-century-entrepreneur.html

Pentland, A., Werner, J. & Bishop, C. (2018). Blockchain+AI+Human. *Open Music*. https://open-music.org/blog/2018/10/3/blockchainaihuman-whitepaper-and-invitation

Rethink Music. (2015). Fair music: Transparency and payment flows in the music industry. *Rethink Music*. http://www.rethink-music.com/research/fair-music-transparency-and-payment-flows-in-the-music-industry

Pitt, I.L. (2010). Superstar effects on royalty income in a performing rights organization. *Journal of Cultural Economics* vol. 34, no. 3, pp. 219–236.

Rosen, S. (1981). The economics of superstars. *American Economic Review*, vol. 71, no. 5, pp. 845–858.

Scherer, F.M., Harhoff, D. & Kukies, J. (2000). Uncertainty and the size distribution of rewards from innovation. *Journal of Evolutionary Economics* vol. 10, pp. 175–200.

Seville, C. (1999). *Literary Copyright Reform in Early Victorian England: The Framing of the 1842 Copyright Act*. Cambridge: Cambridge University Press.

Soundcharts (2019a). Music market focus: Japan [latest stats, trends, & analysis]. 7 January. https://soundcharts.com/blog/japan-music-market-overview

Soundcharts (2019b). *Music Market Focus: China Streaming and Recording Business (1/2)*. 21 May. https://soundcharts.com/blog/chinese-recording-market-streaming

Soundcharts (2019c). Indian music industry analysis: streaming, live industry, bollywood, and more. 22 August. https://soundcharts.com/blog/india-music-market-overview

Throsby, D. (1994). A work-preference model of artist behaviour. In A. Peacock & I. Rizzo (eds.) *Cultural Economics And Cultural Policies*. Dordrecht: Springer, pp. 69–80.

Throsby, D. (2010). *The Economics of Cultural Policy*. Cambridge: Cambridge University Press.

Throsby, D. & Petetskaya, K. (2017). *Making Art Work*. Australia Council for the Arts. https://www.australiacouncil.gov.au/research/making-art-work/

Throsby, D. & Zednik, A. (2011). Multiple job-holding and artistic careers: some empirical evidence. *Cultural Trends* vol. 20, no. 1, pp. 9–24.

UK Music (2017). *Measuring Music Report*. https://www.ukmusic.org/assets/general/Measuring_Music_2017_Final.pdf

UK Music (2019). *Music by Numbers*. https://www.ukmusic.org/assets/general/Music_By_Numbers_2019_Report.pdf

Verboord, M. & Brandellero, A. (2018). The globalization of popular music, 1960–2010: a multilevel analysis of music flows. *Communication Research* vol. 45, no. 4, pp. 603–627.

Wang, A.X. (2020). Meet a tech accelerator's 10 newest bets on the future of music. *Rolling Stone*, 2 February. https://www.rollingstone.com/pro/news/techstars-music-startup-accelerator-2020-946426/?fbclid=IwAR3RIY1DAa83dhniXALISJQigUn_MtUFp8lAvKiSGxYJ5R0kVzm2hQerkhU

Wikström, P. (2012). A typology of music distribution models. *International Journal of Music Business Research* vol. 1, no. 1, p. 7.

Wildman, S. (1995). Trade liberalization and policy for media industries: a theoretical examination of media flows. *Canadian Journal of Communication* vol. 20, no. 3. https://doi.org/10.22230/cjc.1995v20n3a884

WINTEL (2018). *Worldwide Independent Market Report*. http://winformusic.org/files/WINTEL%202018/WINTEL%202018.pdf

Wold, H.O. & Whittle, P. (1957). A model explaining the Pareto distribution of wealth. *Econometrica* vol. 25, no. 4, pp. 591–595.

Wolther, I. (2012). More than just music: the seven dimensions of the Eurovision song contest. *Popular Music* vol. 31, no. 1, pp. 165–171.

Xu, X. & Fu, W.W. (2014). Aggregate bandwagon effects of popularity information on audiences' movie selections. *Journal of Media Economics* vol. 27, no. 4, pp. 215–233.

3 Music entrepreneurs and export readiness

As discussed in Chapter 1, the artist manager is a collaborative partner in the music export process. In this chapter, we examine the music export activities from the artist-manager's perspectives, and their roles in moving towards export readiness. All managers are music entrepreneurs and do most of the heavy lifting when it comes to negotiations, deals and seeking out opportunities. Here we discuss how export readiness can involve a multitude of factors, the combination of which does not guarantee success. If the artist's creative content is the fabric underpinning and continually regenerating the music industry, the manager performs a range of crucial duties that hopefully ensure export readiness.

Entrepreneurial activities operate at various stages of a musician's career. We partially draw upon and have adapted the Next Big Sound's "Artist social stages" in defining our own different stages that also account for assessments of popularity and success (Next Big Sound, 2016). The managers interviewed for this research represent each of the stages. Each stage is defined by the size of audience demographic, sales and digital footprints evident through social media analytics. They are: **Emerging**, where artists are at the beginning or in the early career stages of developing audiences/sales/profile; **Breakthrough**, where artists are at a tipping point, developing threshold opportunities in audiences/sales/profile; **Established**, where artists have an evident and sustainable record in developing audiences/sales/profile; and **Epic**, where artists have an evident and substantial audience/sales/profile.

These stages are not fixed sequentially. For example, a transition from Emerging to Established status is very possible. They also may reflect older place-based hierarchies (local, national, regional or global profiles), where (for example) "Established" or "Epic" artists possess considerable national or global success. However, as Chapter 2 discusses, digital landscapes require consideration of benchmarks (especially social media) that indicate other criteria of success and related revenues that make older staged developmental structures redundant.

Music entrepreneurship

Before focussing on music artist managers as entrepreneurs, the general notion of music entrepreneurship is discussed as it is applicable to both music artist managers, self-managed music artists and other music industry workers operating as exporters. In our Exports Strategies survey, when 75 participant music exporters were asked to identify their role, 56% identified as an artist manager, and 19% identified as a self-managed artist, with the remaining 25% identifying as publishers, agents, bookers and labels.

The notion of the entrepreneur in general has many interpretations. In defining entrepreneurship, Cunningham and Lischeron identify a number of schools of thought (Cunningham and Lischeron, 1991, p. 46) based on assessing personal qualities, recognising opportunities, acting and managing, and reassessing and adapting. These also apply to the music entrepreneur. Zuilenburg and Loeb (2013, pp. 111–112) further identify the following six personality traits of a music entrepreneur: Having people skills and the ability to network and promote oneself, being persistent and thick-skinned and not taking "no" for an answer, strong self-discipline and endurance to continue when the odds are stacked against the entrepreneur, a strong belief in both one's own abilities (self-efficacy) as well as in the venture that is being developed, consistency in everything one does in relation to both the customers and the company, and they must be opportunity obsessed.

Only 2 of the 12 managers interviewed had a music performance background.[1] Irrespective of whether a music entrepreneur has a musical background or not, there has been much discussion on musicians and entrepreneurship in today's fluctuating musical landscape (for example: Scott, 2012; Haynes and Marshall, 2018; Albinsson, 2018; Patten, 2019). Patten writes that the relationships between practitioners working in the creative industries and entrepreneurship "are themselves ardently debated, and definitional and theoretical consensus on both has not been reached" (Patten, 2019, p. 23). In their analysis of musicians operating in the south west of England, Haynes and Marshall argue that they are natural entrepreneurs in having to manage gigs, create content, take risks regarding audience attendance and negotiate their value (Haynes and Marshall, 2018, p. 464). Musicians have always had to forge an existence; for example, this entrepreneurial spirit was evident in Mozart who in 1777 decided to base himself in Vienna and earn a living from commissions, touring, teaching and producing. Haynes and Marshall write of an implicit identity conflict when being labelled "entrepreneurial". While artists associate their work with artistic value in which success is informed by such components as peer esteem, reputation, quality and specialised knowledge, they also are confronted with business activities performed on a daily basis in order to eke out a living. Many contemporary artists see their creative activities as being a continuation of this tradition while musicians begrudgingly acknowledge that they are being "entrepreneurial". In doing so they equate the word with profit only and not artistic value (ibid., p. 468). It is ironic that the term "gig" economy uses the word gig as it is used by musicians in referring to being employed or performing for a job which could involve content creation, is dependent upon context and is a moment in time.

This raises concerns about whether musicians who want to be entrepreneurial can easily transfer their skill set from their daily operations, which in most cases take place in a highly networked environment, to a boundaryless open environment where entrepreneurialism underpins the new creative economy. In his study of Swedish musicians in the non-profit sector, Albinsson (2018, p. 355) notes that entrepreneurial identity is readily embraced by younger musicians whereas older pre-millennial musicians see a separation between freelancing money-making activities and their practice. Much of this boils down to the musician's training. Before the turn of this century, for example in Australia, it was not common for musicians to consider or study business practices. Twenty years on from the turn of the century, an Internet search will show that most contemporary music institutions have some type of music industry content or commitment.

There are many parallels between music industry actors and entrepreneurs with their focus on the need to survive and risk management activities. These include networking, creating contexts, seizing opportunities and deal-making. An important factor to consider is the use of the term "creativity". Chapter 1 refers to Bilton (2007) who writes that the term creativity within the creative economy context is more about process and management; it is economic, rather than about individualism:

> Where once we might have described creativity in terms of idea origination, and innovation as a process of idea implementation, today that distinction looks increasingly untenable. What does "creativity" mean in today's creative economy, and where do we find it? My argument is that creativity is no longer the sole preserve of the traditionally defined creative industry, occupation or department. Creative work and creative workers are having to take on managerial functions. At the same time, managers are beginning to seek recognition for their "creative" contribution. Creativity is accordingly being relocated and redefined, first as something integral to the process of management, second as a brand value which managers and non-managers actively seek to promote to their clients.
>
> (Bilton, 2007, p. 24)

The early 20th-century economic theorist Joseph A. Schumpeter places creativity and innovation at the centre of the entrepreneur's ethos. The entrepreneur forges new pathways, and is a risk-taker who creates new opportunities: "The typical entrepreneur is more self-centred than other types … relies less than they do on tradition … and … consists precisely in breaking up old, and creating new, tradition" (Schumpeter, 1934, p. 70). Haynes and Marshall (2017, p. 477) compare this to the Romantic notion of the artist as hero. If creativity is essential to being an entrepreneur, does that mean musicians are adept or readily able to be entrepreneurs? Excellence in a particular creative endeavour in one field does not necessarily mean that excellence can be achieved in a totally different field, although this can happen. Runco and Jaeger (2012, p. 92) define creativity as being bipartite: It must be "original" and "effective". "Original" can mean novel, unique or divergent, while "effective" refers to appropriateness, usefulness or value (ibid, p. 92). This is similar to the abovementioned relationship to practice; creativity is not necessarily universal, where one can transfer one's creativity to other fields.

It depends on appropriateness and context. This constructivist approach is apposite as "everyone's social reality is intimately interwoven as each [social reality] shapes and is shaped by the other in everyday interactions" (Cunliffe, 2008, p. 124). If a musician happens to be a successful entrepreneur it means, from a Bourdieusian (Bourdieu, 1990) perspective, that the musician has mastered the vocabularies and attributes defined by that field and context. For this reason, this chapter focuses on those music managers who consciously see themselves as having to be entrepreneurial in an ever-changing export industry that is informed by technological change, audience demographics and taste, and new modes of business communication. They construct a reality based on the changing contexts around them. This includes, to paraphrase Bilton (2007), the right mix of people in the team or partnership who work collectively and creatively in situating their product or brand.

While the above discussion includes artists and managers as music entrepreneurs, the remaining discussion deals specifically with managers as music entrepreneurs. In an environment defined by change and uncertainty, music entrepreneurs thrive on networking, flexibility and problem-solving (Schulte-Holthaus, 2019). Ulrich Beck's seminal text, *Risk Society* (1992), provides important background concepts applicable to the music entrepreneur's survival in a world of uncertainty. Beck argues that the breakdown of modern institutions has produced a shift in trust from established institutions and social structures to the individual, who needs to make more choices and be self-reliant:

> Decisions on education, profession, job, place of residence, spouse, number of children and so forth, with all the secondary decisions implied, no longer can be, they must be made.
>
> (Beck, 1992, p. 135)

Beck discusses three dimensions of labour market navigation and its role in defining individualisation: Education, mobility and competition. *Education* provides upward mobility and contributes to regularity frameworks such as various industry sectors stipulating the requirement of a qualification; the educated aspirant has choices to make regarding their career path: "the educated person becomes the producer of his or her own labor [sic] situation, and in this way, of his or her social biography" (ibid., p. 93). *Mobility* removes people from their traditional work patterns: They have to go where the money is; "the labor market, by way of occupational mobility, place of residence or employment, type of employment as well as changes in social location it initiates, reveals itself as the driving force behind the individualisation of people's lives" (ibid., p. 94). *Competition* thrives on individualisation and destroys any sense of community. In order to survive, the individual needs to separate from others, resulting in an "individualisation among equals" (ibid., p. 94). Beck sees these three dimensions as being interconnected. They reinforce each other.

While Beck's discussion on mobility and competition is directly applicable to the music entrepreneur, formalised education is not so applicable. The pathway into the industry from a management perspective is not always clear cut, and is often obtained by chance. When asked what the managers saw as important first steps, many specifically mentioned the importance of getting directly involved, making contacts and developing good relationships: "I don't think they're [qualifications] critical. Entrepreneurial people in business generally from my experience ... don't need formal qualifications" (Interview 1, 2018).

From a formal education perspective, the music export industry is deregulated: Anyone can potentially be an exporter. Entry into the industry is informal via networks, reputation, artistic success, musical demand and marketing. The lack of education pathways in a highly unreliable sector is addressed with Beck's discussion on biography. For Beck, in order to survive in a risk society of uncertainty, biography becomes important: One has to construct or make one's narrative:

> What is demanded is a *vigorous model of action in everyday life*, which puts the ego at its centre, allots and opens up opportunities for actions to it, and permits it in this manner to work through the emerging possibilities of decision and arrangement with respect to one's own biography in a meaningful way ... this means that in order to survive, an *ego-centred world view* must be developed, which turns the relation of ego and world on its head, so to speak, conceiving of and making them useful for the purpose of shaping an individual biography.
>
> (Beck, 1992, p. 136, emphasis added)

This construction of a personal narrative is fundamental to the music entrepreneur. Having a degree from a particular institution is not important; having the contacts and reputation is. The narrative can be based on tours, awards, streams, reviews, networks, etc. To quote Banks et al., "'society' is opened up to individual manipulation and interpretation: it becomes variable and open to the 'articulation of alternatives' [lifestyles, careers, work…]" (Banks et al., 2000, p. 456).

While uncertainty and risk underlie entrepreneurship, entrepreneurs at the same time must generate new activities (Gifford, 2003). Schumpeter, who saw the entrepreneur as an economic (visionary) leader, lists these activities as the following:

1. The production and carrying out of new products or new qualities of products;
2. The introduction of new production methods;
3. The creation of new forms of industrial organisation (for example trustfication);
4. The opening up of new markets; and
5. The opening up of new sources of supply.

(referred to in Becker, Marcus et al., 2011, p. 245)

These align with the second school of thought, outlined above by Cunningham and Lischeron (1991, p. 46), which conforms to Schumpeter's view: *Recognising opportunities*. Further to this and to varying degrees, all the interviewed managers displayed all of Cunningham and Lischeron's schools of thought and Bilton's value-adding approach. Bilton (2009) sees management skills as being integral to recognising these opportunities. Managers must continually insert themselves into the many value chains of the music industry in order to value add (enable or capitalise on a deal):

> Creative work and creative workers are having to take on managerial functions. At the same time, managers are beginning to seek recognition for their "creative" contribution. Creativity is accordingly being relocated and redefined, first as something integral to the process of management, second as a brand value which managers and non-managers actively seek to promote to their clients.
>
> (Bilton, 2009, p. 24)

The essential characteristics of entrepreneurship can be found with the entrepreneur's approach to managing change, utilising resources, collaboration, accessing networks and relying on individualistic approaches. In the following quote, from Banks et al. (2000), the term cultural entrepreneurs is applicable to music entrepreneurs:

> By resourcing and developing networks – simultaneously social and professional – cultural [music] entrepreneurs safeguard existing initiatives, clients and projects while opening up the possibility for the forging of new cultural and economic opportunities – social ties in many ways drive the productive potential of the culture.
>
> (Banks et al., 2000, p. 460)

In a digitised environment that is heavily reliant on fan interaction through the use of social media, career success involves a mixture of various factors. Hughes et al. (2013, p. 77) write that within the Australian context, "contemporary markers of success are not only built on musical ability, but also more explicitly on business acumen and strategic planning". Furthermore, success does not always mean financial success, but can include non-financial success such as achieving specific aesthetic criteria or reputation.

The music entrepreneur management team

The music entrepreneur (be it an artist manager or self-managed artist) reflects the "boundaryless career" (Arthur and Rousseau, 1996) where professionals are unpredictable, no longer tied to any one organisation, able to manage their own career paths, are highly mobile and invest considerably in professional networks (Zwann et al., 2010). They display the essential characteristics of entrepreneurship with their approach to managing change, utilising resources, collaboration, accessing networks and relying on individualistic approaches.

It would be very rare for a manager to work completely alone. The many tasks can be too great and involve many skills. Managers usually have a core team around them as well as specially devised teams for particular events:

> Having a great team around you is important and having as many people as you can that are locally based, or if you are going into a new territory, to gather some of those people if you can.
>
> (Interview 2, 2018)

To establish an international presence (referring back to Bilton's concept of team entrepreneurship mentioned in Chapter 1) a team will be responsible for the following: Touring, defining a niche audience, digital marketing, social media tools, product identity, international networking at industry events, employing international booking agents and publicists and follow-up travel for meetings.

Strategic planning

The reliance only on talent and luck is very rare and risky, as exporting into international territories is highly competitive. Knowing when to launch or promote an artist at showcase or trade fair events is crucial. All managers stressed the importance of planning and not simply turning up somewhere and hoping for the best:

> I've seen bands go overseas without any real strategy before, and they end up playing to nobody, and they think, oh, we can't believe we're playing South by Southwest, but without a strategy in place, and without a clear pathway in how you're going to be playing to whether it be labels, or publicists, or promoters, or festival bookers.
>
> (Interview 3, 2018)

The importance of having someone on the ground in the country intended for export cannot be understated. This could be a booking agent, publicist, co-producer or partner manager. Each territory demands a dedicated strategy involving labels, publicist, etc.:

> we were looking to spread our wings, with our focus being North America, and the UK. I think it's quite challenging to go over, with the eye on the prize of a booking agent. That's what a lot of people are looking for ... We made partnerships with digital distribution, which was ... a key income stream, particularly in North America ... The key thing for us is just establishing a partner that can get us out there on the live frontier. That's the biggest thing you can control in terms of the income streams.
>
> (Interview 2, 2018)

This correlates with the results from the Export Strategy Survey where participants were asked about the importance of having an international partner: 45.65%

said having a local partner at an international event was very important, with 32.61% saying it was important (representing a total of 78.26% of respondents).

In a "born global" culture, the potential to instantaneously access global markets and networks is crucial and can be expressed in many ways: Via a digital presence, establishing international offices, international partners and constant travel. For one manager based in Australia, regular travel is exhausting due to the time and distance, yet the benefits can include reputation consolidation and an intimate understanding of the international area:

> The Australian market is quite small in the scheme of things. It's often very hard for an act to only be popular in Australia and to make a successful living doing that. I think for artists to be successful overseas is a huge thing.
>
> (Interview 5, 2018)

Within the national context, all interviewees acknowledged the difficulty in making a viable local career in the music industry, necessitating an international focus. Five of the 12 managers interviewed have international offices. All engage international agents, or work with someone locally in the country they intend to tour:

> We feel like a physical presence outside of Australia is probably the single most important way for us to benefit the export potential for our Australian artists … It helps us think globally as well as be international in our presence … We're happy to be touring our artists internationally … We get artists into the international markets very early in their careers.
>
> (Interview 6, 2019)

"Psychic distance" is well documented in international business literature. Developed by researchers from Uppsala University (Johanson and Vahlne, 1977), it refers to the subjectively perceived distance between businesses and markets of a given country; because of this, exporters tend to start with the familiar. People or countries are perceived to be more distant the more different their cultures, customs or economic development are (ibid., p. 1). As a result, perceived distance creates uncertainty, evident when managers and artists choose English-speaking countries due to the cultural or language similarities:

> If you're an Australian artist and you're exporting, your immediate ones are going to be English language countries … If you're looking at deals, most of them will cover those territories because they're ultimately the most profitable … the UK, obviously being Commonwealth, it's cheaper from a visa perspective.
>
> (Interview 4, 2017)

With the saturation of northern hemisphere markets for music exports (UK, Europe and the United States), and the growth of Asian, African and Latin American markets as identified by Department of Foreign Affairs and Trade (2019), minimising "psychic distance" presents many real opportunities for music exports. Reducing this cognitive perception is achievable due to digitisation, social media platforms and meeting with stakeholders from these countries at international music market events. However, many of the managers stressed the importance of domestic market events such as Big Sound (Queensland) which enables domestic artists to be exposed to potential opportunities from visiting international industry stakeholders.

Risk and trust

> The centre of risk consciousness lies not in the present but in the future. In the risk society, the past loses the power to determine the present. Its place is taken by the future, thus, something non-existent, invented, fictive as the "cause" of current experience and action.
>
> (Beck, 1992, p. 34)

While financial transactions are obviously fundamental to the entrepreneur and can be clearly defined, the more intangible transactions are also crucial, including reputation building, trust, bartering, sharing and networking. The value of these intangible transactions, while recognised by all interviewees as being significant, was difficult to ascertain. An attempt was made to identify a single event where opportunities could be monetised or traced back to an intangible value input. Interview responses demonstrate the ambiguous and at times vague connection between intangible and tangible outcomes:

> It's hard to put your finger on it. I mean, obviously, there can be business outcomes, immediate or not immediate, and networking outcomes. Sometimes you don't know when that's going to come back into play.
>
> (Interview 7, 2018)

Working in a highly fluid environment means risk management is achieved through personalised contacts, the use of word-of-mouth, engaging with professional networks and relying on professional knowledge and expertise. The number of times a manager returns to various locations or events (national or international) is one example of this: "I spend far more time overseas now. It's so critical, I think, to be seen as someone who's local. So, at the moment, I'm six weeks on and six weeks off" (Interview 8, 2018).

Trust and time enable value creation. The role of time is crucial in developing non-financial exchanges and relationships. Our Exports Strategy Survey showed that it can take up to four years to plan an event or activity. In the "trust economy", trust is important in maintaining customer loyalty, be it for reliability, reputation, quality or service (PricewaterhouseCoopers, 2018). This may be based on building an emerging reputation over time, being in the same place or knowing that someone is of potential value sometime in the future.

All interviewees acknowledge the amount of time it takes to see a return on activities: "Well it's all about contact … Some take 20 years, some take two months" (Interview 9, 2017). The focus on the individual, and trusting how to navigate relationships, can be seen in the following quote where the manager develops an informal relationship with a potential partner. There is no specific plan, but trust in the quality of the relationship, which in turn led to outcomes:

> The first time I went over to the US I met a guy … who works at a record label from Seattle … We met up for the first time and were just catching up, as you do, meeting for the first time, but we established a relationship in that he had flagged that he was interested in the music scene within Melbourne specifically … he flagged an interest in what was going on in Australia as a result of a few artists that had begun to do quite well overseas, and then we kept in touch … Following that I ended up sending him some demos for a band … who last week released their first album … and we've released two EPs with them. That relationship has really broken that band overseas. They played to 1500 people in London a couple of weeks ago, before an album has even come out. So I think that would be one example of how it's been financially beneficial for us and for the band.
>
> (Interview 3, 2018)

Repurposing aptly sums up the necessary skills for a manager in relation to their export activities. A "remix and recontextualisation" approach means they create and maintain value by continually having to seek new opportunities, value add their product with existing value chains and, through trust and reputation, enter into transactions as a co-creator or partner. However, their continual incursions into overseas territories demand a heightened sense of entrepreneurialism, an intuitive acuity for market demand and trusting their judgement as to whether an artist is worth taking a risk or not.

Export activities

A common question when exporting: Is it necessary to first construct a local audience? When 66 artists/artist managers were asked about their national and international activities, 63% of participants engaged in national activities, and 37% engaged in international activities. For a majority of participants, domestic activity provided solid grounding for the development of an international market. However, maintaining a continual presence overseas can exert considerable pressures upon relationships and finances (discussed later in this chapter).

The definition of an export activity is broad. It can range from those that have specific tangible outcomes such as a deal for distribution or streaming to intangible activities that lay the foundations for a potential financial return such as a media appearance, meetings or networking. The export activities listed in Figure 3.1 have been taken from the Sounds Australia surveys given to participants who attended an international industry event (see Chapter 1, Methodology). Figure 3.1 provides a breakdown of all these activities and their percentage level of emphasis.

ANSWER CHOICES	RESPONSES	
International physical or digital sale and distribution of recorded music	82.61%	57
International Streaming (free or paid)	86.96%	60
Engaged in a major recording/licensing deal	28.99%	20
Engaged in an independent recording/licensing deal	55.07%	38
International festival	76.71%	55
International tour or support slot	65.22%	45
International showcase events	82.61%	57
International music market event	56.52%	39
Engaged in a publishing or sub-publishing deal	52.17%	36
International management/co-management	30.46%	21
International TV/film synchronisation placement	53.62%	35
International video gaming synchronisation placement	15.94%	11
Engaged international publicist	63.77%	44
International TV and radio promotion/appearances	50.72%	35
Engaged an international record producer	46.38%	32
International press/media coverage	65.22%	45
Brand partnership/sponsorship/product endorsement	28.99%	20
Re-negotiated existing partnerships	37.68%	26
Conducted business meetings	73.91%	51
Other (please specify)	5.8%	4
Total respondents: 69		

Figure 3.1 Question 16 from the Exports Strategy Survey—Q16: Since 2009 which of the following export strategies have you engaged in?

Being able to export does not always necessarily require a homegrown audience. Yet for Emerging and Breakthrough artists, the relationship between radio and TV airplay, online streaming, achievement recognition such as national awards, access to international industry events and a management/PR team can lay strong foundations for success. While ultimately achieving financial gain is the goal, there are many reasons for exporting. English-speaking countries are the natural choice for many managers due to the cultural or language similarities. The top five activities in Figure 3.1 are international streaming (86.96%), international physical or digital sale and distribution of recorded music (82.61%), attending an international showcase event (82.61%), attending an international festival (79.71%), conducting business meetings (73.91%) and engaging with an international publicist (63.77%).

Each territory, city or region can be uniquely defined. Digital analytics play an essential role in helping managers determine where artists' fan bases are located: "you see something on your streaming platforms that is indicating that, you know, France is actually, really playing a lot of your music" (Interview 1, 2018). Because of streaming's reliance on access-based music services, the relationship between artists, managers, labels (major and indie) and audiences is in flux. "Datafication" (see Chapter 1) is making managers rethink their relationship with labels and international fan development:

> The rules have just completely changed … there's no rules in how you release music. Except if the music is really good and you've got a fan base that is

> really engaged with you, then you can use that platform streaming to help ... amplify that. And that's been one of the most exciting things happening in the last few years. And it's changed to the point that you don't even need a record label anymore. Record labels are, certainly for developing artists, almost redundant to a certain level ... They need you, they need the artists and so that's an exciting turn of events in my opinion.
>
> (Interview 1, 2018)

This is further exemplified by Wikstrom (2013) who argues that incorporating an audience's creativity into a business plan enables strong communication with the artist and peer-to-peer relationships. He describes how the next phase of the music industry will be based on context or doing things with music as exemplified by the UK artist Imogen Heap: "Imogen Heap's Twittering, YouTubing, blogging and what-have-you are more than promotion for upcoming albums and concerts – these activities are all part of an immersive multi-platform Imogen Heap experience" (ibid., p. 251). In similar ways to the interactive gaming industry, such an approach raises ethical issues for managers and labels, and questions the role of authenticity as the focus shifts from a fixed recording to an experience in which the audience engages on a co-creative level. Examples of this can be observed in the early 2000s when artists started to release stems for fans to remix as part of a shared economy business model in which fans have a creative engagement with the artists. Mobile apps or album apps that allow the listener to interact or change the musical form have been gaining in popularity since the late 2000s. The Album app developed by Paterson, 2016, was developed as a format which offered ways to remix the songs and engage in the artwork of the EP. The project investigated "the app as a potential album-release format of the future in an initiative to lure the consumer away from the 'single track download' mentality" (Paterson et al., 2016). Platforms like Patreon also offer ways for artists to engage with their fans and income streams.

Critical are the ancillary digital activities required to get one's product global. Fan development via co-creative experiences, or peer-to-peer relationships, must be added to the music exporter's digital tool kit as a crucial addition needed for a return on investment. In the next section we discuss attendance at international festivals and showcasing, also considered important for the development of an export outcome.

Export readiness

> You need to be ready to export the moment that you start. You're operating internationally from the moment you put a song online and to think otherwise is short-sighted.
>
> (Interview 4, 2017)

Due to the complexity of the music industry and its utilisation of social media, streaming and technological innovation, "music export readiness" cannot be prescriptive or limited to traditional definitions of export. Austrade's "international readiness tool" (Austrade, 2006) asks questions about the current nature of export engagement, the status of domestic market sales, production capacity, product differentiation, financial resources, management support and resources, market research, promotional materials, pricing, payment mechanism and product delivery. Given the fluctuating nature of the music industry due to technological change, the trust placed in international networks and access to globalised markets and communication, the purpose of our interviews with Australian managers was to reassess "export readiness".

Should all Australian artists be looking to export? Export readiness in music has some differences to Austrade's standard requirements for export. For example, while an international competitor analysis is important, it may not be as relevant, as the celebration of diversity and difference in music is a key factor in maintaining cultural and economic vibrancy. Austrade identifies the following key signs: Significant management time and strong management commitment, strength in the domestic market, the resources to succeed, business and export planning and export knowledge and skills. Some Australian musicians (e.g. Gotye, Iggy Azalea and Sia) have bypassed the local market to different extents in favour of international bases, seeking US or European audiences. However, there are some factors that are just as essential, such as staffing, knowing the market, distribution and marketing.

Based on interviews with Australian managers, the following areas have been identified as factors contributing towards export readiness. In a globalised and digitised world, some would say that the playing field has been levelled. But this is not the case. Music export readiness can involve any combination of the components listed below, or just one, as the emergence of the YouTube star has shown. While access to data is now ubiquitous in a "born global" world, the awareness of hidden costs and hurdles will make or break the success of a music export. It is the facilitation and management of that music export within a complex ecosystem of transactions, analytics and many stakeholders. Figure 3.2 lists indicators that help define a music export readiness framework.

Depending on who that target is, having an Australian domestic track record can help. For example, an international partner may research the artist's Australian track record through digital analytics or domestic reviews. But it also can be the case that the sharing of an artist's work via Facebook's friend/fan network bypasses the need to see if the artist has been successful in Australia. Another point of difference is that it is not necessarily a competitive market between Australian artists. There is always room for new artists who have a particular sound.

Challenges and advantages

The most obvious and common challenge for artists, labels and managers is the "tyranny of distance" (Blainey, 1966) for artists based in the southern hemisphere. It can cost between $20,000 and $50,000 to take an Australian artist or band to do a two-week tour or attend an industry event, leading many managers to seek

1. Representation	The three main actors in this space are the artist manager, label and publisher who negotiate all deals. Some artists represent themselves when negotiating deals.
2. Strategic planning and infrastructure:	Having the appropriate management team and an export strategy are essential. This includes market research, management, an international partner, legal support.
3. International networks	Accessing an international team or community of contacts who have market knowledge or can provide access to key stakeholders and support.
4. International industry events and showcasing	Maintaining a presence at these events enables networking, keeping abreast of industry changes and opportunities.
5. Territorial knowledge	Each territory will have its own demands such as visa regulations, appropriate ground support or specialist skills.
6. Financing	Adequate financing is needed to ensure delivery of product, international follow up meetings, follow up tours and media appearances.
7. Promoting and maintaining the story	A narrative or 'buzz", radio and TV broadcast are necessary to be able to get exposure, and maintaining the narrative with backup resources (recordings). This includes repeated airplay and broadcasts, reviews, publicists, tastemakers, influencers and bloggers.
8. Audience/digital footprint	The size of the artists' fans and associated digital analytics such as as their demographics, country and location are important determinants for different career stages (Emerging, Breakthrough, Established, Epic).
9. A "born global" attitude	Dissemination and promotion through streaming services, social media and sharing platforms such as YouTube and Instagram.
10. Domestic activity	Building a strong local or national audience such as awards, touring, airplay social network activities. Attendance at workshops held by Sounds Australia.

Figure 3.2 Export readiness indicators.

bookings through media engagements or follow-up tours to help pay for the investment:

> I think we're at a severe disadvantage … that's because of the strength and power of the media outlets in those countries, and also that's where playlists are made … if we were in LA right now, everyone in the world would know who we are, because all the editors to the websites that make those opinions would be coming to our shows just by virtue of the fact that we're down the road.
>
> (Interview 10, 2018)

To help improve the distance problem, the Australia Council for the Arts has instigated a residency programme based in Nashville, USA, for Australian songwriters, enabling them to immerse themselves into the Nashville music scene (Australia Council, 2019). Some managers have established international offices in the US or UK. Out of a total of 48 respondents from the Exports Strategy Survey who answered a question on challenges, 33 said that travel costs and time were a significant barrier to their export activities (68.75%), while 30 said that costs involved with travel to follow up an export opportunity were a significant barrier (62.5%).[2]

Interviewed managers had mixed responses regarding whether being perceived as an Australia act was an advantage in other territories. Most said yes, with the US market thought to be more open to Australian exports than the UK. In terms of infrastructure, it was noted that the national public youth broadcaster Triple J and other ABC broadcasting programmes helped establish a ground base. These media opportunities provide a "barometer" for national and international observers to monitor:

> [Australia is] a country that people watch. America, in particular, watches Australia. I know a lot of people there will look at the Triple J additions every week, as a bit of a barometer. Australia has a reputation for producing great music but also embracing stuff before other places do. Like, a lot of acts will, kind of, break here before elsewhere. Whereas America, 100%, I know people watch Australia very closely. So, there's an advantage in that sense, definitely.
>
> (Interview 7, 2018)

The cultural value of public media and cultural infrastructure such as the ABC, Triple J and the Australia Council cannot be underestimated. Combined, they provide cultural and economic inputs which stitch together a diverse music industry, providing a valuable measure of activity:

> We have a national radio broadcaster in JJJ and ABC, similarly to what BBC Radio One is for the UK, that creates significant audience spill, which leads to artists, when they get support from those single format radio platforms, particularly when they're government backed and not purely commercially driven types of things … I think that creates a situation where Australian artists can find audiences, and then can use that as leverage to create a bit of a runway for international export opportunities. I would probably say that's one of our main strengths is having that platform.
>
> (Interview 11, 2019)

Case study: Courtney Barnett

One interesting artist to consider in relation to how combinations of industry and state support can be utilised to harness international opportunities is the Melbourne-based singer/songwriter Courtney Barnett. Originally from the northern beaches of Sydney, Barnett arrived in Melbourne in 2008. By 2010, she was playing second guitar in two local bands, subsequently finding and promoting her own gigs in inner-Melbourne pubs such as The Old Bar (*The Australian*, 2015). The former CEO of Australian Independent Record Labels Association (AIR), Nick O'Byrne became her manager in 2011, with Barnett's first EP released in 2012, along with the establishment of her "indie" label, Milk! Records with partner and Melbourne artist Jen Cloher. Barnett's second EP, *How to Carve a Carrot into a Rose* and single "Avant Gardener" were showcased at the CMJ Music Marathon in October 2013. *Pitchfork* magazine named "Avant Gardener" its best new song for 2013, while Stereogum announced *How to Carve a Carrot into a Rose* as its "Album of the week", with favourable reviews in *The Guardian* and *The Times* (ibid.).

Barnett's album, *Sometimes I Sit and Think, and Sometimes I Just Sit*, was released in 2014. It partially derived from an independent label funding grant of $15,000 provided by copyright body PPCA and the Australia Council. The album was released through Mom + Pop Records in the US in 2015 (and Marathon/House Anxiety in the UK) while gaining four Australian Recording Industry Association (ARIA) awards in 2015: Breakthrough Artist, Best Female Artist, Best Independent Release and Best Cover Art. The album was also nominated in the same period at the BRIT Awards and the Grammys (Best New Artist). In 2015, Barnett was also awarded International Pathways funding from the Australia Council ($20,000) for showcasing activity at New York's CMJ Marathon event, coordinated by Sounds Australia. In May 2016, Barnett was the musical guest on the season finale of *Saturday Night Live*'s 41st season, hosted by Fred Armisen, and on *The Tonight Show Starring Jimmy Fallon.* In June 2017, Barnett won the Breakthrough Artist of the Year award at the A2IM Libera Awards in New York.

In some respects, Barnett's career trajectory from inner-city Melbourne pub performances to large international festivals represents an astonishingly quick progression from Emerging to Established artist. Strategising impact across different media, live performance and other industrial events, in hindsight, was essential in allowing audiences in different territories to become fans and build momentum. The local timing of the album release in March 2015, with subsequent release scheduled internationally, set up showcase possibilities:

> It was just so lucky … for it all to happen right there, just couldn't have been better timing for her. And it really came down to timing … if South By [Southwest] had been in April, it wouldn't have worked … There's only a two or three month window … if the record had been not completed by January, then we would have had to put the record out in the back half of the year, and we wouldn't have had that same opportunity. So, yes … seeing an opportunity and just running with it, hard … you're just ready to recognise something when it presents itself.
>
> (O'Byrne, 2018)

For Barnett, South by Southwest (SXSW) provided the opportunity to synchronise plans for further exposure: "Our booking agent was able to bring down every promoter in the country to see her show" (ibid.). South by Southwest organisers awarded Barnett the Developing Act Grulke Prize, awarded to those "who are breaking new ground with their creativity and show the most promise in achieving their career goals" (Baroni, 2015). This was preceded by appearances at CMJ and The Great Escape; yet the SXSW appearance was formulated to synchronise with a range of other activities:

> At that point in time, we had every single partner in place. And it was the week before Courtney's record came out … we could play shows in front of every important press outlet in America, and many internationals … play[ing] 70 shows in front of the world's media the week before your record came out was just too perfect … Our booking agent was able to bring down every promoter in the country to see her show, publicists were able to bring TV bookers down. We did an event with Tumblr … solidify relationships with Pitchfork or Stereogum.
>
> (O'Byrne, 2018)

As a strikingly distinctive writer and performer, Barnett's catalogue of witty and ironic depictions of everyday life laid the foundations for success beyond Australian audiences. Yet her path is also a textbook case in the ways in which the patchwork of state and federal export assistance can work in establishing a solid domestic base before preparing for international forays. This has included involvement as a performer with Victoria's youth music programme The Push, an Australia Council/PPCA grant to perform at SXSW, Sounds Australia support to play at "Aussie BBQ" events at CMJ and The Great Escape, Creative Victoria funds for touring and Victorian state funding through its New Enterprise Incentive Scheme (NEIS) assisting with establishing Milk! Records. For Barnett,

> Government grants gave me creative independence when I was starting out, because it meant I was worrying less about impressing for label and publishing advances, and I was less reliant on taking some big-company sponsorship to fund a tour.
>
> (Barnett cited in Hogan, 2017)

Collaboration—across territories and sectors—is an important feature, particularly if the artist and managers' experiences can assist Emerging artists:

> I think we do lots of things for free, both for ourselves as a company, and also on behalf of other artists. So, one example might be organising Courtney and some other bands in the upcoming Laneway tour. I'm trying to launch the Girls Rock! Adelaide chapter, to come a day early and have Courtney and Cam Cope … there's no financial benefit for any of us to do that, apart from maybe giving back.
>
> (O'Byrne, 2018)

Beyond management, Barnett utilises a team of nine people (tour manager, front of house mixing, foldback mixing, lighting personnel and four band members) for touring. However,

> If you take a further step out, she has three booking agents – one based in North America, one based in the UK, and one based here [in Australia]. And then a UK-based label, an American label, each of those companies with teams of ten or twelve people … Courtney's American publicist has been quite fierce and a big part of her success … [The] managers are the inner sanctum, but going far and wide, hundreds of other people get on board.
>
> (O'Byrne, 2018)

Experiences with Barnett and other acts have provided her manager with firm views about understandings of "export ready":

> I've just never seen anyone build a buzz without a speck of buzz before. Buzz is a bad word … Having success in the domestic market, it makes you a good artist because you've been plying your trade for a while … It's totally feasible, maybe more at a pop level, that you could have fans in a pocket of the internet overseas, that you can build on through an export strategy, without necessarily having fans here. But it's always going to help if there's a story at home.
>
> (O'Byrne, 2018)

For Barnett, Sounds Australia have provided vital complementary functions to various state funding support. Beyond appearances at carefully selected showcase events, the primary benefits of Sounds Australia collaboration have been in networking:

> It's like the spider web analogy, where basically they help you line by line. You're filling in this web until you kind of catch who you need, whether it be a record label for your artist, or not. They've provided 40 or more opportunities for me to draw another line and meet someone else.
>
> (O'Byrne, 2018)

Financial outcomes: Discussion of Export Strategies survey

In this section we provide a window into the activities of music exporters based upon the Export Strategies survey conducted in 2018. Four hundred and five artists and artist managers who had completed the above Sounds Australia survey and attended an international industry event were surveyed about their approaches to and investments in music exporting. The purpose of the survey was to ascertain the time it took to achieve an outcome, the tangible or intangible value of that outcome and the resources and investment required. As it can take time to see a return on investment, participants were asked about their various activities since 2009.

The surveyed participants reported that, on average, most of the international music activities are expected to have financial returns within two years. This response represents the average return, given that they may have participated in selected activities more than once since 2009 or with multiple artists. Activities such as a showcase, international tour, support slot or TV appearance are believed to have potential future profit returns. A large percentage of financial losses were from activities such as hiring an international record producer, international showcase event costs and gaining an international tour or support slot.[3]

All manager interviewees acknowledge the amount of time it takes to see a return on activities: 45% of participants saw a financial return within 12 months; 26.22% within two years; 11.18% within five years; and 0.81% within ten years. This suggests that for most participants involved in export activities since 2009, the average amount of time involved from planning to fruition is four to five years; more than five years is not uncommon:

> I feel like you kind of have to lose about $100,000 touring the USA before you get to break-even point. Like, your first tour with a band might lose $40,000. And your next one might lose thirty, and your next one twenty, and your next … and then you finally break even … But then you also have to do that in Europe, as well. So if you're trying to do it all, kind of, globally, there's, kind of, $200,000 of losses you have to swallow in one way or another, before you can be at a point where you know you're going to make money on a tour.
>
> (Interview 10, 2018)

Apart from revenue received from the sale of goods and services, financing in the industry involves a mixture of sponsorships, donations, grants. Financing provided by family or friends is an example of the "gift economy" which is based on relationships and where there is no expectation of a financial reward but some reciprocity is involved (Klamer, 2003). Klamer provides a general interpretation of a gift as "any 'good', including money, that is transferred, conveyed or transmitted from one party to another when the nature, value and the timing of an equivalent is left undetermined" (ibid., p. 243); the most important gifts are not recorded, such as parenting or volunteering (ibid., p. 244). More than 70% of artists/self-managed artists and 50% of artist managers identified that family/peer financial support was important in realising their music export activities. As one artist noted, "my mom really gave me a little nudge out of the door. In fact, she got a $10,000 loan to buy me my campervan" (Interview 34, 2018).

Both artists and artist managers (93% of those surveyed) believed that government funding is very important. A high level of respondents received government funding, the majority received from the Australia Council for the Arts. Participants stated that their attendance at international industry events was financed by either a federal or state government grant, Export Market Development Grant (EMDG), label, company funds, self-financed, family or peers. Other than government sources, artists and artist managers received most financial assistance from recording labels. Family and publishers were also popular funding sources. Slightly more financial support is received from family than from publishers.

Participants who obtained industry support, received grants and/or private investment, had a higher success rate in achieving outcomes. Of the 28 participants questioned about the importance of government funding, 93% of participants who received government funding showed a high level of satisfaction in achieving goals. Respondents who did not obtain financial assistance had a lower rate of success in setting up and establishing deals. Artists with support from both government and industry had the highest success rate in setting up and establishing deals for export.

The three biggest areas of investment cited were the engagement of an international record producer, international touring and renegotiating existing partnerships. In terms of the financial gain over the ten-year period, participants reported that, as a result of these investments, they were able to receive accumulative amounts from engagement of an international record producer international touring, or renegotiate existing business partnerships. This shows that, while specific activities can be expensive in the short term, it is the combined activities that can enable a financial gain (seen, for example, in the flow-on effects from touring or the combined effects from multiple marketing and investment strategies).

An overarching issue has been the turnaround time to see a return on an opportunity. Planning for an opportunity to eventuate is only the first part of the time involved in exporting. The second part is the waiting time for a return on investment which can on average take about two years; however five years or more is also possible.

> Cash flow is the most difficult part of developing a career … Because it's so much investment of time, and the funnels by which money flows back to artists and then eventually, to managers after that are pretty slow and cumbersome … But the financial realisation for the artist is not until seven or eight months after, and sometimes, nine or ten months for the manager. So, there are huge difficulties, I think, with that.
>
> (Interview 4, 2017)

ANSWER CHOICES	RESPONSES	
Focussing on domestic market	66.67%	6
Unable to get enough funding to follow up	77.78&	7
Band/business broke up	22.22%	2
Couldn't find a market/audience	0.00%	0
Retired	0.00%	0
Had to prioritise other opportunities	44.44%	4
Unable to travel	22.22%	2
Negotiations didn't go as planned	11.11%	1
Other (Please specify)	22.22%	2
Total Responses = 9		

Figure 3.3 Percentage breakdown of reasons for discontinuing exporting.

Those surveyed who identified as no longer exporting (9 out of the 75 participants) gave reasons for discontinuing exporting such as lack of funding and the decision to focus on the domestic market (see Figure 3.3).[4]

Conclusion

The international music industry is a highly competitive landscape which at the same time relies on collaboration and teams. Accessing international audiences requires an entrepreneurial mindset which can fall within the domain of the artist, manager and supporting team. This involves a series of relationships based on partnerships, deals or co-creation activities. In a continually changing music industry environment based on new technologies, new formats for music promotion, fluid audience demographics and multiple industry actors, the music entrepreneur must be adept at managing these. An important focus is maintaining a high degree of communication and trust.

Relevant to this chapter is Bilton's discussion in Chapter 1 of the manager's collaborative approach to team building and partnership where he writes about "a more realistic unit of analysis for creative processes and product … [where] Creative thinking … depends upon a union of contrasting abilities and styles of thinking" (Bilton, 2007, p. 19). We have explored whether a music entrepreneur has the same set of skills as a start-up or inventor entrepreneur. It could be argued that anyone involved in the music industry, either as an artist or industry worker such as a manager, intuitively understands the volatile nature of music. All the interviewed music managers were aware of this volatility and the demands needed to manage constant change. This is aptly summed up by Banks et al. who state that:

> Cultural producers are well equipped to manage risks. In cultural industries the primary value of goods is symbolic and short lived; it is lodged in ephemeral signs, meanings and senses of style … The market is well understood to be volatile, and subjective, and prone to rapid and illogical transformation.
>
> (Banks et al., 2000, p. 455)

Irrespective of having a musical background, the music entrepreneur (be it an artist, manager or artist manager) has the potential to thrive in today's gig economy which is unpredictable, flexible and based on relationships. Indeed, Schumpeter's definition of an entrepreneur as a highly creative, free-wheeling spirit aligns neatly with the romantic concept of the innovative creative artist, in particular the music entrepreneur. Further research is needed as to whether music entrepreneurs have an inbuilt entrepreneurial ethos easily translatable to economic contexts.

Because of the high-risk nature of the music industry itself, export readiness involves a multitude of factors. In a "born global" world, and once business infrastructures are established, it is possible to export totally online, although this can be more of an exception than the norm. Artists are able to export their music to various territories without the need to tour.

Chapters 5 and 6 discuss how policy can greatly aid export readiness in providing infrastructures, grants, subsidies, taxation breaks, support mechanisms and industry incentives to overcome the many challenges, be they distance, touring and promotional costs or international representation such as consular support, attendance at industry events and investing in new technologies that promote Australian music. In the next chapter these transactions are discussed further with respect to the importance of networks and the role of gatekeeping.

Notes

1 In our study, 9 of the 12 managers had a post-secondary qualification of some sort including marketing, music industry, journalism, criminal law and creative arts. Six of these had a post-secondary music business or marketing-related qualification. Three had no post-secondary qualification. The 24 artists whom they managed had no post-secondary music qualification, a qualification in music performance or music production or a qualification in an area outside of music. Of these 24 artists, only 3 artists had a specific music performance or production degree; the remaining musicians had a non-music post-secondary qualification, or no qualifications.

2 Nearly 80% of the Sounds Australia survey respondents considered the relocation of a band to a new market as important to realise a profitable export career.

3 Unfortunately, as the 405 respondents were given the option to skip certain questions, not enough respondents completed the 2 questions relating to financial investment and revenue required to predict the potential financial impact from engaging in export activities. It is also difficult to separate the impact of individual activities, as these activities cross over into different income streams.

4 Appendix 3 provides an artist snapshot of strategies and outcomes; and an artist manager snapshot of strategies and outcomes.

References

AUSTRADE (2006). International readiness indicator. https://www.austrade.gov.au/Australian/Export/Guide-to-exporting/International-Readiness-Indicator

The Australian (2015). Courtney Barnett - The new face of rock. 31 October. http://www.rickyfrench.com/courtney-barnett-the-new-face-of-rock-weekend-australian-magazine-cover-story/

Australia Council for the Arts. (2019). Nashville songwriters' residency. https://www.australiacouncil.gov.au/international/nashville-songwriters-residency/

Albinsson, S. (2018). Musicians as entrepreneurs or entrepreneurs as musicians? *Creativity and Innovation Management* vol. 27, no. 3, pp. 348–357. doi:10.1111/caim.12254.

Banks, M., Lovatt, A., O'Connor, J. & Raffo, C. (2000). Risk and trust in the cultural industries. *Geoforum* vol. 31, pp. 453–464.

Baroni, N., (2015). Courtney Barnett wins SXSW award, adds more Australian tour dates. *Musicfeeds*, 26 March. https://musicfeeds.com.au/news/courtney-barnett-wins-sxsw-award-adds-more-australian-tour-dates/

Beck, U. (1992). *Risk Society Towards a New Modernity*. London: SAGE publishing

Becker, M.C., Knudsen, T., Swedberg, R. & Schumpeter, J.A. (2011). *The Entrepreneur: Classic Texts by Joseph A. Schumpeter*. Stanford, CA: Stanford University Press, p. 245.

Bilton, C. (2007). *Management and Creativity: From Creative Industries to Creative Management*. Oxford: Blackwell.

Bilton, C. (2009). Relocating creativity in advertising: from aesthetic specialisation to strategic integration. In A.C. Pratt & P. Jeffcutt (eds.) *Creativity, Innovation and the Cultural Economy*. London: Routledge, pp. 23–40.

Blainey, G. (1966). *The Tyranny of Distance*. Melbourne: Macmillan.

Bourdieu, P. (1990). *The Logic of Practice*. Stanford, CA: Stanford University Press.

Cunliffe, A.L. (2008). Orientations to social constructionism: relationally responsive social constructionism and its implications for knowledge and learning. *Management Learning* vol. 39, no. 2, pp. 123–139. doi:10.1177/1350507607087578

Cunningham, J.B. & Lischeron, J. (1991). Defining entrepreneurship. *Journal of Small Business Management* vol. 29, no. 1, pp. 45–61. https://www.questia.com/library/journal/1G1-10666908/defining-entrepreneurship

Department of Foreign Affairs and Trade. (2019). Market insights. https://www.dfat.gov.au/trade/engage/economic-diplomacy/Pages/market-insights

Gifford, S. (2003). Risk and uncertainty. In Z.J. Ács & D.B. Audretsch (eds.) *Handbook of Entrepreneurship Research: An Interdisciplinary Survey and Introduction*. New York: Springer, pp. 37–53.

Haynes, J. & Marshall, L. (2017). Reluctant entrepreneurs: musicians and entrepreneurship in the "new" music industry. *British Journal of Sociology* vol. 69, no. 2, pp. 459–482. doi:10.1111/1468-4446.12286.

Hogan, M. (2017). How countries around the world fund music—and why it matters. *Pitchfork*, 26 June. https://pitchfork.com/features/article/how-countries-around-the-world-fund-musicand-why-it-matters/

Hughes, D., Keith, S., Morrow, G., Evans, M. & Crowdy, D. (2013). What constitutes artist success in the Australian music industries? *International Journal of Music Business Research* vol 2, no. 2, pp. 61–80.

Johanson, J. & Vahlne, J. (1977). The internationalization process of the firm—a model of knowledge development and increasing foreign market commitments. *Journal of International Business Studies* vol. 8, no. 1, pp. 23–32. doi:10.1057/palgrave.jibs.8490676.

Klamer, A. (2003). Gift economy. In R. Towse (ed.) *A Handbook of Cultural Economics*. Cheltenham: Edward Elgar, pp. 243–247.

Next Big Sound. (2016). *Artist Social Stages*. https://help.nextbigsound.com/s/article/Artist-Social-Stages-1519949295551

Paterson, J., Toulson, R., Lexer, S., Webster, T., Massey, S. & Ritter, J. (2016). Interactive digital music: enhancing listener engagement with commercial music. *Innovation in Music II*. UK: Future Technology Press.

Patten, T. (2019). Understanding the creative industries entrepreneur: a qualitative study. artivate. *A Journal of Entrepreneurship in the Art* vol. 5, no. 2, pp. 23–42. https://artivate.org/artivate/article/view/55 doi:10.4135/9781526476838

PricewaterhouseCoopers. (2018). The new trust economy. https://www.pwc.com.au/industry/entertainment-and-media-trends-analysis/outlook/2018/the-new-trust-economy.html

Runco, M.A. & Jaeger, G.J. (2012). The standard definition of creativity. *Creativity Research Journal* vol. 24, no. 1, pp. 92–96. doi:10.1080/10400419.2012.650092

Schulte-Holthaus, S. (2019). Entrepreneurship in the creative industries: a literature review and research Agenda. In E. Innerhofer, H. Pechlaner & E. Borin (eds.) *Entrepreneurship in Culture and Creative Industries: Perspectives from Companies and Regions*. Cham, Switzerland: Springer, pp. 99–154.

Schumpeter, J.A. (1934). The theory of economic development: the fundamental phenomenon of economic development. In M.C. Becker, T. Knudsen & R. Swedberg (eds.) *The Entrepreneur: Classic Texts by Joseph A. Schumpeter.* Stanford, CA: Stanford Business Books.

Scott, M. (2012). Cultural entrepreneurs, cultural entrepreneurship: music producers mobilising and converting Bourdieu's alternative capitals. *Poetics* vol 40, no. 3, pp. 237–255.

Wikstrom, P. (2013). *The Music Industry: Music in the Cloud.* Cambridge: Polity Press.

Zuilenburg, V. and Loeb, P. (2013). Personality traits of successful music entrepreneurs. *Acta Academica* vol. 45, no. 1, pp. 100–118.

Zwaan, K., ter Bogt, T.F.M. & Raaijmakers, Q. (2010). Career trajectories of Dutch Pop musicians: a longitudinal study. *Journal of Vocational Behavior* vol. 77, no. 1, pp. 10–20. doi:10.1016/j.jvb.2010.03.004.

4 Networking at music industry export events

Introduction

Chapter 3 discusses the role of music entrepreneurs and their export strategies in order to be export ready. It was shown in Chapter 3 that, in order to manage risk, the ability to network is an important skill. These networks are defined by roles and relationships which can be peer to peer, contractual, professional, community-based, commercial, familial or fan-based. In this chapter we discuss networks in the music export environment of an international music industry event. International market events are a hotbed for networking and gatekeeping. There are many more international market events now; each has become successful in finding its own niche audiences and industry sectors.

This chapter continues with previous references to the interviews with managers and data from the two survey designs discussed in Chapter 1: The Sounds Australia surveys, and the Export Strategies survey. In the Sounds Australia surveys, participants were asked about their experience of a music industry event and opportunities achieved. The events that those interviewed attended were Music Matters, Singapore; Primavera, Spain; Folk Alliance, US; Canadian Music Week (CMW), Canada; Americanafest, US; CMJ, US; MIDEM, France; Reeperbahn, Germany; A2IM, US; Showcase Scotland, UK; Liverpool Sound, UK; The Great Escape, UK; and SXSW, US. The Export Strategy Survey investigated the viability of the participants' music export strategies and allowed us to follow up on the responses obtained from the earlier Sounds Australia survey. There are many types of market events based on different music genres (Americana, Folk Alliance, Classical Next, Jazzahead, Amsterdam Dance Event). "These national and international industry events are valuable for learning and keeping abreast with changes in the industry, as a good snapshot of what's happening around the world" (Interview 2, 2018).

Knowing your networks

A network is defined as "goal-directed behaviour which occurs both inside and outside of an organisation, focussed on creating, cultivating, and utilising interpersonal relationships" (Gibson et al., 2014, p. 146). Movement between these networks is very fluid, relies on personal relationships and often involves a clear demarcation of roles. To varying degrees, professional networking events are based on proximity and similarity (Reagans, 2011, p. 835). Proximity can be physical (for example the same room), virtual (social platforms) or defined kinship (cousin or sibling, etc). Similarity, for example, can be based on common likes, professional interests, working for the same organisation or a common education background.

Bourdieu's forms of capital and their conversion provide a useful backdrop to the value of networks (Bourdieu, 1986). In his famous essay, "The Forms of Capital" (1986), Bourdieu writes that economic capital can be created and transformed from "cultural" and "social" capital as a result of socialisation and class. For Bourdieu, "social capital" is a "credential" referring to the "actual or potential resources which are linked to possession of a durable network of more or less institutionalised relationships of mutual acquaintance and recognition – in other words, membership to a group" (Bourdieu, 1986, p. 249). Conversely, cultural and social capital can be transformed into economic capital. It is here that networks play an important role. Someone with a good reputation, and who is very connected, obviously has high social capital in contrast to a newcomer with no experience or professional relationships. Cultural capital operates on a symbolic level. Bourdieu (ibid., p. 244) identifies three states of cultural capital: "embodied" (being, disposition), "objectified" (goods) and "institutionalised" (qualifications or association with an organisation). Both social and cultural capital play an important role in the music industry in which risk and trust are important drivers (see Chapter 3).

In contrast to traditional linear value chains in which value is added by each participant along the chain, networks disrupt this linearity through their ability for nonlinearity of communication. Their value is informed by opportunity, co-creation, access to information and relationships made through strong and weak ties. Strong ties relate to "frequent, local interactions (and that are relatively more probable to cover a short distance" (Lizardo, 2006, p. 782), connecting people with similar goals and interests. Weak ties are "relatively infrequent extra-local interactions (… more likely to span a larger distance … connecting people to dissimilar others" (ibid., p. 782). These ties are not fixed in that they are open to change due to the comings and goings of participants.

> Luckily, when I was on that trip, other people travelling with me were promoters for music festivals, and they would hook me up with their booking agent friends. So, outside of the actual trade show itself, I just went over and did trips and met people in the industry, and sat down and spoke to them, and told them about who I was and what I was doing.
>
> (Interview 2, 2018)

While strong ties enable actors within a network to exchange and capitalise on information to consolidate their position and status, Ko and Butler (2007) argue that weak ties are important, as occasionality or chance interactions enable new inputs from "outsiders". This helps avoid communication and interaction between like-minded actors where regularity can cause sameness, convention or a "closed shop".

Zwaan et al. (2010, p. 18) found that "the most successful pop musicians had the best professional network whereas ... relatively unsuccessful pop musicians had the smallest network". For the creative industries worker, networks support knowledge, creative energy, industry development, help find new employment opportunities and manage job insecurity (Felton et al., 2010). They provide continuity, are defined by relationships and underpinned by trust. Just as organisations rely on trust, the quasi-institutional nature of networks makes them similar to organisations.

Networks can be complex structures due to their extent of influence, density (participants' connectivity) and centrality (who knows whom) (Aldrich and Zimmer, 1986, p. 13). The professional networks observed at international industry events, discussed later in this chapter, demonstrate these three components. As well as being based on location and similarity, there is a complex mix of values including financial interests and transactions, a participant's reputation, knowledge sharing, goodwill and advocacy. Opportunities can be had in these dynamic environments. Participants become co-creative in sharing values, resulting in value adding on what they already have or know (Lusch and Vargo, 2006).

Lee (2014, p. 141) identifies three factors that define a vibrant professional network culture: A large number of connections to enable the flow of information, key individuals to facilitate information transfer by establishing new connections and the presence of knowledge experts. All networks represent a particular type of transaction in which values are exchanged. These value exchanges create flows which in turn can lead to wealth and opportunity. That wealth can be financial (revenue streams) or non-financial (cultural enrichment, knowledge or reputation building). This is reinforced in our interviews with artist managers. For many music entrepreneurs, networks are the most important factor in developing a successful export strategy. Networks create opportunities for partnerships, establishing deals, building on opportunities and increasing knowledge of current industry trends.

Gatekeepers and intermediaries

There are many theories of gatekeeping from diverse disciplines: Management, journalism, information technology, social networks and communication theory. A brief overview of selected theories is given to provide a context for the later discussion on the international market context.

A gatekeeper controls access to information within a network. Conversely, the gated is an entity or individual who is subjected to a gatekeeping process. Delulius (2015) gives an excellent summary of gatekeeping theory starting with the "father of gatekeeping theory", Kurt Lewin, who, according to Delulius, "approached gatekeeping as just one of many interrelated phenomena that together make up a social field" (Delulius, 2015, p. 4). Astor's (2016, p. 33) summary of music industry contexts ranges from the more traditional approach where access to the industry was controlled by a select few who controlled the production and distribution channels (for example, the major record companies or broadcasting) to the post-punk DIY culture and rise of social media influencers where the traditional power bases are usurped.

Lewin (1947) identified the following components of gatekeeping: Force, channel and section. A force facilitates or constrains the gated. These forces can be positive or negative, and are not fixed and fluctuate. For example, someone who is considered valuable by a gatekeeper will most likely experience a positive force. On the other hand, someone who is out of fashion will most likely endure constraint by a gatekeeper, thereby representing a negative force. Forces can be determined by taste (aesthetic), market demand, policy or ideology. "A channel is defined by the obstacles an item will face: from discovery to use" (Delulius, 2015, p. 7). Each channel is defined by its sections. These are the points through which a decision is made where the gated is positively encouraged or negatively discouraged (constrained). These decision points are determined by gatekeepers. A section is defined by the points "at which decisions are made within a channel" (ibid., p. 6). "Decisions in each section are guided by force". A gate is the point at which a force changes direction from being excluded from a channel or keeping within a channel (ibid., p. 6). In the music industry there are many channels through which a gatekeeper can determine whether a gated individual/entity can move. For the music entrepreneur, identification of these gatekeepers and channels is key. The following quote aptly describes the approach to planning done by music entrepreneurs with "hit lists" in the identification of and access to channels and gatekeepers. "People do their research before they even get to the conference. They already have a hit list of things they want to see and talk to, and they've already made connection to those people beforehand" (Interview 5, 2018).

Shoemaker and Voss (2009) identify five levels of gatekeeping and their forces: "Individual", "communication routines", "organizational", "social institutions" and a "social system" (ibid., Part II). While these five categories apply to journalism and the media industries, they can be seen to be in operation in the music industry, irrespective of whether it is a pre- or post-digital culture. These gatekeeping levels of force have been broadened to include small businesses and other actors in the music industry. The individual level concerns the characteristics of individual gatekeepers, their interpretations, opinions, aesthetics, experiences and expression through social media platforms or product choice. The communicative routines level concerns the repeated practices and routines of a particular profession, interest or lifestyle. These routines constitute the daily "grind" or codes of practice of a profession of repeated activity. The organisational level is an extension of the individual where the organisation becomes the equivalent of the individual. For example, a company is defined by its ethos, values and reputation, all of which have been developed internally through decision-making processes. The social institution level deals with the social forces that have an impact on organisations such as governments, lobby groups or advertising companies. The social system level deals with societal ethos and values which can have an (ideological, cultural, economic or political) impact on organisations' decision-making.

Barzilair-Nahon (2008, p. 1501) applies her gatekeeping model to other types of social networks. These are particularly relevant to the role of digital music platforms with respect to the development of fans, audiences, the rise of independent labels and artists and new means of distribution. Barzilair-Nahon shows that due to social networks, gatekeeping is no longer one way but multidirectional, in which the gated can become a gatekeeper. Gatekeeping "salience" is based on four characteristics: The *relationship* between the gatekeeper and the gated, which can shift between being one way or through frequent exchanges; the *production of information* where the source of information between the gated and gatekeeper is interchangeable; *alternatives* for the gated which provide options to circumvent gatekeepers and/or gatekeeping mechanisms; and the *power relationship* between the gatekeeper and gated where the gated may have its own power in the relationship.

Nahon (2011) introduces "network fuzziness" to describe the unfixed nature of a network's activities of inclusion and exclusion demonstrating a modern-day example of Lewin's forces and channels. "Network fuzziness" is defined by the balance of power in networks, which is continually shifting between stakeholders, in particular between gatekeepers and the gated. This fuzziness is particularly apt when discussing the volatile nature of the music industry and the ability at any one time for a new phenomenon to become popular or "the rage". Nahon (2011) outlines five factors that determine the "fuzziness" of inclusion in/exclusion from a network: Collective patterns of the gated which are continually shifting, increasing integration and interoperability between platforms and applications, dynamism between gatekeeper and gated roles (roles change across networks), interpretation of meaning of gated content (people reinterpret actions, moments to be applicable to their own contexts) and the holistic and interconnectedness of networks (Nahon, 2011, p. 766). These five factors and their transferability show the dynamism of a network's identity due to the introduction and impact of new information into a network. Later in this chapter, it will be shown how this "fuzziness" operates at an international market event where situations and relationships are dynamic and open to change once new information or a new person is introduced into the network, such as a new act that creates excitement. The emergence of the playlist for streaming platforms exemplifies fuzziness of gatekeeping forces.

At the beginning of 2020 Spotify became the world's largest music streaming service with 100 million premium subscribers (FIPP, 2020). However, with so many artists' creative work now more readily retrieved, the born global notion that an artist can be successful by simply uploading onto streaming platforms such as Spotify is not guaranteed. Curated playlists, new platforms and influencers exemplify a seamless transition from the older gatekeeper such as A&R, publishers and broadcasters to the more modern type of gatekeeper. As the following interviewed manager says, it is still a lot of work to break through into these new domains.

> There's a new platform every day. Instagram, Twitter, Facebook, those socials, Snapchat … and then there's learning how to deal with iTunes and Apple and Spotify and how to get your music. A lot of the music that's coming in here on Spotify and all those channels is not coming from here, it's coming from there, from America and England. So you have to get your music onto those American track and playlists to get back into here. It's quite a trip and there's been a lot of complaints lately that there's very few Australian songs in the top 40. And that's because you can get streamed here but you need to get into this worldwide … Because the radio stations are looking at the analytics … it's coming from America. So you've got to get onto those qualified play lists in America and England and things like that. It's quite complicated.
> (Interview 9, 2017)

The relationship between Spotify and the major labels is of particular interest here, with the major labels having shareholdings in Spotify (and other digital platforms). The following quote demonstrates the complex relationship between Spotify and the major labels, clearly showing it's not a level playing field due to holding interests and challenges:

> Tencent Holdings is the majority parent of Tencent Music Entertainment (TME); Tencent is leading a consortium, with TME as a named constituent, that is set to buy 10% (and potentially, eventually, 20%) in Universal Music Group; Universal Music Group still owns a stake (believed to equate to around 3.5%) in TME rival, Spotify; TME and Spotify own single-digit stakes in *each other*, thanks to a "stock swap" agreed in 2017; and UMG's biggest rivals, Warner Music Group and Sony Music Entertainment, both own stakes in TME. Which, remember, is about to own a stake in Universal.
> (Music Business Worldwide, 2020)

This complexity plays out in the following interview with a UK-based music rights consultant in which the shift from an older gatekeeping era dominated by the labels has led to a now more convoluted situation:

> The relationship between the labels and the streaming services is very powerful in London. If you think in terms of Payola and what that used to be at radio, that's now occurring undoubtedly on Spotify … Although Spotify will love to say, "hey, we played an artist from Byron Bay the other day, we put him on the top of our global playlist, we promote talent from everywhere". You look at them over a 6 month period, they're pushing catalogue artists and artists signed to the majors … That gives us a Payola power out of London that you don't have. Sydney, Melbourne, Berlin even, Stockholm even. And that's really bad for plurality and diversity, but it's to our advantage … I think at the moment Spotify is doing a big push around that Guardians of the Galaxy with all its 70s soundtrack. They're just pushing out 70s hits. Again viewed across the year, yes, they played someone from Byron Bay,

> they played someone from Lithuania … But their push is on their relationships with the big spenders at Universal, Sony and Warner. Who are here with direct lines to New York, in the way that you won't find elsewhere.
>
> (Interview 12, 2017)

Aggregators and digital music stores, combined with the newly established curators, have redefined the playing field for aspiring artists in seeking promotion on various platforms in competition with a swathe of new songs and artists. Attracting the attention of a playlist curator is crucial. In 2019, Spotify founder Daniel Ek stated that the number of daily uploads to Spotify is around 40,000 (Music Business Worldwide, 2019). In 2020 Soundcloud reported that while it has over 25 million creators, only 12 million of these creators get heard every month (Music:)ally, 2020). While the Internet is perceived as a leveller and egalitarian, these staggering and sobering statistics show that all the help, from influencing, representation, lobbying, channelling, marketing, etc., is crucial. Being "born global" is not enough; an entrepreneurial perspective is necessary in order to cut through the overcrowded landscape:

> I think if you want to look at an example of this, it's the New Music Friday playlist on Spotify which is quite a sought after premiere opportunity for artists internationally. It's a playlist that's updated every week, it's updated on Friday. It makes a lot of traffic. So if your song is included on that playlist, it's a good way to introduce your music to new people and to acquire some new fans and listeners. Spotify controls that editorially, but that list has been … growing. I think it started as maybe a 20 or 30-song playlist, and I think the US version of the playlist has been well over 100 tracks. That's 100 pieces of music that are brand new that they've selected, plus there are probably thousands of others every week that are submitted that aren't included. The fact that that's happening globally means that it's very busy at home for Australians. You've got all this international music now that's flowing in without any kind of barrier. And in fact, it's expected that it would have an international presence. That then I think makes it harder for local artists to get noticed both at home and abroad. So the challenge of … overcoming the noise and having those opportunities to present a story, that becomes a real challenge. I would say developing a sales story is becoming harder. It kind of follows on from the same principle, but getting spins and getting your playlist spins and getting your playlist count up which is now seen as a key performance indicator in the music industry as the number of plays you've had on something like Spotify, it's harder when you're coming from a smaller market.
>
> (Interview 13, 2018)

Due to the Internet, traditional approaches to gatekeeping are being revised to include new actors such as curators, bloggers, influencers and aggregators (Astor, 2016). If a gatekeeper controls information (Lewin, 1947), then it is implied that the gatekeeper is an arbitrator of power, deciding what is to be distributed or disseminated. If power underlies the role of the gatekeeper, what then is the role of the intermediary? Bourdieu's definition of an intermediary is general and can also be seen to apply to gatekeepers: "All the occupations involving presentation and representation … in all the institutions providing symbolic goods and services … and in cultural production and organisation" (Bourdieu, 1984, p. 359).

Later in this chapter it will be seen that both the gatekeeper and cultural intermediary are present at international music industry events. Sometimes they are clearly separate, but at other times, the distinctions between their roles are more ambiguous. Hesmondhalgh (2006, p. 226) argues that too many use "cultural intermediary" wrongly, referring to Bourdieu's (1984) initial use in reference to tastemakers. For example: Fairchild (2014) mixes a range of roles and figures within the music industries into a "cultural intermediary" field, ranging across policy, industry, promotional, media. As such, there is a need to distinguish between the different roles and activities of those who actively shape public opinion, taste and related notions of innovations and style; produce "cultural jobs [that] directly create performances and texts" (Miller, 2014, p. 25); and perform brokering roles between different fields. This is of particular importance when looking at government export offices such as Sounds Australia at international industry events. Are they gatekeepers or intermediaries? Because export offices are "selling" their knowledge and providing access to networks at these international events which are attended by key stakeholders with control to markets, media and industry sectors, they also fit with Miller's assertion that they are also gatekeepers: "determining who and what counts as cultural" (ibid., p. 26).

Maquire and Mathews (2012) see the intermediary as someone who

> construct[s] value, by framing how others (end consumers, as well as other market actors including other cultural intermediaries) engage with goods, affecting and effecting others' orientations towards those goods as legitimate—with "goods" understood to include material products as well as services, ideas and behaviours.
>
> (ibid., 2012, p. 552)

Whereas the original definition of the gatekeeper is someone who controls and decides on value, for our research the intermediary is seen as someone who facilitates or creates value.

Bypassing gatekeepers

A powerful example of bypassing gatekeepers can be seen in the rise of the unknown artist who reaches fame independently from traditional gatekeeping pathways. Barzilai-Nahon's (2008) gatekeeping theory accounts for the rise of the "YouTube star" phenomenon where artists (usually millennials) bypass the established gatekeeping pathways and directly connect with online audiences. For Barzilai-Nahon, there are multiple pathways once someone provides new information into a network, involving or bypassing different stages of gatekeeping. For example, the "YouTube star" relies on communities discovering and sharing amongst themselves to a point that the fan base is in the tens of millions, attracting interest from sponsors, major labels, broadcasters and other key industry actors such as influencers. In a very general sense, the fan base here is also a gatekeeper, where each fan decides on whether the information should be shared: "Fans want to be able to have discovered something on their own. They want to have the ownership, to say: Hey, I'm the reason this is so successful" (Petridis, 2014). This is a useful example of value co-creation where "once it was seen as a linear process, the value chain is increasingly viewed as networked and distributed to other parties" (Choi and Burnes, 2013, p. 39). The multiple sharing of content, be it direct or repurposed, becomes a nonlinear process in which all parties identify through co-creation, creating networks within networks. Kibby (2000) succinctly sums up this sense of co-creation with the following:

> The ritual exchange of information online allows fans a feeling of community between themselves and between them and the performer, facilitating a belief in a commonality, although they are dispersed geographically and disparate in needs and experiences. An electronic place in which to "gather" enables a direct link between fans, and even makes possible a direct connection between fans and performers. The link benefits not only the fans, but also the performer and the record company, in that it provides a connection to a central focus of the performer and the producer, the marketplace.
>
> (Kibby, 2000, p. 91)

The rise of Australian artist Troye Sivan exemplifies gatekeeping bypassing co-creation, a feeling of community and how contemporary networks can be utilised to build larger audiences. Sivan's initial fan base was constructed via appearances on *Australian Idol* in 2006. With the release of his single "Happy Little Pill" and later the debut album *Blue Neighbourhood* in 2015 (EMI and Capitol), his loyal fan base helped him achieve Established artist status, with both releases reaching number one on iTunes. By uploading his music on YouTube, he actively developed a social media network of fans and friends with whom he interacted, discussing issues such as his coming out. "He sparked his career online, expressed his deepest truths to thousands of viewers, and received enormous support from the loyal fanbase he has built over the past decade through the web" (Ampersand, 2019). Through his direct communication about personal issues, fans identified with him: "The reason why I love Troye is because he is such an inspiration to me … and he is such a genuine person" (Don't bore us, 2018). In a 2018 interview Sivan talks about this direct personal relationship: "I just want to provide for a young audience what I felt was lacking when I was a kid … which was representation of someone living their life" (Bruner, 2018). In July 2020, Sivan had 17,000,000 listeners on Spotify (Spotify, 2020). His highly active engagement with audiences can be seen with the following statistic sample: 9,362,997 Twitter followers (Trackanalytics,

2020a), 7,180,000 YouTube subscribers (Trackanalytics, 2020b) and 11,200,000 Instagram followers (Instagram, 2020).

International market events: An overview

> There are a lot of conferences and showcase events around the world and unfortunately a lot of the young Australian bands go to these events before they're ready. So they spend all their money and they go to these events and nothing happens because they're not ready. They don't have a network of people, it's not that easy. You go to South by Southwest, it's 2,000 bands. Unless you're well connected or you're very special, you're not even going to see the light of day.
>
> (Interview 9, 2017)

International music market events consist of trade fairs, conferences, showcases and/or festivals and are not new to export strategies for the music industry. These industry events have long been seen as crucial in the development of an export strategy, as the primary forums containing key stakeholders, gatekeepers and intermediaries, bringing people together into one space. Strong and weak ties do exist despite the fact that everyone is in the same room. These industry events occur over a short time period where everyone has a role and purpose. All interviewed managers stressed the importance of repeated networking by continually maintaining a presence at these events. Considering the distance and time involved for Australian-based managers, the international events enable time and travel costs to be saved in meeting potential partners, promotors, publicists, labels, etc.:

> [They are] very important. Yes, I mean critical. I mean you know, they bring a lot of people together in the one place. They can often be very noisy, loud events where you're struggling to get heard but if you do get heard and you do seem to have a moment then that can be enormously influential. And we've had some moments at South By Southwest and the Great Escape and things like that. Where you know, they really get a project properly off the ground and running.
>
> (Interview 1, 2018)

Being selected to showcase at an international event presents huge opportunities for artists and bands. They have the chance to perform in front of industry professionals, network and attend conference panels, speed dating and other networking events. However, getting industry professionals to come to an artist's showcase involves considerable investment: Travel expenses such as accommodation, flights and ground transport, freight for instruments and additional backline equipment. All these are paid for by the artist(s) including associated marketing and promotional activities independent to the festival's contractual commitments with these artists. For many of our industry interviewees, these events were crucial in developing an international career:

> I must have attended ten or 12 of them before I first took an artist to one ... I was really lucky to work for an organisation where it was part of my job to try and help other people export, before I had to do it myself, so I got to see it time and time again, how it would work. I thought we really were able to strategically launch my artists' career from two or three events.
>
> (Interview 9, 2017)

All events have their own communities and networks which are formed over years of attendance. One manager travels to international events on average five times a year, with each visit involving months or weeks of accommodation: "It's very important to be [at] and go to these conferences and just keep up with what's going on" (Interview 9, 2017).

A number of events were attended by the authors in order to directly observe export offices, Australian artists and related industry workers. Export offices provide an invaluable service of brokering introductions for delegates including newcomers with elite industry professionals. They facilitate business meetings between delegates with other industry professionals to help create new opportunities and fulfil export goals. The following three event observations provide a window into their activities and ambience.

SXSW, USA: March 2017

South by Southwest (SXSW) began in 1986 with 40 artists performing, 5 stages, a festival and conference. In 2018, it had 2,057 bands perform on 100 stages: "It started as a music festival and conference with the idea of giving artists a platform to perform in-front of the industry and to network" (Interview 15, 2016). The event has expanded to include film, education and interactive sectors in order to provide a platform for all creative industries. Given the sheer scale of the event, many SXSW veterans give the advice to not just show up without doing your homework:

> I've been attending SXSW in Austin Texas for over 10 years. In the early years it was very slow in terms of business for me. It took time to build my network, but also build my business to the point where I could add value to others. This has now well and truly paid off.
>
> (Interview 14, 2018)

There are many established communities within SXSW that have developed over time. It is difficult for newcomers to navigate their way through, with export offices assisting:

> Export offices are really helpful for bands at SXSW. Certain export offices do it better than others, depending on their strategies and budget. In fact it's more important for the export offices to provide artists with support and help navigate through these events and new markets, than writing a cheque.
>
> (Interview 15, 2016)

SXSW also attracts a large public audience to the festival and events held throughout Austin. Accommodation is very expensive and high in demand with an overwhelming number of showcases, events, parties and panel sessions. In 2018, there were 75,098 conference attendees, 4,967 conference speakers and 4,035 media participants; 2,057 bands performed on 100 music stages, with 455 film screenings and 10,000 VR screenings (SXSW, 2018). There was a total of 2,147 conference sessions with 102 countries being represented by registrants (SXSW, 2018). Overall, the 2018 event saw approximately 432,500 people participating in the conferences and festivals (SWSX, Event Statistics, 2018).

MIDEM, France: June 2016

Launched in 1967, MIDEM has been a leading event for the international music industry. The market event is mostly associated with making international and territorial deals in licensing and publishing. MIDEM takes place in a conference centre consisting of stands, panels and seminars. The panel sessions included new innovations in music delivery, copyright, presenting new research. New technology was often discussed with music technology start-up events or new innovations such as blockchain. The event is not based on a showcasing model; however performances occur at events throughout venues around Cannes.

It was observed that Australian labels and publishers were introduced to international actors who could assist in creating new networks and potential new business partnerships by the Sounds Australia team. There were many "invitation-only" events, creating a level of exclusivity within established relationships and networks. There was generally an open atmosphere at the conference with just an undercurrent of a quasi-elite. For example, it was commented by one attendee that some of the more powerful industry actors never leave the hotel rooms, preferring to have meetings there and only attending evening sessions for drinks.

> I would consider MIDEM [is] now for publishers; I really don't think it's delivering to anyone else than publishers. Others, you can go there and you can learn a few things, but it's still very, very heavily publisher-driven.
>
> (Interview 16, 2018)

The Great Escape, UK: May 2016

The Great Escape is a festival, showcase event and conference that occupies the city of Brighton with multiple simultaneous events. As a festival, it selects (curates) artists that it thinks are appropriate to its programming agenda. Given its size and spread across the city, it was apparent that it would be hard for a band to come to an event like this with no assistance and support, especially all the way from Australia. It also hosts a pre-festival panel for managers and industry organised with several export offices, providing network opportunities before the event. As with all of the other industry events, the panel sessions provide valuable information about music exporting, aspects of and trends emerging in the industry:

> We went to The Great Escape in 2015 … Our primary goal in going there was to get a booking agent and to get a record label to sign [artist] for the UK and Europe, and we achieved both of those things from going there.
>
> (Interview 2, 2018)

Observation at these key events continually reinforced the following themes and priorities related to successful navigation of a new market: A digital publicist is essential in a new market; international acclaim can feed into narratives of success for domestic market consumption; local agents and publicists possess the required knowledge to place acts in front of key gatekeepers; festival bookers use showcase events as a "one-stop shop" for booking and signing talent; and appearances at one showcase event can lead to a snowballing effect of multiple offers of showcasing, festival and touring activities.

Showcase events are a major part of an international market event in which selected bands are given the opportunity to perform in front of industry professionals. Artists can apply to showcase or are invited by the market event. There are showcasing events held every month all over the world across different genres and niches. The events help build international teams around artists and help contribute to export success.

Sounds Australia, networking and showcasing

For Australian artists, managers and industry workers, access to these international industry events has been greatly aided by Sounds Australia, Australia's national export platform, established in 2009. Sounds Australia is a joint initiative of the Australia Council for the Arts and APRA/AMCOS. It provides support at international showcase market events, supported by State governments and other music industry bodies.

The Sounds Australia stand provides delegates with somewhere to work, relax and request assistance. The team directs delegates to opportunities, panels or people who can help with specific goals. One of Sounds Australia's main aims is to assist industry and artists attending international market events. In doing so, Sounds Australia provides a range of services and support that are essential for the music exporter. These are showcases with technical support, networking, invited lunches, networking and organising meetings, legal and visa advice and speed dating meetings

If networking is seen as the fundamental activity for making deals and creating opportunities, the role of Sounds Australia is pivotal in facilitating networking between Australian artists, industry workers and international stakeholders.

> They can tap into some of the major players in the industry and put our young managers and our young bands in front of them, or get them to come and see the show, perhaps. So they build up that respect.
>
> (Interview 9, 2017)

Sounds Australia is recognised as a market leader in bringing artists, companies and managers to key overseas markets, strategising about the best combination of events for Australian acts and adopting a collaborative approach in working with Australian music sectors and States in presenting a national structure to international territories. It has proven its worth in assisting the music industry by developing important business relationships and providing support for exporting artists.

In order to cut through the networking complexity, various State organisations use intervention strategies where artists, managers, labels, agents, etc., are placed in specially constructed environments such as showcase events and speed dating. Sounds Australia's "AUSSIE BBQ" event is full of international industry professionals including labels, publishers, agents, festival bookers, managers and artists. Bands are provided with professional backline, sound and stage technical support. This enables a professional performance for the band to put their best foot forward. The AUSSIE BBQ has become a successful example of how an export office can assist its artists in providing access to networks and gatekeepers. Chapter 5 discusses Sounds Australia's approach to supporting Australian music exporters in more detail.

The intensity of international events

International industry events demonstrate a wide array of transactions that are not simply defined by attaining a deal. As a temporary cluster (Henn and Bathelt, 2015, p. 105) they are a complex space for networking, influencing, gatekeeping, collaboration and knowledge sharing. They provide excellent insights into cultural mediation when all stakeholders are in the same place.

Shoemaker and Voss's five levels of gatekeeping, discussed earlier, can be applied to an international music festival, where there are a number of events happening simultaneously (Shoemaker and Voss, 2009). At the individual level, the musical taste of a consumer or a particular demographic exemplifies personal gatekeeping where the fan selects which act to attend. Specific technical requirements for a performance opportunity venue that specialises in a particular style and fast turnaround of acts are an example of routine gatekeeping: If the wrong technology is used, then the operators of that technology will reject the work as it will slow down or disrupt the process. Organisational gatekeeping can be the decisions made by a peer review committee (for example, a festival's programming decisions). At the institutional level, the many industry and showcasing events exemplify their exogeneous nature, where external participants convene at one particular event. At the cultural level, the programming will reflect the changing times and emerging trends. Within any of these levels one can find intersections. For example, the musician who only likes a particular technology for a reverb sound is an example of routine, but also can exemplify cultural gatekeeping in that the technology used represents a particular sound and style.

Janssen and Verboord (2015, p. 3) identify seven types of activities underpinning the mediation of cultural products. They are gatekeeping, co-creation, networking, selling/marketing, distributing, evaluation and policy frameworks. These can all be seen to be in operation at market events. Cultural, social and economic capital conversions are rife with the desire to make a deal, lay the foundations for a future deal or share knowledge with the intention of planning a deal. Reputation, legitimacy, data analytics, impact of digitisation, audience responses, taste and value creation all come into play at these short-term events. These events show how strong and weak network links operate. They are sites for different types of networking, information exchange, co-creation and gatekeeping. While everyone is in the same space, there are levels of access, knowledge exchange and deal-making.

> there's been probably four times in the last eight or nine years where we went in spirit [South By Southwest] with the goal of an artist being you know, really, really hotly, sort of, pursued by labels. And so then to … be in a position where we put them in front of publishers and booking agents and promoters that could potentially also work with them. And we've had … some significant moments like that where an act has gone in and they're unsigned … unpublished. And they came out with like five or six record deal offers, publishing offers. A bunch of agents wanting to work with them and promoters talking about how they'd be really keen to put them on at a festival.
>
> (Interview 1, 2018)

Networking opportunities provided by international industry events enable manager/entrepreneurs to be strategic, adapt to challenges, be flexible and collaborate on projects with limited resources (Schulte-Holthaus, 2019). The cumulative effect of networking and its positive impacts at international industry events are commonly recognised and seen as a value intangible input. Of the 45 participants in the Export Strategies survey, when asked what had the most impact on their export activities at international industry events, 51% said networking was the most positive; 41% surveyed had attended between one and five international market events; with 21% having attended over 15 international market events. Fifty-nine percent of respondents engaged in export activities primarily through existing networks:

> So, I think that's absolutely integral: if you're at that point where you've just kind of started, but there's also that point … where you've got a bit of the plan in place … It can help you finish the plan. By connecting you with other people … And I think all managers at all levels use those platforms like Sounds Australia … if you're a young manager and you, literally, have no idea, to be able to go into those places with that wrapped and meet the people in the industry. And start learning about the market from the ground up. There's nothing else, really, like it that exists. And, the fact that everyone has equal footing within those programmes. And everyone has the same access to people is just phenomenal.
>
> (Interview 8, 2018)

All managers stressed the importance of repeated networking by continually maintaining a presence at international events seeking exposure and visibility, attracting booking agents, label deals or digital distribution revenue streams. Finding booking agents was a common priority, particularly in the US. This helped finance further opportunities:

> I was keen to hook a booking agent, because the performance fee is very integral for us … We didn't get any label deals, so we made partnerships with digital distribution, which was good, a key income stream, particularly in North America … The key thing for us is just establishing a partner that can get us out there on the live frontier. That's the biggest thing you can control in terms of the income streams.
>
> (Interview 2, 2018)

Bathelt and Schuldt (2008) argue that international industry gatherings have become central nodes connecting the global industry and provide all actors with access to new technologies, market trends and potential partners. All of the manager interviews and surveyed participants confirm their value. The Sounds Australia survey found that after attending an international music market event, 60% of participants achieved their goals and objectives, while 74% gained opportunities after attending an event.

Lampel and Meyer (2008, p. 1027) call these "field-configuring events" (FCE) that have six characteristics: They assemble in one location actors from diverse professional, organisational and geographical backgrounds; they have limited duration, normally running from a few hours to a few days; they provide unstructured opportunities for face-to-face social interaction; they include ceremonial and dramaturgical activities; they are occasions for information exchange and collective sense-making; and they generate social and reputational resources that can be deployed elsewhere and for other purposes.

An important aspect of international events is the creation or arbitration of a global "buzz" which occurs within a densely knit web of specialists, and where specialised information and knowledge flows cannot be ignored (Bathelt and Schuldt, 2008, p. 864); "Global buzz generates openness and swift access to external knowledge pools, embedded in a variety of different industry settings and/or world regions" (ibid.). The notion of "buzz" is key to these events, enabling disruption of codified communication protocols found within strong ties. Caves (2000, p. 181) describes buzz as "a critical mass of favorable, or at least involved discussion" where word of mouth is a powerful transmitter for creative goods, and is free and rich in information. It is "treasured among those who promote the sale of creative goods. It is also a check on them, because it mobilises many involved persons' judgments on the worth of creative works that are subjects of serious promotional investments" (Caves, 2000, p. 181). This kind of language is not uncommon for the managers we interviewed, with one manager observing that "there was so much buzz on them around the world that everyone flew in literally just to try and sign them" (Interview 1, 2018).

This is reinforced by recent network theory which differentiates performance from success (Barabási, 2018). While performance is determined by the ability of the "performer" and can be measured (for example revenue streams), success is open to variability and determined by a community or network's assessment of that performer. Creating a buzz is key to success. It generates a sense of salience where an artist becomes valuable to other gatekeepers and their networks:

> So, I emailed, I picked 12 labels and publishers and a lawyer, two lawyers that I thought were all people that would maybe would like what he was doing. And I sent them a personal email to say "hey, we've just signed this artist" and kept it really vague. And it was quite remarkable. I actually didn't expect the response to be as strong but they came back, every single person was like responding within two or three days and saying wow, this is actually extraordinary … [and] We really, really love to see him, can you send up the dates of his shows at South By? And these people started talking about him and by the time we go to South By, there was about 150 or 160 people that were actually all going up and saying "so you're managing [artist]?"
>
> (Interview 1, 2018)

As intermediaries, Sounds Australia plays a number of vital roles at these events. Sounds Australia is recognised by all interviewed managers as being an important export resource. In essence, they provide access to gatekeepers through all their activities. As one artist manager states, Sounds Australia "generally, [are] providing a platform to do business, and … able to participate in that, has been really wonderful" (Interview 10, 2018).

> I think [showcase events are] particularly important at the beginning of an artist's career, when there's heat and an artist is exciting, it's a marketplace for those artists. It's a place where different stakeholders can come and join the team, join the artist, managers can build teams around their artists.
>
> (Interview 11, 2019)

It can be argued that Sounds Australia can be seen as a gatekeeper as well as an intermediary. This is unavoidable. As cultural representatives and through their representation of Australian export interests, they perform brokering roles in these industry environments. Sounds Australia is conscious of this potential ambiguity which is why they do not select artists to showcase. Any Australian artist selected by a festival is automatically given the chance to showcase. All interviewed managers are aware that access to these networks, while at times fortuitous, can be strategically managed. It starts with the artist's narrative, creating a story which enables product differentiation and promotion. These become the drivers for success as the artist's reputation and narrative become salient, increasing in value each time a new gatekeeper (curator, influencer, critic, booking agent, etc.) picks up the artist, thereby enabling access to a new network of sphere of influence.

> There was so much buzz … around the world that everyone flew in literally just to try and sign them. And so we sat in a hotel, we never left the hotel

> and just took meetings for five days straight with different people who were pitching to sign them.
>
> (Interview 1, 2018)

There have been many instances when a circuit breaker is needed where the artist accesses a network from a different point such as going abroad and getting established there. This is where the industry events are crucial in providing access to these networks:

> I think a good example of this is … the British band that I manage. They're in the UK, their home territory; they've done a bunch of touring. They were doing okay-size shows. They weren't getting any radio play and it wasn't really profitable just yet. But we took them over to do a showcase at a festival called Eurosonic which is like the South by Southwest of Europe. It's held in the Netherlands … The band went there, played some shows, got some incredible press coverage. That led to them putting out their first single from the album. When we put it out globally, the Netherlands was the territory that reacted the most. Radio started playing the song there, and the band's career really started to grow in the Netherlands before it grew in the UK in a really significant way.
>
> (Interview 13, 2018)

Conclusion

The rise of digital platforms means that gatekeeping can occur on every level of a network and is multidirectional. In many ways, the international industry events represent an intersection of gatekeeping theories depending on who the gatekeeper and gated are at any particular time, and across individual, institutional, governmental or functional levels.

The volatility of a network, either within a temporary cluster such as an industry event or through more long-term relationships, presents many opportunities for aspiring artists and managers. The international events enable networks and participating gatekeepers to maintain their identity. Repeated attendance maintains strong ties which are perpetuated beyond the short-term time period of that event.

International industry events, in being highly charged temporary clusters, are excellent examples of gatekeeping, network fuzziness and the role of strong and weak ties. Strong ties can be formidable for newcomers due to familiarity amongst returning actors. However, if an artist can create a buzz, the networks become energised to the point at which that buzz, in being a weak tie, can have impact on the decision-making processes of various stakeholders. Suddenly, the gated becomes very salient:

> This is where the build [of] your story comes to fruition, because if you build your story, the grant providers also see the success that's coming, they do hitch their ticket to a successful band. We were really lucky. We had. Almost

> to the tune of $30,000 dollars in terms of international grants and then also got a recording grant.
>
> (Interview 2, 2018)

All networks have their access points either formally such as through membership, or informally through contacts or reputation. This chapter discusses the volatility that can be associated with a network. Implicit in this chapter's discussion is the articulation of power and who controls that power. In the older model, the articulation of power was very clear as power was mostly one-directional. The Internet and DIY strategies adopted to access the industry have challenged the older one-way power stream into one that is multidirectional. While this is arguably a positive move towards a more decentralised model, there are still fundamental problems about power and control such as being included in highly prized curated playlists.

The power relationship between the gated and gatekeeper is not always fixed which is why "having one's finger on the pulse" is so important. New buzzes have the potential to challenge existing power relations within a network. In their study of talent buyers in Boston, Massachusetts, night clubs, Foster, Borghatti and Jones (2011) found that the more original a band's content, the more that talent buyers maintain close ties with each other in sharing information, but do not have close ties with the bands. Conversely, if the content of a band is more familiar, then the talent buyers adopt an arms-length perspective with each other, but foster close ties with the bands. This continual shift between the familiar and unfamiliar exemplifies the fluctuating nature of networking and the constant threat of the new to a network's stability. Competition and collaboration exist side by side. It is why the closed space of an international market event presents many insights into the arbitration of information and access to power.

Governments and industry have understood this volatility with the provision of incentives, grants, representation and special events to enable artists and managers better access to a music industry network and its gatekeepers. The emergence and importance of international industry events are one example of this conscious access, which can be closed and fixed through familiarity, but also provides a fantastic opportunity for the gated to gain access. The policies underpinning access to industry networks are developed in later chapters.

References

Aldrich, H. & Zimmer, C. (1986). Entrepreneurship through social networks. In D.L. Sexton and R.W. Smiler (eds.) *The Art and Science of Entrepreneurship*. Cambridge, MA: Ballinger, pp. 3–23.

Ampersand (2019). Troye Sivan: authentic artistry in the age of social media. 18 February. http://www.ampersandla.com/troye-sivan-authentic-artistry-in-the-age-of-social-media/

Astor, P. (2016). What is gatekeeping? In P. Rutter (ed.) *Music Industry Handbook*. London: Taylor & Francis, pp. 33–39.

Barabási, A. (2018). *The Formula: The Universal Laws of Success*. New York: Little, Brown and Company.

Barzilai-Nahon, K. (2008). Toward a theory of network gatekeeping: a framework for exploring information control. *Journal of the American Society for Information Science and Technology* vol. 59, no. 9, pp. 1493–1512. doi:10.1002/asi.20857.

Bathelt, H. & Schuldt, N. (2008). Between luminaires and meat grinders: international trade fairs as temporary clusters. *Regional Studies* vol. 42, pp. 853–868. doi:10.1080/00343400701543298.

Bourdieu, P. (1984). *Distinction. A Social Critique of the Judgment of Taste*. London: Routledge.

Bourdieu, P. (1986). The forms of capital. In J. Richardson (ed.) 1987. *Handbook of Theory and Research for the Sociology of Education*. New York: Greenwood, pp. 241–258.

Bruner, R. (2018). Troye Sivan is the perfect pop star for 2018. 23 August. https://time.com/5375715/troye-sivan-2018/

Caves, R.E. (2000). *Creative Industries*. Harvard: Harvard University Press.

Choi, H. & Burnes, B. (2013). The internet and value co-creation: the case of the popular music industry. *Prometheus* vol. 31, no. 1, pp. 35–53. doi:10.1080/08109028.2013.774595.

Delulius, D. (2015). Gatekeeping theory from social fields to social networks. *Communication Research Trends* vol. 34, no. 1, pp. 4–23.

Don't Bore Us (2018). Dear Troye Sivane. 29 August. https://www.facebook.com/dontboreus/videos/342833042952889/

Fairchild, C. (2014). Popular music. In J.S. Maguire & J. Matthews (eds.) *The Cultural Intermediaries Reader*. London: SAGE, pp. 125–133.

Felton, E., Collis, C. & Graham, P. (2010). Making connections: creative industries networks in outer-suburban locations. *Australian Geographer* vol. 41, no. 1, pp. 57–70. doi:10.1080/00049180903535576.

FIPP (2020). Chart of the week: the world's most popular music streaming services. 17 February. https://www.fipp.com/news/insightnews/chart-week-world-most-popular-music-streaming-services

Foster, P., Borgatti, S.P. & Jones, C. (2011). Gatekeeper search and selection strategies: relational and network governance in a cultural market. *Poetics* vol. 39, no. 4, pp. 247–265. doi:10.1016/j.poetic.2011.05.004.

Gibson, C., Hardy, J.H. III & Buckley, M.R. (2014). Understanding the role of networking in organizations. *Career Development International* vol. 19, no. 2, pp. 146–161. doi:10.1108/cdi-09-2013-0111.

Henn, S. & Bathelt, H. (2015). Knowledge generation and field reproduction in temporary clusters and the role of business conferences. *Geoforum* vol. 58, pp. 104–113. doi:10.1016/j.geoforum.2014.10.015.

Hesmondhalgh, D. (2006). Bourdieu, the media and cultural production. *Media, Culture & Society* vol. 28, no. 2, pp. 211–231.

Ingham, T. (2019). Nearly 40,000 tracks are now being added to spotify every single day. *Music Business Worldwide*, 19 April. https://www.musicbusinessworldwide.com/nearly-40000-tracks-are-now-being-added-to-spotify-every-single-day/

Ingham, T. (2020). Tencent, set to control 10% of universal, also owns 9.1% of spotify – but Daniel Ek has the final say on firm's stake.*Music Business Worldwide*, 10 February. https://www.musicbusinessworldwide.com/tencent-set-to-control-10-of-universal-also-owns-9-1-of-spotify-but-daniel-ek-has-the-final-say-on-firms-stake/

Instagram. (2020). *Troysivane*. https://www.instagram.com/troyesivan/

Janssen, S. & Verboord, M. (2015). Cultural mediators and gatekeepers. In *International Encyclopedia of the Social Sciences and Behavioral Sciences*, Second Edition. pp. 440–446. doi:10.1016/B978-0-08-097086-8.10424-6.

Ko, S. & Butler, J.E. (2007). Creativity: a key link to entrepreneurial behavior. *Business Horizons* vol. 50, no. 5, pp. 365–372. doi:10.1016/j.bushor.2007.03.002.

Kibby, M. (2000). Home on the page: a virtual place of music community. *Popular Music* vol. 19, no. 1, pp. 91–100.

Lampel, J. & Meyer, A.D. (2008). Field-configuring events as structuring mechanisms: how conferences, ceremonies, and trade shows constitute new technologies, industries, and markets. *Journal of Management Studies* vol. 45, no. 6, pp. 1025–1035. https://doi.org/10.1111/j.1467-6486.2008.00787.x

Lee, M. (2014). Fostering connectivity: a social network analysis of entrepreneurs in creative industries. *International Journal of Cultural Policy* vol. 21, no. 2, pp. 139–152. doi:10.1080/10286632.2014.891021.

Lewin, K. (1947). Frontiers in group dynamics: II. Channels of group life; social planning and action research. *Human Relations* vol. 1, no. 2, pp. 143–153. doi:10.1177/001872674700100201

Lizardo, O. (2006). How cultural tastes shape personal networks. *American Sociological Review* vol. 71, no. 5, pp. 778–807. doi:10.1177/000312240607100504

Lusch, R.F. & Vargo, S.L. (2006). Service-dominant logic: reactions, reflections and refinements. *Marketing Theory* vol. 6, no. 3, pp. 281–288. doi:10.1177/1470593106066781

Maguire, J.S. & Matthews, J. (2012). Are we all cultural intermediaries now? an introduction to cultural intermediaries in context. *European Journal of Cultural Studies* vol. 15, no. 5, pp. 551–562. doi:10.1177/1367549412445762.

Miller, T. (2014). Cultural work and creative industries. In J.S. Maguire & J. Matthews (eds.) *The Cultural Intermediaries Reader*. London: SAGE, pp. 5–33.

Music:)ally. (2020). 12m SoundCloud creators get heard every month (but 13m don't). 3 June. https://musically.com/2020/06/03/12m-soundcloud-creators-get-heard-every-month-but-13m-dont/

Nahon, K. (2011). Fuzziness of inclusion/exclusion in networks. *International Journal of Communications* vol. 5, pp. 756–772

Petridis, A. (2014). Streaming in: the new wave of pop stars created by youtube. 21 February. https://www.theguardian.com/music/2014/feb/20/ward-alvord-days-boyce-avenue-youtube-pop-stars

Reagans, R. (2011). Close encounters: analyzing how social similarity and propinquity contribute to strong network connections. *Organization Science* vol. 22, no. 4, pp. 835–849. doi:10.1287/orsc.1100.0587.

Schulte-Holthaus, S. (2019). Passion and performance in entrepreneurial contexts: an interest-based approach. *The Journal of Entrepreneurship* vol. 28, no. 2, pp. 201–222. doi:10.1177/0971355719851895.

Shoemaker, P. & Vos, T. (2009). *Gatekeeping Theory*. London: Routledge. https://doi.org/10.4324/9780203931653

Smith, C. (2020). 16 amazing SoundCloud statistics. 1 July. https://expandedramblings.com/index.php/soundcloud-statistics/

Spotify. (2020). Troye Sivane. https://open.spotify.com/artist/3WGpXCj9YhhfX11TToZcXP

SXSW. (2018). Event statistics. https://explore.sxsw.com/hubfs/Hosted%20Files/2018-SXSW-Event-Stats-April-2018.pdf

Trackanalytics. (2020a). https://www.trackalytics.com/twitter/profile/troyesivan/

Trackanalytics. (2020b). https://www.trackalytics.com/youtube/user/troyesivan18/

Zwaan, K., Ter Bogt, T.F.m. & Raaijmakers, Q. (2010). Career trajectories of Dutch Pop musicians: a longitudinal study. *Journal of Vocational Behavior* vol. 77, no. 1, pp. 10–20. doi:10.1016/j.jvb.2010.03.004.

5 Case study

Australia

Introduction

We have examined the changing landscapes for the music industries, and music export in particular, in prior chapters. Here we begin to examine the specific national contexts of music exports, and related government and industrial positioning. In this chapter, we examine the broader histories of Australian music export initiatives that reveal a gradual recognition of its potential, and since the 1980s, have also aligned with senses of cultural identity.

Australian music export policy, like much of music/cultural policy more broadly, reflects the governance history of a settler society that has borrowed widely and often from the British Westminster system, with attendant arts policy machinery, funding models and discourses. Australian policy contexts share much with other Commonwealth nations such as New Zealand and Canada. Citing McCaughey (2005), Craik (2007, p. 35) notes the larger nations (e.g. Germany, France, the Scandinavian countries) where arts/culture is "a core priority for government policy and expenditure … and those for whom it is a footnote or *marginal* responsibility (Canada, Australia, New Zealand, Singapore and Switzerland)". Yet as this book shows in the following chapter, this is changing, where nations notice particular comparative advantages in promoting popular music in other territories and have invested accordingly.

Post-war Australia was primarily known for "excellence" in opera and classical music; Joan Sutherland, Percy Grainger, Peter Sculthorpe, Margaret Sutherland and others enjoyed extensive domestic and international careers. By the 1960s, popular music had obtained a foothold, especially in UK markets:

> Australasian artists such as The Seekers, The Bee Gees, Frank Ifield, The Easybeats, John Rowles and Rolf Harris have achieved international success. The forecast growth of the music industry in Australasia … should parallel the great expansion of growth predicted by the leaders of the industry and closely related to the enormous investment and talent which is available to bring about an expanded acceptance by the world's people of the pleasure available to them through the media of music.
>
> (Frederick C. Marks, Festival Records Australia and New Zealand delegate, cited in Marks, 1969, p. 230)

For all of Mr Marks' enthusiasm, the Festival Records Manager noted the historical problems facing both Australia and New Zealand popular music: The large distances from other key markets; the small population sizes of both nations; the intrusion of government in terms of tax, trade and public broadcasting policies; and the high costs of production and distribution (ibid., pp. 233–235). This comment—uttered in 1969—predicts much later concerns from Australian labels and managers about the challenges in later decades.

In this chapter we examine the emergence of different strands of policies and regulations as successive governments since the 1970s began to acknowledge how popular music might accord with wider political and industrial ambitions. This included a parallel acknowledgement of the potential of music exports, which reveals a sharper profile in industry and government thinking in the 1980s. The rest of the chapter is devoted to examining the development of Sounds Australia, the nation's export programme, and its contemporary operations. In particular, we will look at how Sounds Australia operates in the same ways or differently from its overseas counterparts, and how Australia's music export programme became embroiled in wider cultural funding battles and debates in Australian politics. Sounds Australia is offered here as an extended case study that prefigures similar examinations in Chapter 6 which looks at the governance and operational contexts of other leading music export nations.

Policy histories

While the federal Whitlam (Labor) and Fraser (Liberal/National) governments of the 1970s had expanded the range of arts activities within Australian government structures and funding, the real policy work to accommodate popular music within traditional funding structures began in the 1980s. A 1986 House of Representatives' report, *Patronage, Power and the Muse: Inquiry into Commonwealth Assistance to the Arts*, acknowledged that "cultural value is not limited to any narrow range of activities" (Breen, 1999, p. 101). This opened funding support for "contemporary" music, with report recommendations for training, education and recording assistance, along with a blank tape levy to fund Australian composers (ibid., pp. 101–102). A later Australian Trade Commission report recommending export assistance seemed sensible to then (Labor) federal Minister for Trade, John Dawkins: "There is a depth of talent in the Australian music industry which, given expert advice and marketing assistance, can, I am confident, earn valuable export dollars for Australia" (cited in Breen, 1993, p. 75).

Arguably the world's first cultural policy programme (preceding the Blair Government's UK Creative Industries Taskforce of 1997), the Keating Labor Government's *Creative Nation* was a bold vision that connected media and other technological industries with a less traditional arts policy. It also heralded a decisive shift from *culture* to *creativity* as the defining locus of support and policy formation (see Throsby, 2015). In announcing a new suite of Cultural Industry Development funding, the Prime Minister situated cultural exports as a prominent means to link interdependent discourses:

> Australia stands to benefit greatly from sharing the best of its culture with the rest of the world. First of all, there is the economic argument. Cultural industries create wealth and provide employment, but there is only so much economic sustenance which a population of 17 million can provide. For the Australian cultural industries to flourish, they must look out towards the markets of the world … A confident international projection of Australia's culture will greatly enlarge and enhance our national life: it will improve our domestic employment rates, our balance of trade, our position in the world and our understanding of what it is to be Australian. Culture is one of Australia's most intelligent exports.
>
> (Keating, 1995, pp. 4, 6)

While the Labor governments of Hawke (1983–1991) and Keating (1991–1996) maintained support for the high arts, the recognition of popular culture's potential (such as gaming, the book and music industries) was harnessed to an explicit international outlook that was expected to simultaneously assist GDP and the formations of a new national identity. In 2007, Jennifer Craik established a typology of policy models as a means of identifying much larger shifts of intent in policy directions, and the extent of federal resources attached to them. For Craik, Australia was moving from a "Patron" model (with the older shibboleths of "excellence" and "international standards") towards some forms of the "Architect" model (incorporating elements of industry assistance) (Craik, 2007, p. 81) (we return to elements of the Craik typology in the next chapter).

The Labor Government backed an Export Development Strategy from Austrade in 1986, arguing that traditional support at music trade fairs like MIDEM, complemented by more targeted activities, should produce results. In the same year, Export Music Australia (EMA) was launched to promote Australian popular music in select markets, co-funded by APRA, AMCOS and ARIA. In time, EMA would produce an Export Market Development Grant Scheme, export marketing guides, workshops and industry fairs. This timed well with Ausmusic, the government-funded body established in 1988 to oversee education, training, policy and advocacy. However, substantial conflict about policies (and their implementation) between Ausmusic, Austrade, industry sectors and government departments (Breen, 1999, pp. 81–87; 160–161) prohibited a truly coordinated series of strategies that could be effective. In addition, statistics on outcomes diverged enormously. MIDEM coordinator for Australian participants, Phil Tripp, estimated $63m royalties for nine companies as a result of their presence at MIDEM in Cannes in 1988, while Austrade in the same period estimated returns of $1m per year from export investments (ibid., pp. 85–86). The problems in deploying a reliable economic method are evident in a 1987 *Economic Evaluation* of the Australian industry, which stated exports to be worth $18m in 1984/85 (Hoegh Guldberg, 1987, p. 129) that included musical instruments, "recorders and reproducers", and "other" recording media (ibid.).

In 1997, a federal government initiative, Contemporary Music Export Marketing Advances, offered loans for bands and management for promotional activities overseas (Elder, 1997). Two *Sydney Morning Herald* articles in 1997 revealed the diversity of opinions about the increased drive to supporting export initiatives. Advertising the Pacific Circle Convention, a "fair, festival *and* convention" of Australian talent and the local music industry, promoter/manager Michael Chugg spoke of the need to lure key recording company and promotion executives to Australia "to show what's going on here" (cited in Martin 1997, p. 13). Chugg cited the recent international successes of Peter Andre, Silverchair, Savage Garden and Deni Hines as reasons why ARIA was providing $4 million in support (ibid.). In the same year, the newspaper's music editor Bruce Elder remained deeply sceptical of the federal government's recent Contemporary Music Export Marketing Advance scheme:

> The biggest problem with government initiatives in pop and rock is that, as a general principle, they do not work. Popular music is one of the last bastions of laissez-faire capitalism. It succeeds in the marketplace (which most people in the record industry believe is the only aesthetic criterion) because of a mixture of accessibility, style, hype and marketing.
>
> (Elder, 1997, p. 17)

The export sector (in general) is one of the most scrutinised: Between 1977 and 2008, 12 reviews were conducted by different internal and external bodies (Commonwealth of Australia, 2008, p. 38). In 2005, Austrade announced renewed efforts to tackle the US and British markets, with an increased presence at events such as South by Southwest (with the claim of ten acts achieving international label signings after attendance) and a new Manchester office established (Eliezer 2005, p. 18). By 2008, Austrade pointed to successes: "its 60 international offices helped broker 211 music deals in 2007, up from 114 in 2006 and 68 in 2005" (Eliezer, 2008, p. 21). In 2007–2008, 131 artists/businesses received an Export Music Development Grant, with Austrade administering $3.4m to the music industry (Murfett, 2008, p. 1). Further, "In 2008–09, 98 music industry exporters received $3.08 million in EMDG grants. These companies generated around $8.64 million in exports" (Austrade, 2010, np).

However, the Australian Music Office (established in 2005 in London, Los Angeles and Frankfurt) services were criticised for seemingly duplicating expertise to little effect (Murfett, 2008, p. 1). Concerns were beginning to be expressed in public about a perceived lack of coordination between the Australian Music Office, which also charged artists and managers for their "matchmakers" services that did not amount to more than "superficial" support, according to one artist manager (ibid.). After a review and restructure, the offices were closed in 2011. In addition, the defeat of the Keating Labor Government in 1996 saw the incoming Howard Coalition Government end Ausmusic funding. In hindsight, it has been argued that the Australian Music Office concept was not fully appreciative of the particular needs of cultural industry exports:

> I think the problems there were that it was very much run like any other industry, except this is an industry that didn't have money to invest in the same way. People in meats and wine are used to paying for that kind of service. There was no way an artist's manager was going to pay an unknown

> person in government something like $140 an hour to maybe set up some meetings. There's nothing about that you could get across the line.
>
> (Interview 16, 2018)

In 2008, the Australia Council announced its "Track Record" programme, providing successful manager applicants with $40,000 over two years to develop the international profile of their bands. This was deemed to be part of a wider export development push, "responding to current global interest and demand in rock/pop and Indigenous music from Australia" (Australia Council, 2008).

The lack of industry coordination was confirmed in a 2005 report, *Let's Get The Show on the Road*, that outlined the obstacles to a "cohesive contemporary industry", emphasising the lack of coordination between Australian States, with a "highly fragmented" music sector that was failing to present a unified voice to government (Allen Consulting Group, 2005, pp. v–vi). However, external contingencies began to produce some agreement within music sectors and broader government policy, reflected in a range of reports assessing technological, cultural and industrial change. The Rudd Labor Government's 2010 *Strategic Contemporary Music Industry Plan* saw the need to "encourage ongoing exposure and increased diversity of Australian contemporary music across various platforms" (Commonwealth of Australia, 2010, p. 12), and sought views on "financial support to assist new and emerging artists and bands to produce broadcast-ready, and commercially viable, products for radio" (ibid.). A 2012 *Convergence Review* proposed that major media companies ("content service providers") pay into a "converged content production fund"; Australian contemporary music would be one of the beneficiaries in the production of new local content for a platform age (Commonwealth of Australia, 2012, pp. ix–xii). In the same year, a review of the Australia Council found that both Canada (0.156%) and New Zealand (0.198%) spent more than Australia (0.084%) on arts/culture (Trainor and James, 2012, p. 22), and that the considerable lack of funding for "contemporary" music should be addressed by a new funding stream of $15b for "unfunded excellence" (ibid.).

Sounds Australia was

> … instigated by the Australia Council for the Arts in 2008, and it became a joint partnership between them and APRA. I think what's important to note is that our creation came out of the market development section of [the] Council.
>
> (Interview 16, 2018)

Originally conceived as an appointed role within the Australia Council, Millgate's position was ultimately (and literally) situated closer to industry sectors, with the office created within APRA AMCOS's Sydney building.

As the Gillard Labor Government was preparing its own update to the Keating Government's *Creative Nation*, Australian music sectors made clear that further investment was required for export activity to match the scale and purpose of overseas competitors. Succeeding Peter Garrett as Arts Minister, Labor veteran Simon Crean released *Creative Australia* in 2013. Those on the Minister's advisory committee stated that Crean wanted a "joining the dots, bringing culture into contact with the 'education revolution', with technology and innovation, and with its role in binding the social fabric of the nation" (Bakhshi and Cunningham, 2016, p. 7). While much of the policy document simply re-heated existing cultural programmes and visions (Homan, 2018), the internationalisation of Australian content was re-emphasised. Sounds Australia was regarded as part of a set of initiatives driving "cultural diplomacy and the creative economy" (Australian Government, 2013, p. 117), with the added obligation of popular music to assist in growing connections between Australia and Asia in the "Asian Century" (ibid.). $1.75m was provided for Sounds Australia for four years (part of the funding had begun in 2012).

Government lobbying also derived from a recognition that more could be done in articulating an Australian voice within particular markets:

> When I used to go to South by Southwest, you'd watch a manager … It's very isolating, but I think there was this idea that if I introduced you to this person, they'd run off with you, but now there's this amazing camaraderie. You can see the managers supporting each other … It's all by example, everyone walking through the doors together; it's so intangible, but it's effective and contagious. You can start to see that people knew where the Australians were.
>
> (Australian export manager cited in Homan et al., 2016, p. 67)

> We went to play in Nashville in 2006 and went to this terrific festival called the Americana Festival, which is where they divide their music up to try and brand themselves. So country music is a dirty word for the Americana folks, because when they say "Americana", they're talking about the traditional people, you know, the Johnny Cashes and Willie Nelsons and all of those people, plus the roots and blues end of the spectrum. Country music is now the "Nashville pop" thing, you know, Keith Urban and Taylor Swift and all that sort of stuff. Anyway, of course we don't make that differentiation here, because it's just all country; it's just that pop's at one end and the roots thing's at the other. So I went to this festival and saw all these amazing people who were performing under this Americana banner, and I thought to myself, (a) gee, I'd love to come here and play, but (b) this is where Australian country artists, or a lot of them anyway, should be focussing their attention, 'cause it was a growing event and a growing genre.
>
> (Australian artist cited in Homan et al., 2016, p. 67)

Yet history seemed to be repeating. As with *Creative Nation*, much of *Creative Australia* was not implemented due to the demise of the Gillard Government, and the disinterest shown by the incoming Abbott Coalition Government. The new conservative Arts Minister, George Brandis, had promised before the 2013 election to eradicate "fashionable" cultural funding, with "the pursuit of excellence across all of the artistic genres [to] be the central value of cultural policy under a Coalition Government" (Brandis, 2013). Beyond re-shaping funding in highly controversial ways (see, for example, Eltham and Verhoeven, 2015; Mendelssohn, 2015), Sounds Australia's funding was not renewed within the Minister's new Catalyst fund in May 2016, where "organisations like Sounds Australia were invited to apply for a share of $12 million per year over four years" (Carter, 2016). After considerable media reportage and lobbying by industry bodies, by November a new Arts Minister, Mitch Fifield, had found $1.16m for Sounds Australia over four years (Crittenden, 2016).

With the 2019 election looming, Labor and Coalition parties promised bipartisan commitment to furthering the potential of Sounds Australia. In October 2018, the Labor Opposition announced a "new Sounds Australia" that with the existing Live Music Office would have a combined budget of $10m over three years if elected (Shorten, 2018). In March 2019, the Coalition government announced a further "$1.6 million to expand the [Sounds Australia] program to assist the Australian music industry to capitalise on emerging markets in Asia" as part of a $30.9m "Australian Music Industry Package" (Fifield, 2019). The bipartisanship was partly facilitated by submissions and hearings of a federal parliament *Inquiry into the Australian Music Industry* in 2018. Central industry bodies, including ARIA and APRA AMCOS, spoke to the need for a further concentration on exports performance.[1] Of the Inquiry Report's 16 recommendations, 3 focused upon exports:

- "The committee recommends that the Australian Government invest in Sounds Australia to enable it to expand its music exports program" [Recommendation 8];
- "The committee recommends that the Australian Government implement policy to prioritise and promote the use of Australian music and the hiring of Australian artists for government activities, events, and promotions, both in Australia and at Australian-hosted functions and events overseas" [Recommendation 9]; and
- "The committee recommends that the Department of Foreign Affairs and Trade work with the United States of America to develop mutually beneficial visa arrangements that allow artists from both countries to more easily showcase and tour" [Recommendation 10] (Commonwealth of Australia, 2019, pp. xviii–xix).

The call for an expanded Sounds Australia was also placed within the context of a local industry goal of "gaining a five per cent market share of the global music market by 2030", where this "would generate a $5 billion export market" (ibid., p. 60). This was based on ARIA CEO Dan Rosen extending the authors' estimation of local exports to be $195 million, that "is 20 per cent of the Australian music industry's revenue. So we need to switch it around by 2030, where exports are 80 per cent" (Eliezer, 2019). This represents much wider collective ambitions for the country. It is now pertinent to examine the recent operations of Sounds Australia in terms of their industrial and national ambitions, the allocation and uses of resources and their position within the global circuit of other national schemes and activities.

Sounds Australia

Beginning with initial operational funding of $50,000 from the Australia Council in 2009 to a budget of $931,890 in 2018, Sounds Australia has received over $7m in financial and in-kind support to date. Its stated roles are to:

- Provide the best possible environment for Australian artists at international showcase events;
- Provide industry value-added networking and business matching opportunities at international events and centralise export strategy across national, State and Territory funding agencies and industry bodies to reduce the duplication of available resources;
- Raise the profile and visibility of Australian artists and industry in key international markets; and
- Facilitate the introduction of buyers and sellers of Australian music (Sounds Australia, 2018a).

In similar ways to other case study nations examined in the next chapter, Sounds Australia invests its resources heavily in the showcase/trade fair model. This includes a range of activities that are specific to particular artists, managers and companies that emphasises industry-wide sharing of knowledge.

According to its Executive Producer Millie Millgate, in its 10-year history, Sounds Australia has showcased 1,708 Australian acts and coordinated 176 B2B networking events, 39 trade stands and 15,274 meeting opportunities. Its staff have been involved in 22 panel presentations, and organised 115 Australian speakers at international conference events; since 2009, Sounds Australia has been involved in 80 different international events, in 69 different cities and across 25 countries (ibid.). For example, Australian showcase nights are offered at the Folk Alliance International in North America; an Australian pavilion stand is offered at Jazzahead in Bremen and Classical:NEXT in Rotterdam; and in 2019, 33 Australian artists performed at The Great Escape, the primary showcase event in the UK. At South by Southwest, an Australia House was established in 2018 to present acts over five days and nights in Austin. There is also a large annual presence at the Reeperbahn Festival in Hamburg.

In addition, Sounds Australia has hosted a range of veteran and emerging acts at the Americanafest in Nashville, and at Music Matters, Asia's prominent independent music festival. Based on expressions of interest, a delegation is also taken to A2IM, the "Indie Week" conference held annually in New York. Sounds Australia staff also attend the annual BIGSOUND Festival in Brisbane and have led in events where Australia has been nominated as the "spotlight" country at Canadian Music Week (2015), The Great Escape (2010, 2019) and the Reeperbahn Festival (2019).

Sounds Australia does not select artists for particular showcase or promotional events; the organisation becomes involved once an act has been invited to perform. Instead, the organisation is activated upon an artist or manager's presence or acceptance to an international event or strategy:

> What works I think incredibly well with our initiative over other territories is that we have nothing to do with the artists being selected, and it's something we try to remain distant; the less we have to do with that, the better … We've been asked, but the more arm's length we are, the better. I've looked at initiatives [in other countries] who are backing their best horses attempting to filter locally, and then push … but if a festival booker in Brighton, or Austin, or Toronto has decided that "this artist might do well in our market", that's when we step in, when they then come to us. To me, that's a much more effective way of making that decision. Once you're committed, then … we get involved with export training, with information, what state and federal funds they can go for.
>
> (Interview 17, 2009)

Domestically, Sounds Australia coordinates information sessions in each State for artists, labels and managers interested in export activity, with an emphasis upon expectations and preparedness to be "export ready".

The project undertook to observe Sounds Australia at key events; authors observed their staff at A2IM, The Great Escape, MIDEM and Reeperbahn, while also conducting interviews with other national export staff and attendees. We observed the general flows of traffic through events, where attendees were primarily juggling many activities throughout one day, according to their industry roles: Business meetings, managing a showcase for their performer, attending a panel presentation for market reconnaissance, gauging the related market and regulatory contexts of the host country, scoping media opportunities, scoping licensing opportunities, etc. This included Sounds Australia activities such as "speed networking" for businesses, business stand representations, networking receptions, Australian market briefings or the distribution of Australian marketing materials or digital start-up sessions. Alternatively, Sounds Australia will facilitate specific market reconnaissance meetings for Australian managers (e.g. "Meet the Canadians"; Irish networking breakfast).

In our observations of Sounds Australia's presence at key events, it was clear that Millie Millgate enjoyed an enviable reputation among other national export staff. This has been earned by Millgate's collegiality with other national stand staff and managers, and her accumulation of knowledge about the international flows of personnel, genres and gatekeepers (and it is rare for the same senior export manager to remain in the role for ten years, an unusually long period). This uniquely places Millgate to observe trends in national policy, and the evolution of showcase work tied to other activities.

Previous incarnations of export assistance—the Australian Music Office work in locations such as Los Angeles in the 1980s, for example—have described their primary task to be that of "matchmakers" (see above). For Australian industry personnel, Millgate exemplifies the "intermediary" model (Negus, 2002) of harnessing industry knowledge and different elements of a global network where applicable. According to one artist manager:

> I think that on a very personal level having [Sounds Australia] people in those markets at those big showcases, when the managers have problems or wobbles, or don't know what to do about something, that sort of friendly person from home is actually really, really important, and I think they do a really good job of that.
>
> (Interview 18, 2018)

Budget considerations, mixed with the "hands-on" approach of the Sounds Australia team, also means that they are more likely to perform on-the-ground duties themselves:

> Other [national schemes], they just would never think to deal directly with a venue … They'd want to put someone on the ground locally who will know … It means you've got a relationship with the artist that is very, very personal and very close.
>
> (Interview 16, 2018)

This seemed very different from the fee-for-service model favoured by the federal governments of the 1980s and 1990s.

That nations (and by extension, music export offices and programmes) are engaged in competition within "attention economies", and related goals of improved export revenues, is at times implicit and explicit. However, we observed high levels of cooperation between export office staff at showcase events, supported by the comments of various staff interviewed. Beyond competitive instincts, there was acknowledgement that at times shared resources and expertise could benefit all parties:

> So we'd help out the Canadians and then when you go back to Canada or the U.S. or whatever, the Canadians would say "come along to the party". And then you're meeting up with all the different ones, so we became part of the gang. And I can remember for Australia we did Liverpool Sound City, we were all in the same physical space, the Australians were downstairs, we were upstairs. So we said, rather than one competing with the other, why don't we do an exchange? Like, I'll pay for the beer, you pay for the barbeque. It will be a Brazilian band, an Australian band, Brazilian band, Australian band. And in Millie's case it works really well because she doesn't have ego, she's not like "no, no, no", it's okay, so it works … We do these things almost out

> of poverty, we have to be inventive to find new means of attracting publics and so on.
>
> (Interview 19, 2016)

This reminds us of the different hierarchies of support available to export administrators, contingent upon the emphasis and related funding within national cultural budgets. Yet it also reinforces another intangible factor at play: A much broader desire to see artists succeed, irrespective of their national origins.

While State governments had always interacted with Sounds Australia, collaboration is also gradually increasing with other federal government sectors. For example, in 2018, Sounds Australia assisted Tourism Australia's "G'Day USA" programme and Austrade to provide an Australia House platform at South by Southwest, which included the use of celebrity chefs and film stars promoting Australian food parallel to the music offerings (Interview 20, 2018).

Governance and funding

Within ten days of assuming the Executive Producer position in the newly formed Sounds Australia in 2009, Millgate was at MIDEM, providing a good opportunity to assess different national models. The UK's setup was a potential template to follow, although its foundations in trade-related funding and ambitions did not fully accord with Australian operations. It is interesting that Sounds Australia does not regard itself as an "export office" (with accompanying direct funding of overseas activities, selection of artists and oversight of various domestic grant funding) as it is understood in countries such as Sweden, but as a "branding exercise":

> It was set up as an overarching umbrella that everyone could come in under. Maybe that's partly why the model evolved that way. It was about, it's there for everyone to access. Even to the point where I think there were a couple of artists who put Sounds Australia on their CDs and on their flyers just because they were going to be part of the umbrella. The language is around creating a logo and an identity that would have this national org [sic] feel. But no-one ever used the words "export office"; no-one used "export body".
>
> (Interview 16, 2018)

The relative lack of funding (compared to similar UK, Canadian or Scandinavian organisations) in its early years provided the organisation with decisions about how to allocate scarce resources. After a year with only one employee, in late 2010, an Export Music Coordinator position was established. In the first ten years, "It feels like it's been hand-to-hand combat" (Interview 21, 2018) with the organisation covering the central showcase events with few staff and related resources. It also forced them to make hard choices about what is feasible, particularly in making annual judgements about whether key global showcase events have retained their prominence and use to Australian artists. In relation, this also meant judgements about which territories—and genres—in which to concentrate resources.

This could include the ability undertake more reconnaissance trips to emerging events and markets, and to significantly widen the scope of activity in genres (see discussion below):

> It's great, we're doing bits of jazz and classical. But if it had significant resources, it could actually sit down with the classical sector and spend the time to say, "what is the opportunity for Australian contemporary art music internationally?"
>
> (Interview 21, 2018)

In 2013, an Export Music Producer position was funded, and a Digital Export Producer role was created in 2018 by re-allocating existing funds. The staff expansion to four positions remains low in relation to international export offices, but it did enable the team to consider training staff expertise upon other markets such as Asia and South America. This was acknowledged in the Sounds Australia submission to the 2018 Australian Parliament *Inquiry into the Australian Music Industry*, where it was argued that further resourcing would allow it:

> to develop a boutique in-bound buyers program specifically targeted to support Australia's folk, jazz, contemporary classical, blues, roots and world music genres … to host hand-picked international programmers and festival bookers as part of a curated VIP offering … with a combination of existing local music festivals, regional performing venues, tourism associations and attractions, State governments and local councils across Australia.
>
> (Sounds Australia, 2018a, p. 19)

The Sounds Australia team have made understandable choices about "core" and "secondary" markets based on available resources, the primary markets for Australian exports and the dominant locations of the showcase model. The above proposed strategy aligns with countries such as Brazil, who have in the past invested in in-bound programmes to promote artists and labels who may not directly align with existing international showcase circuits.

Longer debates also form part of decisions about how best to support artists and the suitability of grant funding to address long-term industry needs. Further resourcing of managers, both to assist their experiences in bringing acts to market, and in growing the number of experienced managers, was regarded as a problem across the Australian industry. One industry veteran argued that "There is a dearth of managers in Australia – it's the hardest job outside of crew" (Morrison, 2018). Local resources are available to Australian managers for learning their craft (e.g. AAM/APRA AMCOS mentorship programmes; State programmes such as the Fast Track Fellowship and Music Passport grants through Creative Victoria). For one interviewee:

> It's about this obsession with resourcing bands to go, rather than resourcing the managers to have the business done. Another challenge for that is being

> able to be in the market longer than just coming through on a tour or whatever, and actually immersing yourself wherever it is to build deep relationships and networks.
>
> (Interview 18, 2018)

Another music manager interviewed believed that managers should be consulted more on the prioritisation of market choices. Greater emphasis upon both training and supporting managers for international engagement would reflect concurrent shifts in the funding structures of other nations. For example, the UK Music Managers Forum partners with Arts Council England in the Accelerator Programme for Music Managers, allowing managers to apply for up to £15,000 that includes training and mentoring components. This need was acknowledged in the Sounds Australia submission to the 2018 Australian Parliament Inquiry into the Australian Music Industry:

> the addition of subsidised targeted trade missions for managers, with a concentration on relationship building, market education and demonstrations of the latest technology and service platforms, undertaken explicitly without artists involved, would allow managers to advance their own international networks and increase skill capacity.
>
> (Sounds Australia, 2018a, p. 18)

A subsequent recommendation of the Inquiry was to "invest in initiatives aimed at training and supporting artists and industry professionals to grow and develop their businesses", which included the need to reinstate funding for the Australian Music Industry Network's CONTROL[2] programme for managers; and the Australia Council's International Music Makers and Music Managers fund (Commonwealth of Australia, 2019, p. ix).

State–industry collaborations

The development of artist managers (see Chapters 3 and 4) is one of a number of issues relating to how the music industries arrange themselves across seven State governments/territories situated within a federal government system. Prior to the formation of a national export organisation, Australian State governments were engaging in some forms of export activity. Queensland is thought to have first assembled a policy linking arts and trade strategies:

> Trade Queensland had some pretty great initiatives. They had engaged a company in the US to work with them and had two Queensland acts every year on the MUSEXPO showcase. They had the same deal in place with the Great Escape [UK event] and two Queensland artists would be on the Great Escape, and they also had the same with Music Matters (Singapore event],

> but I think just one artist. They also engaged a publicist that would work with those artists in the region, and they also had funding quarantined for showcase event participation. And they also contributed some inbound to BIGSOUND, bringing additional key buyers in … the funding for the acts came from Arts Queensland.
>
> (Interview 16, 2018)

Western Australia also began funding expeditions to SXSW, and Victoria started to support international tours (ibid.).

In its ten-year history, Sounds Australia has been primarily funded through a combination of state (Australia Council, Department of Communications and the Arts, Department of Foreign Affairs and Trade, NSW, Queensland, South Australia and Victorian governments) and industry (APRA AMCOS, PPCA, AMPAL, AMIN) sectors. Where relevant, industry and Australian State bodies have worked together at specific events and locations, such as AMPAL with MIDEM in Cannes, AIR/PPCA with A2IM in New York and the Australian Music Centre with Classical:Next and Jazzahead!. APRA AMCOS has been crucial in providing infrastructural support (including office space), and the Australian Music Industry Network (AMIN) assists in working across State and industry sectors, with the Australian Association of Managers (AAM) liaising with Australian artist managers.

Some Department of Foreign and Trade (DFAT) funding and in-kind support (such as the use of High Commission offices) have also been provided for work in emerging markets and related events. DFAT currently funds a trade mission to South America and has worked with Sounds Australia across a number of different countries, including the London High Commission and offices in Los Angeles, New York, Houston, Chile, Brazil, Argentina and Berlin. It has been suggested that greater branding strategies with DFAT and a range of related Australian products and media, "where music fits in with that as the soundtrack of export" (Interview 18, 2018), could be explored.

As discussed above, Sounds Australia's activities are not directly aligned with a specific grant scheme. Beyond invitations to international showcase events, artists, managers and companies are encouraged to examine the range of assistance available across federal, State and Territory schemes (see Figure 5.1). This has imposed expectations upon Sounds Australia that it perhaps cannot deliver:

> It's very much become now, "we need to see what you're doing for Victorian artists", for New South Wales artists, for Queensland artists. It's a much harder sell; we're very much a round peg in their square funding models. And it's really hard as a national body to … Everything we do and speak are in national terms, and so to really start to draw out, "okay, this is what's going to happen exactly for Victorian artists…"
>
> (Interview 16, 2018)

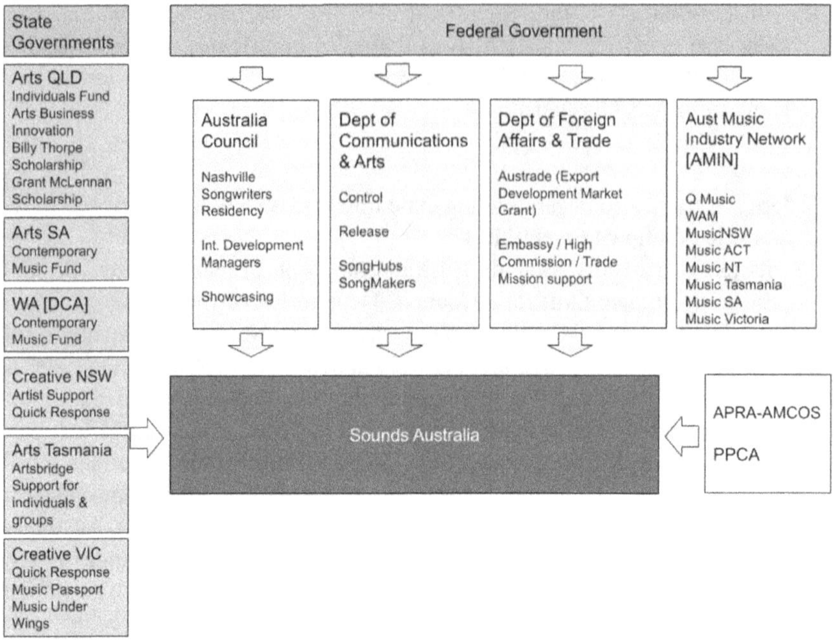

Figure 5.1 Sounds Australia: Governmental/industry funding relationships.

Nation, identity, sounds

As briefly discussed in Chapter 1, national export strategies (to differing extents) draw upon existing global understandings of particular national markers of identity. At the larger showcase events (Reeperbahn, South by Southwest, Primavera, Music Matters, The Great Escape), "THE AUSSIE BBQ" nights have been established by Sounds Australia as distinctive events that draw upon Australian branding that is readily identifiable. They have proven to be an effective drawcard at particular events:

> THE AUSSIE BBQ started as an idea in 2003 to throw together a little BBQ for the Australian bands at South by Southwest Music Festival. It has now grown to become an international circuit of shows that includes Argentina, Austin, Barcelona, Brazil, Brighton, Chile, Kansas City, London, Nashville and Singapore. In most instances, THE AUSSIE BBQ showcases are full band performances rather than solo artists. Back line is shared, changeovers are extremely tight and Australian-Style Hot Dogs aka "Aussie Tacos" are served.
> (Sounds Australia, 2018b)

As noted in Chapter 1, "culture" and notions of local identity are almost invariably invoked by governments in cultural policy announcements or plans, increasingly married to economic goals. The problems in articulating a cohesive national identity through particular artists, or even a genre, have been discussed elsewhere (e.g. Turner, 1992; Homan et al., 2016). Yet as one music writer has observed, "the Australian musical export [is] reshaping stereotypes of a sunburnt country where sweaty bands once played rock 'n' roll in pubs carpeted with sawdust" (Brandle, 2016), with Australian acts finding overseas markets across pop, indie and mainstream rock, progressive rock, country and electronic-pop. For Sounds Australia, this becomes

> … a more compelling conversation now with a commercial sponsor, because we can actually show, and we can talk about certain acts. You've got a Vance Joy or a Chet Faker or a Flume or a Courtney Barnett to reference, whereas starting out you don't have those things.
>
> (Interview 16, 2018)

At the same time, the organisation recognises that problems remain in terms of profile:

> I've just got back from Jazzahead in Germany, and … You go overseas and people go, "oh, you're Australian", but they don't know what that means … If you're in the UK, fair enough, you know what it means, or if you're one of the Commonwealth countries. But you even go to certain parts of America and … they're familiar with *Crocodile Dundee*, and that's about it. If you're talking about actual music and culture and you start talking about the artists that they might know, they go, "oh, are they Australian?". Politically, no idea. They would have no idea of the politics of Australia. Us being in these markets is just … As a little country, you're just trying to jump up at the table of … Sitting around the family table of nine kids and you're the four-year-old who's just trying to get fed. You're just jumping up.
>
> (Interview 20, 2018)

Rather than promoting a settled idea of an "Australian sound", Sounds Australia have instead attempted to construct a series of embodiments of nation, and national structures in relation to successes, where governments and publics have to be made aware of the difficulties local artists face in complex global markets:

> I constantly go back to a lot of the sporting analogy, but it's almost … Do you remember when Australia Post let you write telegrams to your favourite sports heroes? I think of our artists in that same vein. You want people championing them and really cheering for them because they're out there, but you're not going to get this big wave of general public cheering for Alex Lahey. It's just not going to happen.
>
> (Interview 16, 2018)

In a forum discussion on global understandings of "Australian" popular music at the BigSound festival in 2014, it is interesting that *industrial* contexts were highlighted, rather than an argument for the connection of particular sounds to ways of life. The discussants—artist managers, recording label executives and festival owners—believed that Australians' ability to deliver good live performances (in relation to international acts), and the relative isolation of Australia provided a good "incubator", where by the time overseas audiences were "finding" Australian artists, they had considerable experience playing to large venues and working out their recordings/sounds (Radio National, 2014). As discussed below, one means of evading constructions of "the national" as a framing mechanism for exports is to instead investigate the various local scenes and exchanges that are providing innovation.

Measuring outcomes

Music export activity forms part of longer debates about the effectiveness of export promotion schemes, and the role of Austrade in Australian contexts (cf. Brewer, 2008). As with much activity in the creative industries, industries and governments have experienced difficulties in properly assessing Sounds Australia's relationships with existing industrial networks, and accounting for its impact within the range of activities designed to bring artists to market:

> You know that we've created situations and environments where people have met who otherwise would not have met, and it might not have happened then. But it's that third and fourth year where you can draw a line and go, I know how that's happened, and I know how that happened, and I know how that happened [as outcomes] … when people are at an event together, and you've both been at a number now, you're all on an equal playing field. It doesn't matter if you're the first-time manager of your act, you're standing there in exactly the same position. And you're having conversations with other Australians that you never would get if you tried to cold-call them here. And as a community, there's a real cultural community of Australian industry that are exporting. It's really intangible, I don't know how you … But I think it's made them very formidable in that place to do business.
>
> (Interview 16, 2018)

While much has been done in constituting a sense of national cohesion, difficulties remain in terms of placating various stakeholders and funding partners. A recurring problem is that networked State grants don't often accommodate an organisation such as Sounds Australia. For one State funding organisation, there was no recognition of Sounds Australia as a body that interlinked multiple sectors and activities—that it *facilitated* cultural outputs, rather than *producing* them:

> The feedback we got for this last round from them … "it seems like you're travelling around the world networking and you haven't created any new works" … I really have no words for this. This feedback is absurd.
>
> (ibid.)

As examined in Chapters 3 and 4, repetition (of media promotions, live performances, courting targeted markets) is a key feature of export strategies that are usually determined by longer-term engagements. Another State funder on one grant round informed Sounds Australia that "we want to see something new; we just don't want you to do the same thing again" in relation to the core activities (ibid.). This is complicated further by particular expectations by independent States directly relating to outcomes for *their* home-grown artists.

Such opinions speak to continual misunderstandings of the primary facilitation role of Sounds Australia, which we also examine in relation to other national schemes in Chapter 7. The organisation "directs traffic" for a wide range of industry activities and actors. Yet problems remain in making connections to the range of business meetings, showcase performances, scoping visits, "speed networking" and business stand representations. As artists and managers have pointed out elsewhere in this book, these activities often do not have immediate outcomes or cultural/economic benefits; these might be evident years later. While strong industry representations in recent years have enabled Sounds Australia's budget to be defended as a series of business investments to federal governments, the wider issues of discussing value (in ways that are different to the usual music industries' definitions) still remain to some extent.

Scenes and genres

Some interviewees reflected on the kinds of domestic infrastructure required to ensure that Australian acts are sufficiently equipped to explore overseas territories. The ability of the national public broadcaster's youth station, Triple J, to "break" acts, especially for the under-30s and teen markets, has been discussed elsewhere (e.g. Lancaster, 2018). For many managers, national tours are not viable without solid Triple J airplay. One interviewee believed that such "Triple J bands" worked well overseas, as they had time to develop experiences and strategies, and displayed readily evident "indie" credentials (Interview 20, 2018). This reflected the maturity of local rock and pop, particularly in "indie" scenes constructed within the larger Australian capital cities. Conversely, the relative lack of scenes for other genres was provided as one of the reasons for less visibility, and by extension, international success.

The immigration policies of Australia after the Second World War have provided diverse mixtures of sounds and micro-scenes that have drawn upon city populations of mainly southern European migrants (Scott Maxwell, 2008). More recent arrivals, however, have implications for shifts in genre, where it is perceived as a potential export strength: "We would maybe know that there's a great hip hop scene in Africa and Sudan, because there's a huge Sudanese population in Melbourne, there are those kinds of tie-ins that are more likely to happen" (Interview 20, 2018). Local hip hop scenes reflect the inflections of African styles, in turn providing the potential for migrants to lead innovations that can be transferred to international scenes. Interesting translocal music is evident, for example in the Amaru Tribe, a group of Australian, Colombian, Argentinian, Chilean and

Venezuelan musicians based in Melbourne, and their genre of "Cumbia Oceanica", and Takudzwa "Tkay" Maidza, a Zimbabwean-born Australian singer-songwriter and rapper.

How to translate the Indigenous music sector into meaningful export activity has long featured in policy discussions. Making the case for the cultural, social and economic benefits of improved visibility of Indigenous performers and communities, a 2008 report argued for international marketing strategies in conjunction with Austrade so that Indigenous exports could align with the then-Commonwealth *Strategic Contemporary Music Industry Plan.* This included improving business skills, and strategies to increase exposure through the "development of strategic international and domestic touring circuits" (Cultural Ministers Council, 2008, p. 12). In addition, the 2013 *Creative Australia* report noted that the Aboriginal and Torres Strait Islander Music Office, co-funded by the Australasian Performing Right Association and the Australia Council, provided "coordinated and centralised support to assist Aboriginal and Torres Strait Islander musicians by driving initiatives with key stakeholders to overcome barriers, address the engagement gap and increase market penetration" (Australian Government, 2013, p. 86).

As a 2019 election promise (part of its Australian Music Industry Package), the Coalition Government has provided $2.7m for its Indigenous Contemporary Music programme, "to establish a national development program for Indigenous musicians and bands for touring, recording and planning effective touring circuits" (Fifield, 2019).[3]

> There's a great scene in the new *Gurrumul* film where he's playing at a New York record store, and you just see people walk in and going, "I don't know who this guy is, but it sounds [amazing]" ... They literally stopped filing through the records and just ... And within ten minutes, you've got everyone just around him, just watching him. He was like a three-piece band; he was phenomenal.
>
> (Interview 20, 2018)[4]

In January 2016, Sounds Australia announced the position of First Nations Export Producer, with Leah Flanagan, a Darwin-based Alyawarre singer-songwriter, to "provide decision-making, advice, engagement and guidance to Sounds Australia's export strategy, ensuring cultural protocols and processes in promoting Indigenous artists internationally is practiced" (Sounds Australia, 2016), with plans to establish a First Nations international bursary programme. Historically, Yothu Yindi (1990s) and Gurrumul (2000s) have proved the exceptions as Indigenous acts with significant international audiences and recording sales. Sounds Australia has assisted a new generation of Indigenous performers at international showcases including Gurrumul, Mojo Juju, Dobby and A.B. Original. With other performers (Briggs, Baker Boy, Thelma Plum) also finding national audiences, hip hop in particular seems rich in export potential. The additional funding delivered to Sounds Australia in 2019 provides the organisation with the means to address the specific federal government brief "to assist the Australian music industry to capitalise on emerging markets in Asia" (Fifield, 2019).

Future challenges

In this section we briefly outline the challenges confronting Sounds Australia, ranging across related cultural sectors and activities. Much of what is discussed here arguably also speaks to issues for other creative industries and is explored too in the following chapter examining other national programmes and activities.

Tourism

In relation to common complaints that industry sectors can be poor at working with each other, how the music export sector can leverage input from across other government and industry sectors has been little explored. An Australia Council report indicated that arts tourism has increased for visitors to Australia in the past five years, growing at a higher rate than international tourism overall (Australia Council, 2018). While visits to museums and galleries were the highest reported activity, festival attendance had grown by 61% since 2013 (ibid., p. 5). While there were no data provided as to types of festival attendance, such statistics point to the potential for music festivals to be considered as an important part of export strategies. The report also cited 2016 Screen Australia data revealing "that around 230,000 international tourists are estimated to visit or extend their stay in Australia each year as a result of viewing Australian film and TV content" (ibid., p. 7). Similar research is required in assessing the extent to which music influences the choices (and perceptions of Australian music) for in-bound tourists. Unlike other countries (e.g. New Zealand, United Kingdom, Canada) Australia lacks a cohesive branding strategy linking its music export activities with tourism and related plans.

Technologies

In relation to ongoing "datafication" and the implications for reconnaissance discussed in Chapter 1, several interviewees observed that Sounds Australia's "hands-on" reputation and presentational emphasis upon live performances and showcases should be increasingly matched with an emphasis upon digital curation. For example, digital shifts also have implications for traditional presentational modes:

> I think Sounds Australia has been built around export of the live product. Obviously, people have done subsequent deals on other types of rights and recording and publishing, but the shopfront is the live performance. I think now that [Digital Export Producer] Dom Alessio is in the team and looking at how to program recordings into playlists, the shop front is going to be the sound recording.
>
> (Interview 21, 2018)

In relation, the website as "shop front" could evolve as a more holistic centre for multiple channels of information, and also as national site of branding and discovery:

> Our website was very much done as a resource for exporting artists going out. Where do I find funding? What are the due dates for things? Where do I find visa information? … I think we've got the potential to change that now, because there's an understanding of Sounds Australia and that's where you will be introduced to these artists … I think there's definitely options for us to create a content-type discovery portal.
>
> (Interview 16, 2018)

Such options also have to consider other audiences for the site apart from aspiring artists, and the extent to which the web can be utilised for promotion to international territories. As with much of this chapter, how and where resources can be allocated to this—parallel to discussions about how much Sounds Australia should engage with activities usually allocated to labels—remain in play, particularly as data about enduring and breaking markets become more accessible.

Conclusion

Established in 2009, Sounds Australia has evolved in a different form to other national export programmes. Like many other national schemes, it has steered clear of "picking winners" to present on global promotional circuits; unlike other programmes, it has no input or control of related funding measures designed to assist artists or managers. Recent funding battles—where it was implicated in wider federal government moves to radically realign priorities and reduce arts funding overall—have seen the organisation achieve increases and some stability of funding after strong industry intervention.

Continual anxiety about the certainty of even short-term funding has perhaps led to less reflection on Sounds Australia's structure and the potential for doing things differently; its staff are clearly comfortable in fulfilling a series of intermediary roles based upon specialist expertise, including deep knowledge of different markets (and their related intermediaries). And, as with other national contexts, concrete outcomes could be better defined and explained. Other possibilities could be countenanced. For example, are there synergistic benefits to be gained through greater involvement in funding decisions, bringing their experience in different definitions of "export ready" to bear on funding applicants at the Australia Council and State government levels? Some of the more innovative grants emphasising track records rewarding momentum and experience in export spaces existing elsewhere (see Chapter 7) are not evident within Australian structures. In relation, advantages may accrue in attempting a more streamlined funding model where expertise is shared across governmental tiers and is more apparent to aspiring artists. As a national project, Sounds Australia is arguably hampered in not exercising its expertise through a nationally recognised export body incorporating all stakeholders, aggravated by the nation's tripartite system of governance and funding. However, an expanded set of aims and activities also requires an accompanying will of the States and federal governments to restructure in the name of greater collaboration.

In relation, the organisation is also at the centre of much greater ambitions for Australian popular music, with plans to capture 5% of the global music sector by 2030, equating to a "$146 billion industry" including recording, live music and publishing revenues "that would mean an A$7.3 billion music export market" (Eliezer, 2019), as noted above. For one industry figure, growth is to be achieved by pursuing structural reform that involves greater state–industry partnerships, and firmer strategies that proceed well beyond singular artist successes:

> [Sounds Australia] needs to now grow up, and be let loose a bit, and established as an entity that has the right mix of investment and stakeholder representation. Part of that would be cross-government relationships. You ensure that this thing has connections into all of the right government agencies and portfolios, the right breadth of stakeholder representation and investment. So I do think the model going forward should still be co-industry-government investment.
>
> (Interview 22, 2018)

This would see Sounds Australia moving closer to other overseas models in entrenching a cross-portfolio approach to strategy and resources. The ambitious economic targets have been partly based upon the consistent growth evidenced by other national export programmes:

> As I've said ad nauseam, look at Sweden. It'd be nice to be looking at, what's the potential to move closer to being a net exporter? Maybe that's unrealistic from where we sit now, but you need a bit of a sense of where you want to get to in order to move the dial. I think the gap is being clear on that vision and working out, how am I going to get there? And then, what's it going to cost? A failure at government level is to get all excited and proud because we have one artist doing exceptionally well overseas and riding the back of that. That's not the right thing to be excited about.
>
> (ibid.)

This is also related to an acknowledgement that domestic structures (and goals) are more strategically aligned with international arrangements. It is instructive that the Labor Opposition's 2019 election platform included not only the provision of greater funding for Sounds Australia, but that it would be merged with the federal Live Music Office in recognition of the importance of the live sector to artist development. Imposing a sense of "the national" in terms of shared goals and interlinked structures remains a challenge.

One interpretation of the findings of our *Born Global* industry report placed music exports on a wider footing, with Australia as a land of "Beef, coal and hot tracks" (Qian, 2019). This can be regarded as a victory of sorts for the local industries, who have persistently briefed federal governments that popular music possesses the same potential as (for example) the beef or wine industries. Returning to Craik's (2007) observation of arts/cultural funding as historically a "marginal" concern for the state, the local music industries have shared other national rhetorics in emphasising export support as a series of investment strategies. Future challenges remain in ensuring that Australian music export activity is not bracketed off as simply a series of commercial exchanges, but that its more complex components as symbolic production are recognised beyond its commodity forms.

Notes

1 The authors also provided a submission based on interim findings derived from the Australian Research Council Linkage grant project, including a presentation to the Inquiry committee at the December 2018 hearings held in Melbourne. Both the submission and presentation focused on providing economic contexts for Sounds Australia's performance in relation to other major export nations, which were case studies in the project.

2 The CONTROL programme was funded from 2011 to 2017.

3 Prime Minister Scott Morrison rearranged ministerial departments in late 2019. The former Department of Communications and the Arts was incorporated into a new Department of Infrastructure, Transport, Regional Development and Communications. From February 2020, Minister Paul Fletcher's new title was Minister for Communications, Cyber Safety and the Arts. Beyond the announcement press release, there is no information to be found on the new Department's website about the Indigenous music funding.

4 Geoffrey Gurrumul Yunupingu was an Elcho Island musician who won ARIA awards for his recordings in 2008, 2011, 2014, 2015 and 2018. He had previous careers with Yothu Yindi and the Saltwater Band. Yunupingu died in 2017. A documentary of his life, *Gurrumul*, was directed by Paul Damien Williams and distributed by Madman Films in 2018. The film features Yunupingu working with fans of his work, including Sting.

References

Allen Consulting Group (2005). *Let's Get This Show on the Road*. Sydney: Allen Consulting Group.

Austrade (2010). *Export Market Development Grants Fact Sheet: Music Industry*. Canberra: Austrade.

Australia Council (2008). Five music managers on track to international success. 12 December. https://www.australiacouncil.gov.au/news/media-centre/media-releases/five-music-managers-on-track-to-international-success/

Australia Council (2018). *International Arts Tourism: Connecting Cultures*. Strawberry Hills: Australia Council for the Arts.

Australian Government (2013). *Creative Australia*. Canberra: Commonwealth of Australia.

Bakhshi, H. & Cunningham, S. (2016). *Cultural Policy in the Time of the Creative Industries*. London: NESTA.

Brandis, G. (2013). Taking arts to the next level. *The Australian*, 5 September. http://www.theaustralian.com.au/arts/opinion/taking-arts-to-the-next-level/story-fn9n9z9n-1226710602311

Brandle, L. (2016). Australia's new generation of global stars: Lars Brandle studies the form guide. *Musicology Australia*, 1 April. http://musicaustralia.org.au/2016/04/australias-new-generation-of-global-stars-lars-brandle-studies-the-form-guide/

Breen, M. (1993). Making music local. In T. Bennett, S. Frith, L. Grossberg, J. Shepherd & G. Turner (eds.) *Rock and Popular Music: Politics, Policies, Institutions*. London: Routledge, pp. 67–82.

Breen, M. (1999). *Rock Dogs: Politics and the Australian Music Industry*. Sydney: Pluto Press.

Brewer, P. (2008). Australia's export promotion program: is it effective? *Australian Journal of Management* vol. 34, no. 1, pp. 125–142.

Carter, L. (2016). Sounds Australia: music industry condemns decision to strip funding from hit-making agency. *ABC News*, 11 May. https://www.abc.net.au/news/2016-05-11/sounds-australia-denied-federal-government-funding-grant/7406186

Commonwealth of Australia (2008). *Winning in World Markets: Review of the Export Market Development Grants Scheme*. Canberra: Department of Foreign Affairs and Trade.

Commonwealth of Australia (2010). *Strategic Contemporary Music Industry Plan*. Canberra: Department of the Environment, Water, Heritage and the Arts.

Commonwealth of Australia (2012). *Convergence Review Final Report*. Canberra: Department of Broadband, Communications and the Digital Economy. http://www.dbcde.gov.au/__data/assets/pdf_file/0007/147733/Convergence_Review: Final_Report.pdf

Commonwealth of Australia (2019). *Report on the Inquiry Into the Australian Music Industry*. Canberra: House of Representatives Standing Committee on Communications and the Arts.

Craik, J. (2007). *Re-Visioning Arts and Cultural Policy: Current Impasses and Future Directions*. Canberra: ANU e-press, Australian National University.

Crittenden, J. (2016). Government restores sounds Australia funding. *Contemporary Music Roundtable*, 21 November. https://musicaustralia.org.au/2016/11/government-restores-sounds-australia-funding/

Cultural Ministers Council (2008). *Indigenous Contemporary Music Action Plan: Towards a Stronger Indigenous Contemporary Music Sector*. Canberra: Commonwealth of Australia.

Elder, B. (1997). Garden path. *The Sydney Morning Herald*, 24 July, p. 17.

Eliezer, C. (2005). Aussie government to boost music exports. *Billboard*, 30 April, p. 18.

Eliezer, C. (2008). Austrade helps acts to synch and swim to U.S. *Billboard*, 30 April, p. 21.

Eliezer, C. (2019). How the Australian music industry can level up internationally. *Beat*, 18 September. https://www.beat.com.au/how-the-australian-music-industry-can-level-up-internationally/

Eltham, B. & Verhoeven, D. (2015). Philosophy versus evidence is no way to orchestrate cultural policy. *The Conversation*, 29 May. http://www.theconversation.com/philosophy-vs-evidence-is-no-way-to-orchestrate-cultural-policy-42487

Fifield, M. (2019). More live music, more opportunities for Australia's musicians. *Ministerial Press Release*, 30 March. https://www.mitchfifield.com/2019/03/more-live-music-more-opportunities-for-australias-musicians/

Hoegh Guldberg, H. (1987). *The Australian Music Industry: An Economic Evaluation*. North Sydney: Australia Council.

Homan, S. (2018). The music nation: popular music and Australian cultural policy. In D. Rowe, G. Turner & E. Waterton (eds.) *Making Culture: Commercialisation, Transnationalism, and the State of 'Nationing' in Contemporary Australia.* Abingdon: Routledge, pp. 51–63.

Homan, S., Cloonan, M. & Cattermole, J. (2016). *Popular Music and the State: Policy Notes*. New York: Routledge.

Keating, P.J. (1995). Exports from a creative nation. *Media International Australia* vol. 76, pp. 4–6.

Lancaster, B. (2018). In the era of music streaming, do bands still rely on Triple J to launch a career? *The Guardian*, 30 September. https://www.theguardian.com/australia-news/2018/sep/30/in-the-era-of-music-streaming-do-bands-still-rely-on-triple-j-to-launch-a-career

Marks, F. (1969). Australia and New Zealand. In P. Ackerman & L. Zhito (eds.) *Therapie Complete Report of the First International Music Industry Conference*. New York: Billboard, pp. 230–235.

Martin, L. (1997). Circle to unearth next band of gold. *The Sydney Morning Herald*, 4 March, p. 13.

McCaughey, C. (2005). *Comparisons of Arts Funding in Selected Countries: Preliminary Findings*. Ottawa: Canada Council for the Arts.

Mendelssohn, J. (2015). Arm's length? Forget it – it's back to the menzies era for arts funding. *The Conversation*, 13 May. http://www.theconversation.com/arms-length-forget-it-its-back-to-the-menzies-era-for-arts-funding-41743

Morrison, L. (2018. It's time the government stopped neglecting Australia's music industry. *The Guardian*, 30 November. https://www.theguardian.com/music/2018/nov/30/its-time-the-government-stopped-neglecting-australias-music-industry

Murfett, A. (2008). Austrade plays a sour note in music industry. *The Sydney Morning Herald*, 21 April. https://www.smh.com.au/business/austrade-plays-a-sour-note-in-music-industry-20080420-27eu.html

Negus, K. (2002). The work of cultural intermediaries and the enduring distance between production and consumption. *Cultural Studies* vol. 16, no. 4, pp. 501–515.

Qian, J. (2019). Beef, coal, and hot tracks: Aus music exports earn $195 million each year. *ArtsHub*, 12 July. https://www.artshub.com.au/news-article/news/research-and-data/jinghua-qian/beef-coal-and-hot-tracks-aus-music-exports-earn-195-million-each-year-258375

Radio National (2014). *The future of Australian music. Big Ideas Program, ABC Radio.* 20 October. Retrieved from: http://www.abc.net.au/radionational/programs/bigideas/the-future-of-australian-music/5815208

Scott-Maxwell, A. (2008). Localising global sounds: world music and multicultural influences in Australia. In S. Homan & T. Mitchell (eds.) *Sounds of Then, Sounds of Now: Popular Music in Australia*. Hobart: ACYS Publishing, pp. 73–92.

Shorten, B. (2018). Labor will turn up the volume on Australian music. Bill Shorten MP web site. *Australian Labor Party Press Release*, 30 November. https://www.billshorten.com.au/_labor_will_turn_the_volume_up_on_australian_music_friday_30_november_2018

Sounds Australia (2016). Sounds Australia welcomes Leah Flanagan and Larry Heath. *Sounds Australia Facebook Site*, 16 January. https://www.facebook.com/AustMusicWeek/posts/great-news-sounds-australia-welcomes-leah-flanagan-larry-heath/1442182002629486/

Sounds Australia (2018a). *Submission No. 95 to Inquiry Into the Australian Music Industry*. Canberra: Standing Committee on the Communications and the Arts, House of Representatives.

Sounds Australia (2018b). *What is the Aussie BBQ? Sounds Australia Web Site*. http://www.soundsaustralia.com.au/index.php/showcase/aussie-bbq/

Throsby, D. (2015). The cultural industries as a sector of the economy. In K. Oakley & J. O'Connor (eds.) *The Routledge Companion to the Cultural Industries*. Abingdon: Routledge, pp. 56–69.

Trainor, G. & James, A. (2012). *Review of the Australia Council*. Canberra: Department of Regional Australia, Local Government, Arts and Sport.

Turner, G. (1992). Australian popular music and its contexts. In P. Hayward (ed.) *From Pop to Punk to Postmodernism: Popular Music and Australian Culture from the 1960s to the 1990s*. Sydney: Allen & Unwin, pp. 11–24.

6 National case studies, export schemes and policies

Introduction: Models and mechanisms

In the last chapter we examined the development of Sounds Australia and histories of state and industry strategies, including the related challenges of coordinating multiple industry bodies, government and industry sectors, and the particular challenges facing Australian artists, labels and managers. In this chapter we explore other national export schemes, with a particular focus upon leading export nations including Canada, the United Kingdom, France, South Korea, Sweden, Finland and Norway. Drawing on interviews with key industry and export office managers, these case study nations are analysed for their differences in funding/organisational structures, aims and the extent and types of industry–state relationships. As with Chapter 5, the relationships between singular export schemes and domestic music/cultural funding are also explored.

Funding histories reveal sustained state support for classical/art music in the main, with gradual support for folk and other musics of importance to nations or regions (Shuker, 2008). Since the 1980s, nations have been increasingly amenable to supporting local performances and recordings of popular music, often as exercises to boost national identities (see Wallis and Malm, 1984). Early (1970s and 1980s) models of national export assistance entailed selective arms of the state working to boost sales and visibility that were often linked to wider promotional activities of the nation. This comprised funding of selected artists for particular market promotion, and particular market raids or reconnaissance tours, often with artists, managers and recording companies working with and through embassies, foreign affairs or trade departments. Key global promotional events remained influential; for example, a deal was struck at MIDEM in 1971 for Dutch band Shocking Blue to tour Hungary, and to be part of an "artist exchange" with Britain (Ackerman, 1971, p. 70).

According to Laing (2003, p. 199), national music export agencies existed as long ago as 1962 (the Netherlands); other early adopters included Australia in 1988, and France and Sweden in 1993. The gradual emergence of (popular) music export offices was acknowledgement by the state that popular culture (especially the film and television industries) contained possibilities in assisting trade bottom lines. Provided with the right forms of support and promotion, cultural trade imbalances could be corrected: By 2006, "Korea had become one of only a handful of nations that consume more locally produced cultural content than foreign content" (Jang and Paik, 2012, p. 200).

In Australia, for example, industry export guides were published along with burgeoning lines of funding support, part of wider Austrade initiatives to significantly bolster economic returns, principally through increased sales/activity in Europe and the US (McLeay, 2006). For Finland, the promise of an internationalisation of local stars and profits raised new questions for musicians in dealing with industries and the state (Mäkelä, 2008). While France and the United Kingdom have long engaged in export support, it is the smaller and mid-scale nations (ranked by consumption and production) that have been most concerned with export infrastructure. For African nations, real problems remain in transferring overseas success into discernible local industry growth (Laing, 2009), while Europe (primarily Germany, the United Kingdom and France) retains recording sales dominance (Moon et al., 2010). However, as discussed in earlier chapters, the extent to which some aspects of globalisation and digitalisation have changed "international trade in cultural products [which] is vertical between center and peripheral nations" (ibid., p. 381) becomes an interesting prospect. The shift to increasing seeking export revenue has also accelerated with debates about the scope and contexts of the "creative" industries. Organisations have also been formed to engender regional responses to export challenges. For example, the Nordic Music Export Program (NOMEX), a Nordic collaborative venture of the export offices of Finland, Sweden, Norway, Denmark and Iceland, operated between 2008 and 2016 on internal and external services and promotions for export agency members.

In this chapter we take up some of the broader governmental issues and models proposed in Chapter 1, in examining specific national policy, regulation and governance (Freedman, 2008). This requires proceeding beyond the examination of various industrial "gatekeepers" (Caves, 2000), although they certainly exist within local, national and regional export contexts. We noted Littoz-Monnet's (2007) policy models of "Liberal" (arm's length, low state financial involvement), "Dirigiste" (strong intervention, public subsidies) and "Federal" (municipal/regional governance empowerment). In Australian contexts, Craik (2007, p. 81) offers a more expansive global template of cultural objectives and funding mechanisms that is very useful for exploring music export arrangements:

- Facilitator (US): Diversity; tax expenditures and incentives;
- Patron (UK, Australia): Excellence, international standards; arm's length, peer evaluation;
- Architect (France): Social welfare, industry assistance; Ministry of Culture;
- Engineer (former Soviet countries): Political education, national culture; government ownership of artistic production;
- Elite Nurturer (Australia): Selective elite development; direct government funding.

Rather than engage directly with producers, the "Facilitator" model is "hands-off" in creating a range of indirect measures, particularly in ensuring that different cultural producers can survive commercially (ibid., pp. 1–2). This is often done through tax relief or appeals to philanthropic support. A central aim is diversity of funding sources beyond the state, although measuring benefits is more difficult (ibid., p. 81). The "Patron" model, typically adopted by the United Kingdom and other Commonwealth countries, provides direct funding in the name of "cultural excellence" and ensuring national production is in accord with "international standards" (ibid.). It is traditional, too, in primarily ensuring that "elite" arts (classical music, opera, ballet) and heritage forms have a (subsidised) role in the marketplace. In relation, the "Architect" model is "a more interventionist approach in which the rhetoric and aims of arts and cultural policy might be broadly aligned with social welfare and national culture objectives" (ibid., p. 1). In contrast, nations which assumed ownership of cultural production (the "Engineer" model) have done so in order to achieve specific national priorities that may overlap with other political objectives and spheres of government. This model is aligned with Eastern bloc countries, where there is little difference between producer and state objectives (ibid.). The "Elite Nurturer" model is one where "governments select a small number of elite cultural organisations to receive a one-line budget and/or other generous subsidies" (ibid., p. 2). While this has applied to traditional Patron funding (ringfencing support for loss-making producers and insulating them from commercial considerations), this model has interesting prospects for music export contacts when considering how nations are re-shaping alliances with industries and assessing how to reward good track records of success.

Changes in national contexts and global shifts in economic conditions have resulted in a more complicated landscape of objectives and mechanisms. For example, more recent government interventions in Australia have seen some components of federal (and individual State) arts budgets move away from arm's-length processes to "Elite Nurturer" status through Ministerial fiat (Mendelssohn, 2015; Homan, 2016). Further, all western nations (with the exception of the US) have arguably moved to a Ministry of Culture model with components of industry assistance ("Architect" model). While "mix and match" approaches have become more common, nations that have engaged with "Elite Nurturer" and "Engineer" models have shown greater interest in (and funding for) arts/cultural policies (Craik, 2007, p. 35) and to different ends.

Music export activities provide an excellent means by which to examine how such models now operate, and perhaps, how they reflect much broader shifts in uses of public expenditure. In this chapter, we propose modifications of Craik's model to usefully determine differences in current export policies of the seven case study nations we examined; as we explore below, overlaps do exist between models and activities, primarily in the ways in which all of our case nations now deploy some forms of industry assistance. We could also extend the "Engineer" concept to include other strands of "national culture", for example, in the strong ways in which music exports come to be at least partly based on the global branding of music/cultural heritage in the United Kingdom and France. As another example, Scandinavian countries conceive of "international standards" as a useful metric by which to infuse export goals with national identity, and are increasingly willing to directly fund individual successes.

Irrespective of ideological bent and historical patterns of governance, contemporary governments are continually assessing the types and extent of state support for music exports. The following examination of the different forms this takes is not primarily done to assess efficacy, but to examine different forms of relationships between musicians, managers, arts administrators, Ministers and industry sectors.

The Patron model: United Kingdom

The Patron model resembles more traditional arts models in the provision of government funding at arm's length to recipient bodies and activities. Within the contexts of national export funding, this has primarily entailed increased funding to national export agencies or schemes. While Australia and the United Kingdom remain good examples of the Patron model, both countries have sought to work more with their music industries, arguably moving closer to the Canadian model of increasing collaboration with companies and industry sectors.

Much of the governmental machinery might still resemble "arm's-length" processes, yet the Patron model is also increasingly delivered with more acute policy goals. While the United Kingdom enjoys a mature local infrastructure, with the nation a net exporter of popular music, successive Conservative UK governments have emphasised increasing cultural export targets. The *UK Creative Industries Strategy* (2014) and the Trade and Investment Ministry (UKTI) announced an ambitious set of goals for the cultural industries: "to more than double exports to £1 trillion by 2020"; "to double creative industries services exports by 2020 to £31 billion"; and "to increase the UK's share of the global market for inbound foreign direct investment (FDI) in creative industries by 50 percent by 2020" (UKTI, 2014). The UK model comprises an interesting mix of Patron (Arts Council, UKTI) and industry (PRS, BPI) funding that aligns activities to specific expertise and knowledge, with the state as primary funder, but working with industry agencies in allocation.

Via overlapping responsibilities and funding, this mixed model potentially sees a British act obtain funding from the Momentum scheme (funded by the PRS Foundation) for domestic development, achieve PRS funding for an international showcase and then receive Music Export Growth Export Scheme (MEGS) funding for more intensive, global activity based upon prior financial returns. This "business plan application" model is based upon how "a little bit of money" allows acts to scale up their ambitions as a "natural progression" toward international market success (Interview 23, 2016). Catfish and the Bottlemen provide a good example in first obtaining international showcase funding for performances at South by Southwest before obtaining MEGS funding to exploit label and management interest in the United States.

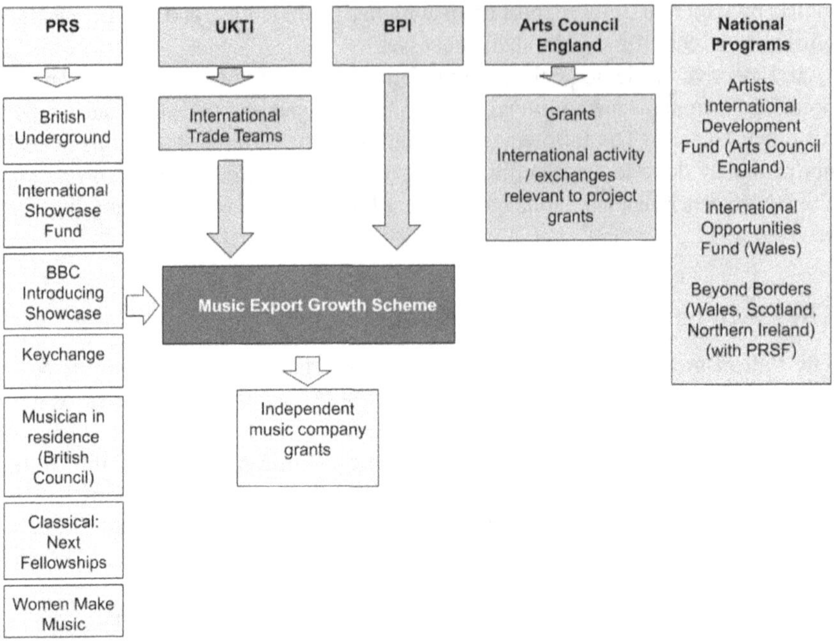

Figure 6.1 Music export funding: United Kingdom.

Funded by the UK Trade and Investment Board (UKTI) and managed by the British Phonogram Industry (BPI), the Music Export Growth Scheme (MEGS) was launched in 2014 with £250,000 to fund international touring and promotion. In 2018, £319,244 funded similar activities. From 2014 to 2018, MEGS (in partnership with BPI) has distributed over £3,000,000, supporting 201 music export projects/acts (BPI, 2018). Artists are eligible for up to £50,000 funding, which can cover no more than 70% of activities:

> With the trade shows, we estimate that for our Los Angeles one, we do between £2m to £4m in deals, and that can be for up to 12 months later … we're building relationships that can provide dividends through the next few years … but how you put a value on that is very difficult.
>
> (Interview 24, 2017)

The MEGS scheme is designed for artists "that have had their first success in the UK and are ready to try and break into an overseas market"; companies "are eligible to apply if you are a UK-based music company with a turnover of less than €50 million and fewer than 250 employees, as per the EU definition of an SME" (BPI, 2019). Applications are assessed by BPI, UKTI and a music industry panel that evaluates *inter alia* domestic track records, existing support and marketing/touring plans (BPI, 2019). UK musicians also have access to the

PRS International Showcase Fund for promotion at international showcase festivals and events. Other export-focused funding exists across the International Showcasing Fund and Artists' International Development Fund (Arts Council/British Council), Beyond Borders programme (Arts Council/PRS) and British Underground.

An interesting aspect of the British model is the formation of British Underground, a creative production company that provides agency functions aligning with other sector investments. Jointly funded by PRS and Arts Council England, the company assists artists "outside the mainstream" across an assortment of global showcase, artist development and networking events:

> What the Arts Council's role is as a public funder, is to almost correct market imbalance or encourage research and development or kickstart something happening, which may not be happening ... It's another way of investing. They are moving towards a focus on diversity and niche genres, rather than just "indie band X".
>
> (Interview 25, 2017)

Through its Horizons programme, British Underground have also been useful in coordinating and branding various national activities within a "British music" banner at events such as WOMEX. UKTI also provides support for trade mission activities related to key showcase events (e.g. Jazzahead, The Great Escape, India Music Mission) (Harris, Hart and Payne, 2016). International song-writing camps are also funded and organised by UKTI, the Music Publishers Association (MPA) and the British Academy of Songwriters, Composers and Authors (BASCA) (ibid.). To address the lack of representation and access to funded opportunities, the PRS Foundation established the Women Make Music grant in 2011 which includes funded projects that increase the profile of female artists. While this tweaked Patron model is regarded as a successful platform of collaboration, those interviewed believed more could be done. In particular, some argued that quick-release funds could be increased for emerging acts, labels and managers to enable access to micro-finance regional/national activity, and that the state should increasingly view music like the film and television industries, where funding of R&D (especially tax breaks for national production) can provide larger returns. Many, in effect, argued a transition to Facilitator/Architect models.

How the existing model will fare with the predicted regulatory and trade problems related to Britain's proposed withdrawal from the European Union is much discussed. UK music sectors have warned that "Brexit" has dire implications, primarily for passport/visa arrangements for touring musicians, changed copyright structures, the possibility of new trade tariffs and increased costs and bureaucratic systems for music tourists and musicians both entering and leaving countries (e.g. UK Music, 2018b; Hann, 2019). A 2018 UK Music report assessed further blockages to the domestic "talent pipeline": A decline in music education, particularly at state schools; a decline in music venues; and lack of finance options for emerging artists at the start of their careers (UK Music, 2018b, pp. 3–15).

The Architect model: France

France represents the best example of a social welfare model driven by government funding and intense levels of industry involvement; a "strong sense of cultural mission has traditionally taken the form of direct state intervention ... even after more than a decade of decentralization ... central government still intervenes energetically in the arts" (Loosely, 2001, p. 1). Beyond longstanding support for classical music since the 1950s, some forms of popular music support were established in the 1970s by Minister of Culture, Jack Lang, with an emphasis on local organisations and councils and the "management of legislative and tax tools intended to boost musical creation and diffusion" (French Coalition for Cultural Diversity, 2008, p. 39). This was also driven by a broader "cultural democracy approach" (Perrin, 2017, p. 11) that incorporated "contemporary" arts and cultural activities, including "non-classical" music. An historic approach—that culture cannot be solely reduced to its economic terms and functions—is summarised in Lang's assertion of "economy and culture, same fight" (cited in Perrin, 2017, p. 9).

France has two tax measures of significance for music. A 3.5% tax on nearly all variety show tickets collected by the Centre National des Variétés, de la Chanson et du Jazz (CNV) (with the exception of classical, religious and traditional music) is redistributed to performing arts companies to fund other forms of support. Since 2006, the country has operated a tax credit mechanism for the recording industry that

> represents 20% of the total amount of expenses for development and digitization, with a ceiling set at €350,000 per recording, for a total that cannot exceed €500,000. In 2006, this measure benefited 47 enterprises for a total amount of 2.7 million euros.
>
> (Coalition française pour la diversité culturelle, 2008, p. 42)

This is partly designed to compensate for expenses related to digitisation. Programmes/funding are available to enhance content creation and exchange in overseas territories, including the Fund for Cultural and Artistic Exchange for the French Overseas Territories (FEAC); "Outside the walls", a one- to three-month programme for artists to stay abroad; and touring and concerts abroad to support the promotion of SACEM repertoire internationally (up to 30% of the artistic budget).

The country has a rich patchwork of peak industry organisations, government departments, regional agencies and institutes, and is vocal in a range of European and international industry debates (e.g. content diversity, cultural taxes, content protections/quotas, the role of global digital platforms). Key bodies of this industry network—SACEM (the collection society for composers), CNV (live music support fund), SCPP (society for producers of phonograms and videograms), SPPF (French sound recording producers partnership), FCM (musical support fund) and ADAMI (collection society for recordings and performance)—provide approximately 50% of the Bureau's funding (Le Bureau

Export, 2015). PRODISS (the national union of producers, broadcasters and theatres) also contributes to central policy discussions in ensuring live performance/touring provides a "springboard" for international exposure. The French institutes and the Alliances Françaises form components of the wider cultural network that are centrally funded.

Le Bureau Export de la Musique Française was established in 1993, initially funded by labels and publishers, with later funding also provided by the national government. Initially established to assist the visibility of French recordings and concerts and related sales, the organisation has 30 staff working across Paris and its current international offices in Berlin, London, New York and Sao Paulo. Their office in Japan was closed in 2016, and they are currently researching offices in Asia and Los Angeles, so they are on "both sides of the states with access to Canada and Mexico" (Interview 26, 2017). The English and German offices are the largest, with five staff working across communications, relations with partners and in contact with French professionals.

Le Bureau Export provides a broad intermediary role, working with music businesses to develop strategies, provide promotional resources and advice and build relationships with international festivals and showcase market events. Funding programmes are provided upon the condition of co-label/businesses investment:

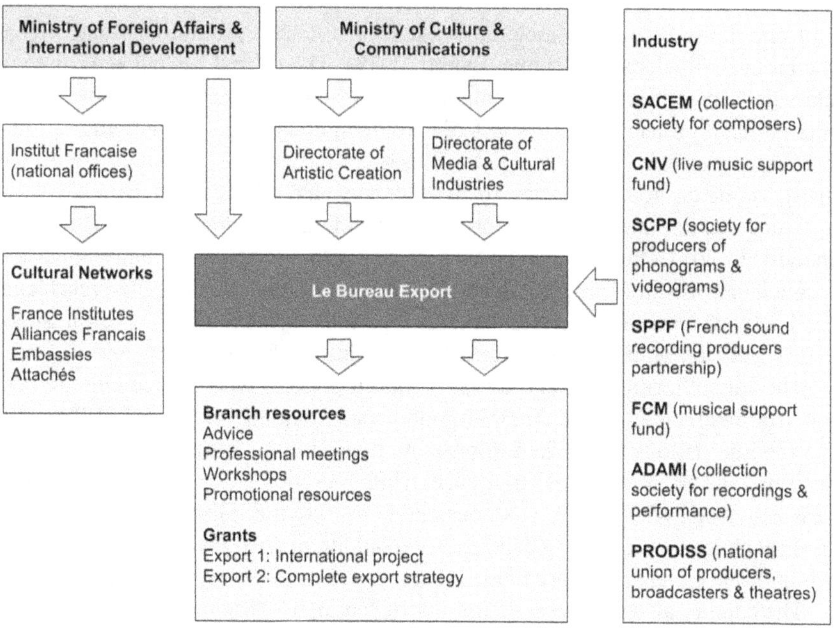

Figure 6.2 Music export funding: France.

> It used to be that we provided funding to support projects—for example promotion funds, touring funds, mobility, or marketing—now we only have one much bigger project fund. If you want to have, for example … a PR in the States, to spread your sounds, you can ask for half of the money of the salary of the person you will engage there.
>
> (Interview 26, 2017)

The Bureau receives approximately €4.5m per year (ibid.) from combinations of industry, Ministry of Culture and Foreign Office funding. In 2014, the Bureau supported 145 artists across showcase events and tours, facilitated 1,256 individual meetings/speed meetings between 141 French professionals and 164 international professionals from 32 countries and stated that 280 artists benefited from engagement with Bureau staff (Le Bureau Export, 2015). Past promotions have played upon organising themes for different market emphasises, such as "Chic Schnack" (Germany), "Francomusics", "France Rocks in the USA", "Frecho", "French Music UK" and "Oui Love" (Britain) (ibid.). "Made in France" promotions have also been developed for Germany, the United States, Japan and the United Kingdom. Applicants for funding must meet at least one of the eligibility criteria for funding: That they are signed with a French phonograph producer or with a distribution licence for export to a French phonographic producer; their publisher is French and/or their works are listed in the repertoire of SACEM; or the producer of their shows is French (Le Bureau Export, 2017). In 2019, the Bureau provided assistance across contemporary, classical and jazz genres, including "personalised advice", "professional meetings", "export workshops", and "promotion" events and marketing resources, including "Made in France" promotions, and "What the France" playlists (Le Bureau Export, 2019). The central funded activities are classified under "Export 1 (contemporary, classical and jazz): development of an international project"; and "Export 2" ("contemporary, classical and jazz") "supports a complete export strategy developed around an internationally confirmed artist, in one or more territories, [over] several years" (ibid., np).

France retains much of the export–embassy linkages evident in 1970s and 1980s models. In 2011 *Culturesfrance* was replaced with a strategy to "unify under the single label, 'Institut français', the diverse structures that compose the French cultural network: institutes, centres, cultural departments of embassies" (Perrin, 2016, p. 22). Both the Ministry of Foreign Affairs and Institut Français work with different "territorial authorities" on coordinated cultural policies with French cultural networks abroad, including "cultural promotion and branding" (ibid., p. 28). Through the Institut, nations are invited to promote their cultural wares through "cultural seasons" and "cultural years" in France, while "'French seasons' abroad are regularly organised with partner countries and constitute multidisciplinary showcases for French arts and culture" (ibid., p. 29). In addition, artist residency programmes within France and abroad are funded to increase European engagement.

The country also has looser definitions of "national" production. Export Bureau assistance is available for artists outside France who qualify through the artist or production being defined as French, and where royalties flow back to France:

> Some artists chose to move to where they want their art to be better promoted. Artists move to Paris because they have more support to export, they are thinking about creating and where they want their audience to be. If, for example, they don't have the means to create where they are from, then they can come to France to make music, for example [from] some parts of Africa.
> (Interview 26, 2017)

The welfarist model remains a central component of ambitions and funding,[1] driven by the Secretariat, Heritage, Artistic Creation divisions and organisational emphasis upon the French language within the Ministry of Culture and Communication. Yet the Media and Cultural Industries Directorate, formed in 2010, signalled moves to broader support to industries, entrepreneurs and the "digital revolution". In relation to music, four staff in the Directorate are engaged across legal, tax and industry development work. The service works in "building its financial devices for the industry, and it can concern all levels of entrepreneurs. You have the small, the middle and the major companies" (Interview 27, 2017). Calls for additional funding of the export office were answered with an increase of €500,000 funding in 2016; an additional €100,000 in 2017; and a further €800,000 in 2018 (Ministry of Culture, 2018). The 2018 budget for the Bureau was €2.7m (Nyssen, 2018).

In July 2015, an industry white paper published by *Tous pour la musique* (2015) contained 21 recommendations to improve music exports, including increases in state funding, regulatory reform (improving processes for touring, visas, etc), greater communication/coordination between industry and state organisations, broadening the Bureau's services to include the recording and management sectors and an increase in the number of branch offices. This reflected similar calls within other nations to address wider regulatory problems beyond funding mechanisms, including better integration of sectors and strategies, the need for a National Music Centre at the centre of such coordination, and the provision of data (Maistre, 2017). Further Architect measures were evident in the 2018 national budget, announcing €1m to fund cultural entrepreneurship initiatives including start-ups and the professionalisation of entrepreneurs (Ministry of Culture, 2018).

The Engineer model: South Korea

The Engineer model is best represented by the policies and structure of South Korea. The country has experienced remarkable growth, rising from the 33rd largest recorded music market in 2005 to the 11th largest in 2012, and was ranked 6th in 2017 (IFPI, 2018, p. 11). However, its share in music markets accounted for only 2% of global music (KOCCA, 2016). As with other Asian music nations, South Korea enjoys the advantages of a considerable Asian market on its doorstep, while retaining significant language barriers in gaining entry to English-speaking markets. For Asian markets, the practice of "twinning" (replicating) acts for different markets, or integrating band members from other nations, is not uncommon (Messerlin and Shin, 2013). For US and European markets, the nature of pop star production has been argued to work against older notions of authenticity prevalent within the music industries (Shin and Kim, 2013). Some acts have achieved success on live circuits in the US; more sustained recording success has been achieved in Japan and China.

In several ways, South Korea arguably prefigured the latest turn to more considered export policies, with music at the centre of the "Korean Wave" strategy established in the early 1990s encompassing other cultural industries (drama, television, film, dance, video) and food culture. The development of local pop through extended television networks (and TV talent programmes) from the late 1980s has allowed early local pop acts (such as Seo Taiji and Boys) to inform later national acts (H.O.T.; BoA; Girls' Generation; Big Bang). The enormous global success of Psy's "Gangnam Style" in 2012 (over 2 billion YouTube views; reaching no. 2 on the US *Billboard* charts; see St. Michel, 2017) prefigured significant gains in 2012 (global tours by TVXQ, Super Junior, Beast, Girls Generation, 2PM, CNBlue and Infinite) and in 2013, where "the number of Korean bands participating at SXSW increased from 4 in 2011 to 10 in 2013"; among the ten bands, seven went on to tour in the US (KOCCA, 2013). An earlier agreement signed with Google provided a K-pop channel on YouTube, with six K-pop concerts broadcast live (ibid.).

Popular music has been argued to be the leading cultural form in making the "Korean Wave" prominent across broader promotional strategies:

> We use k-pop as the big content to start talking about Korean culture – we bring the k-pop first, then we talk about other things, like movies. People think we have only k-pop, and only the dancing groups, the boys … we have a lot genres, it doesn't always equal k-pop – hip hop, punk and EDM [are now evident] … Unlike the American market, we train our artists very hard and they are well trained.
>
> (Interview 28, 2016)

In 2014, Korean cultural exports, led by popular music and television drama, increased by 8.4% to an equivalent of $US6.16b, 2.3% higher than the country's total export growth in 2013 (Zhang, 2016). In 2016, global revenue from K-pop was estimated to be $US4.7b (Soesmanto, 2018). By 2016, the South Korean government could boast that it had moved from 7th to 6th place in global export volumes, with various plans for youth training, stadium construction and content creation centres based on K-pop success (Korean Culture and Information Service, 2017). In 2017, popular music accounted for 6.1% of all cultural exports, producing $US38,491,000 (out of a total of $US63.1 hundred million) (KOTRA, 2017, np). The "music industry accounted for the highest percentage of marketing and publicity spending (14.3%)" (ibid.). In 2018, the supergroup BTS became the first South Korean act to achieve a gold sales certification from the RIAA in the US (IFPI, 2018, p. 23).

Several factors have been noted for continued export success: The unique "pop factory" assembly line evident within core multimedia entertainment firms producing pop acts, the high popularity of local TV talent franchises in launching local careers, the liberalisation of Asian music markets (Oh, 2013) and the high emphasis placed by managers and recording companies upon social media strategies and fan interaction (Jang and Paik, 2012). It has been suggested that a different form of economic intermediary relationship is at work, with large companies "vertically integrating in-house the process of artist selection, musical and performance training, image making, song writing, management, contracting, and album production and growing into large domineering entertainment empires" (Shin and Kim, 2013, p. 260). The role of such core companies as JYP Entertainment and Star Museum (SM) combines some aspects of Motown-like production systems with an instinctive in-house production model that is distinctively Asian (Negus, 2015). The coordination of live and audiovisual content is more complex, with a range of activities and sites (e.g. YouTube) outside governmental and company control (Oh, 2013). It is a unique arrangement where "the Korean government is both omnipresent and minimal: universally engaged to naturalize the neoliberal principles and maximally disengaged by having private talent agencies enact its policies" (Kim, 2017, p. 530). The "total management strategy" of Korean music companies in discovering and preparing artists for potential stardom has been represented by the government as a complete in-house system.

The South Korean model has been recognised as "one of the most salient examples of intervention into the cultural economy both nationally and internationally, with structured symbiosis linking the economic interests of major businesses with the state" (Negus, 2015, pp. 12–13). The Cultural Industries Directorate was established within the Kim Young Sam Government in 1993 with renewed emphasis upon international promotion. The Basic Law for Cultural Industries' Promotion was enacted in 1999, further explicitly outlining the role of the state in investment and planning (Lee, 2013). In the early 2000s, Korean expansion focused upon the Japanese market. Indeed, K-pop policies aligned with broader state policies of expansion, including seeking free trade agreements with various

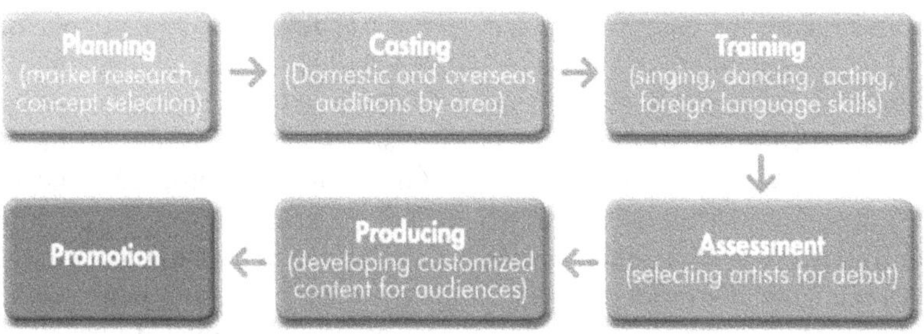

Figure 6.3 Korean artist development structure. Source: Korean Culture and Information Service, 2011, p. 38.

nations (Kim, 2017). K-Pop was viewed equally as both cultural export and "item of tourist destination" (ibid., p. 529).

Government strategies and policies are situated across several departmental responsibilities. In relation to Figure 6.4, the following can be noted for their particular relevance to music exports. The Music Industry Team is located within the Bureau of Popular Culture in the Korean Creative Content Agency (KOCCA), and is responsible for album production, pioneering new markets, organising the Seoul International Music Fair (MU:CON), hosting global showcases, the participation of music businesses and musicians at international music festivals, promotion and marketing, live music concerts and the discovery and development of new musicians ("K-rookies"). They are supported by and work with the Bureau of Global Business in relation to marketing and promotional activities. Broader policy considerations (such as industry strategies, cultural/content industries policy and R&D) are provided through the Bureaus of Cultural Policy and Content Policy, including international exchange and national cultural branding. The Korean Trade Investment Promotion Agency (KOTRA) leads the penetration of new markets for knowledge-intensive industries, including the content industries.

The Ministry of Culture, Sport and Tourism's five-year plan for the music released in 2009 emphasised enhanced international competitiveness for K-pop, along with domestic support. For example, the Global Music Showcase programme funded Korea-centric promotional events in China, incorporating fashion and animation with music promotion, and an Original Sound Track Video Music Festival (KOCCA, 2010, p. 492). The showcase funding also prioritised B2B opportunities and networks with international agencies and was designed to ensure a Korean presence at the global circuit of showcase events, including Music Matters, South by Southwest and Canada Music Week. There has been more recent emphasis upon businesses and musicians "achieving noticeable business deals" from state support (KOCCA, 2015, p. 373).

KOCCA was established in 2009. It has oversight of broadcasting, gaming, music, comics, animation, licensing/merchandising, fashion, "next-generation content", "culture technology R&D" and human resource development (to "train content creators") that also includes the CKL business support centre and academy (KOCCA, 2018a). "Overseas expansion" is a core concern, providing local support prior to "global market entry", including hosting export and trade fairs and roadshows (ibid.). A broader goal is to "develop Korea into one of the world's top five content powerhouses" (KOCCA, 2018b, p. 2). According to 2017 government literature, KOCCA's music funding includes concerts, translation, export marketing and festivals, social media promotion, hosting of the Seoul International Music Fair, collaboration with international producers and musicians, business networking and SME support (financial, taxation advice). The central activities are "recruiting K-rookies" (emerging musicians) and project and concert support. For example, in 2013, the first year of the programme, six acts were selected to perform with other K-pop artists, and provided financial support for album production (KOCCA, 2014, p. 482). The programme has evolved to include assistance with broadcast and digital platform promotion. For more

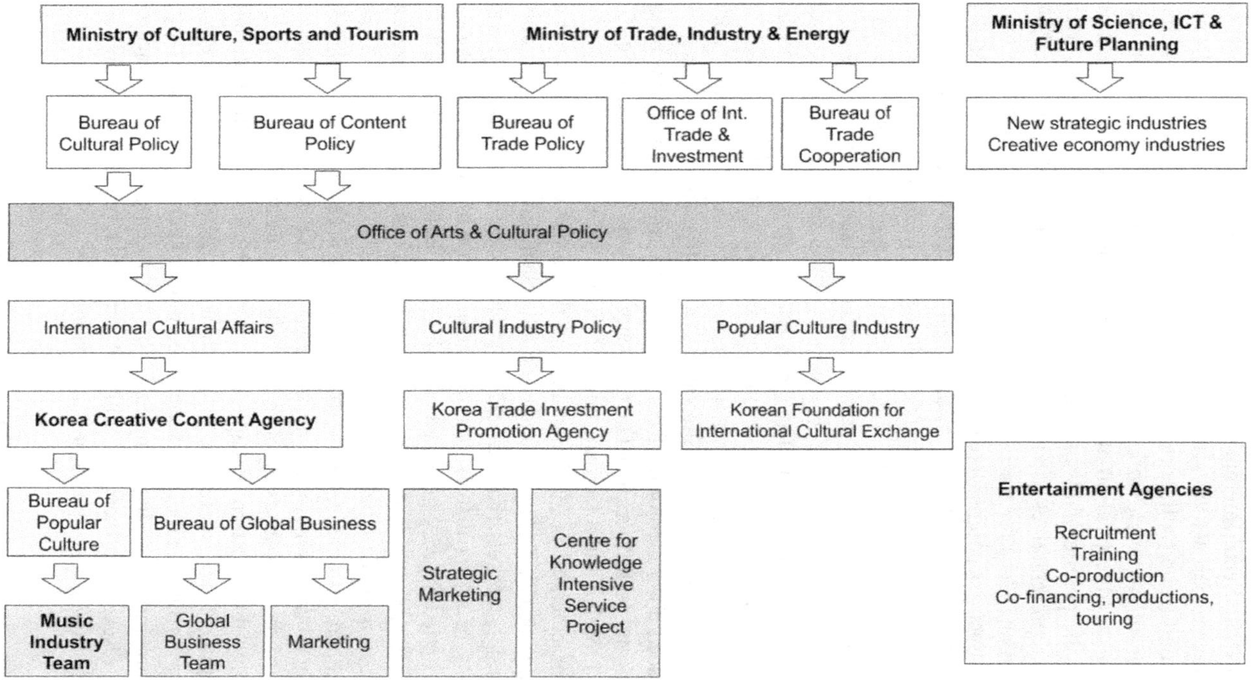

Figure 6.4 South Korea cultural export structure. Source: Derived from Ministry, agency and bureau literature.

established artists, K-pop global showcase performances and tours of artists have been funded in partnerships with larger entertainment firms, primarily playing across Asia and the US.

MU:CON, the Seoul International Music Fair, has also been a central component of Korean export activity. Its 2014 fair, for example, incorporated a business exchange, song camp (collaborations between ten international songwriters and eight Korean songwriters), workshops, a conference and MU:CON Choice (masterclasses, selected festival promotional choices) (KOCCA, 2015). This event is designed as the premier showcase for South Korean artists; in 2013, MU:CON hosted "878 representatives of 310 music businesses from 20 countries, 7,444 participants and attendees for the conference, showcases and networking events. In addition, 21 business booths were set up and 304 consultative meetings took place" (KOCCA, 2013, p. 438). As part of the larger event, "MU:CON Live" musicians in 2018 performed before "65 music industry professionals from 18 countries, which could lead to the chance to perform at some of the world's major music festivals", receiving funding to participate in overseas festivals (Bang, 2018). KOCCA also provides funding for presences at key showcase events, including MIDEM, South by Southwest, The Great Escape, Music Matters and Canadian Music Week, including business-to-business meetings. In 2013, KOCCA support also included direct financial assistance to music producers for album production and subsidising concert venue hire (KOCCA, 2013). By 2014, greater emphasis was placed upon mentoring from and working with international producers, songwriters and performers at MU:CON, with the song camp producing 13 songs between 10 foreign and 8 Korean songwriters (KOCCA, 2015, p. 373).

Concerns emerged in 2014 that beyond the larger enterprises (such as SM Entertainment and YG Entertainment) smaller SMEs and artists were not faring well in foreign markets (KOCCA, 2014). This could be rectified by widening the diversity of artists that to date had been "too narrowly focusing on dance music performed by well-groomed idol singers" (ibid., p. 52). Similarly, it was argued that there was scope for expansion across rock, hip hop, jazz and traditional Korean music (ibid.). Funding structures have become more complex with recent and sustained Chinese investment in Korea's cultural industries; the "accumulated investment on the music industry is KRW 529 billion, accounting for 26.9% of the total investment in the cultural industries" (KOCCA, 2016, p. 134). Beyond the injection of capital, Korean firms such as SM Entertainment have benefitted from greater access to Chinese markets (ibid.). More recently, KOCCA has provided more resources in building expertise in the IT components of the cultural industries, including Start Up Con, a conference and concert event; increasing research partnerships with VR and other "next-generation" content; and other forms of start-up business incubation.

The Elite Nurturer model: Canada, South Korea, Sweden

As discussed above, given its recurring emphasis on selective collaborations with specialist larger entertainment companies, South Korea also provides an example of the Elite Nurturer model working in tandem with Architect mechanisms. Some western nations have also revealed aspects of this model, or at least nodding aspirations to it. Components of Canada's Architect model are accompanied by funding streams designed to broker (selective) long-term relationships with appropriate companies of international standing. The Canada Music Fund (derived from FACTOR funding) is a market leader in this respect through its Support for Eligible Music Companies grant programme, where the "company" definition can apply to labels, publishers, distributors or artist managers. The programme funds business development (activities leading to company expansion of the development of new territories) and business travel activities "that support the marketing and promotion of the company and its services, as well as domestic and international travel to support the company's development objectives" (FACTOR, 2019). The Canada Music Fund also offers the Music Entrepreneur: Aid to Canadian Music Publishing Firms "to support the development of Canadian songwriters/composers and the promotion of new Canadian musical works in Canada and abroad". Both grant funds acknowledged the need to grow domestic expertise:

> It's all well and good to develop our artists, but if there's no industry to support, what you're doing is exporting your artists either into the major label system, or outside the country altogether, which is not our intention.
>
> (Interview 29, 2017)

In breaking with traditional artist-centric grants, such funding forms amount to the opposite of "excellence" discourses of typical Patron mechanisms; instead, a steady progression to export expertise and accompanying track record is rewarded.

While Sweden possesses a mixture of Patron (Arts Council, Arts Grant, Culture Fund, Foreign Affairs) and Architect (Export Music Sweden, comprising rights, musician and recording associations) mechanisms, it has also attempted other assistance forms. The country has in some instances led innovations in creating production hubs that emphasise exports of songs and sounds as much as artists. Denniz PoP (who died in 1998), Jacob Schulze, Kristian Lundin and Max Martin are internationally known as pop songwriters for an assortment of global artists, constructing a pop aesthetic that cuts across genre and national boundaries. These writers, and the "next generation", are a central part of the country being regarded as the "low-key Nashville of the Nordics, a hit-making heavyweight that's one of the world's biggest exporters of music relative to the size of its economy" (O'Kane, 2018). There is a belief that the country's first-mover advantages in some spheres of digital platforms (both Spotify and Soundcloud were developed in Sweden) has had ancillary benefits in music promotion:

> I think another very big contributing fact is the fact that Spotify started in Sweden and is the major streaming service, and the major private consumer service these days. I'm pretty sure that helps too, because the marketers and the record companies and the publishers, they've had a lot of time to practice

> how to perfectly master the art of marketing music in a streaming service environment, as opposed to maybe Germany, where you still have a 70% physical market, or Japan for that instance.
>
> (Interview 30, 2016)

Song-writing has been an important component of international success, including Max Martin, RedOne, Avicii, Swedish House Mafia, Robyn or Lykke Li (MXD, 2016): "We have more superstars in the world of songwriting than we do superstar artists" (ibid.).

Such concentrations of individual talent, it has been argued, are couched in deeper structures. For the national government, not only should small to medium SMEs seek to export; "born global" industries "such as IT, computer gaming, music, design and trade, start-up enterprises are global from the very beginning" (Government Offices of Sweden, 2015, p. 15). This necessitated more intensive assistance for such industries, including strengthening Sweden's image abroad to attract talent and investment (ibid.), and earlier positioning of the music industry at the forefront of new (digital) business models that overlapped with other industries (Government Offices of Sweden, 2012). Further aspects of the welfare model (artist financial support), combined with technological innovation and solid education and broadcasting structures, have allowed particular genres and acts to stand out (Swedish Institute, 2019).

One interviewee noted the irony in the country's comparative success resulting in less annual funding for export activities to their Scandinavian counterparts:

> We have more funding now than when I started, but still compared to Music Finland or Music Norway, we're a really small organisation, at least moneywise … It's easier to go to the government and say that, "hey, we're just one-third of Sweden and we have a pretty similar society, why aren't our export figures similar?". Whereas, we're like number one and they say "well, that's a great job, continue".
>
> (Interview 31, 2017)

The Facilitator model

Few tax or similar mechanisms exist within the case study nations to support export activity (or domestic growth in general). France has longstanding tax mechanisms which warrant the added descriptor of Facilitator. The country has two tax measures that have significance for music. A 3.5% tax on nearly all variety show tickets collected by the Centre National des Variétés, de la Chanson et du Jazz (CNV) (with the exception of classical, religious and traditional music) is redistributed to performing arts companies to fund other forms of support. Since 2006, the country has operated a tax credit mechanism for the recording industry that

> represents 20% of the total amount of expenses for development and digitization, with a ceiling set at €350,000 per recording, for a total that cannot

> exceed €500,000. In 2006, this measure benefited 47 enterprises for a total amount of 2.7 million euros.
>
> (Coalition française pour la diversité culturelle, 2008)

This is partly designed to compensate for expenses related to digitisation.

Several case nations (South Korea, Canada, Australia, Sweden) have deployed media (radio, television, digital platform) quotas as production incentives. Other incentive measures are appearing in national/industry policy documents, particularly in the promotion of diversity of sounds and platforms. Canadian music administrators have pointed to several threats to existing funding structures: Broadcasting revenues (that assist in funding FACTOR programmes) are in decline, and they perceive no clear strategy to deal with digital platforms. As traditional media revenues recede, it is argued that "big streaming suppliers like Spotify should contribute, but Government didn't give themselves the jurisdiction to include within broadcasting [earlier], so now it's hard" (Interview 32, 2017). In response to concerns across the media and cultural industries, the Government of Canada announced a review of the *Broadcasting Act* and the *Telecommunications Act* in June 2018, including funding of content creation and modernisation of regulation to reflect contemporary digital media landscapes.

The economic and cultural case

It has been argued that "the pattern of trade in cultural products seems to support the hypothesis that the relative size of the domestic market matters" (Marvasti, 1994, p. 136). This is certainly evident in the continuing dominance of the foundational centres of pop, country, rock, hip hop (the US, the UK) and the larger domestic markets of Germany and Japan to also figure in overall consumption/production. Yet our case nations confirm the ability of smaller domestic markets to make real gains through sustained production/export support and national branding exercises.

Nations are also increasingly aligning export goals with related economic and cultural outcomes. For South Korea, multiple benefits and activities are aligned with K-pop production. Tourism and nation branding have been important, related drivers of music policy; the "Dynamic Korea" (2002), "Korea Sparkling" (2007) and "Korea Be Inspired" (2010) campaigns preceded later *Hallyu* efforts (Um, 2014). Funding has also been made periodically available for K-pop promotion to synchronise with Olympic Games events (e.g. the PyeongChang Winter Olympics in 2016). There are interesting connections between other growth sectors, tourism and "music hub" policies. In 2016, the "Platform Chang-dong 61" entertainment district (in north-eastern Seoul) opened, incorporating music, fashion and food retail, and recording studios, workshop and exhibition spaces for musicians (Se-jeong, 2016). The Seoul Metropolitan Government has plans for a K-pop museum and a 20,000 seat Seoul Arena stadium for completion by 2020 (ibid.). It has also been argued that K-pop can be indirectly exported through the rise in Korean electronic games (Messerlin and Shin, 2013, p. 14).

For the United Kingdom, implicit and explicit benefits include "soft power" and tourism outcomes. The cultural industries are regarded as one of the national assets for the United Kingdom as trade competition increases:

> The inexorable rise in peer-to-peer cultural contact, the ever increasing economic importance of commercial culture and the realisation that governments gain a "licence to operate" in the international arena partly through their nation's cultural credibility and cultural credentials, will combine to force cultural relations up the political agenda. There is likely to be more investment in attempting to measure the benefits of getting cultural relations right – however long-term and diffuse those benefits may be – and the costs of getting them wrong.
>
> (British Council, 2013a, p. 34)

Popular music is seen to play an increasing role in the United Kingdom's "soft power" globally: "DJ Goldierocks presents Selector, a weekly radio show of new UK music broadcast in 33 countries. For UK Now she travelled widely around China, building networks for the show and hosting talks and workshops" (British Council, 2013b, p. 21).

In many cases, music industry sectors have formed joint tickets in arguing for the economic benefits of export funding. One estimate argues that Korea enjoys a return of 5:1 on its K-pop investment (Kirk, 2016). In 2017, "the international revenues of the French music industry accounted for 283 million euros", an increase of 6.7% with growth in publishing (€54m) and live performance (€72.8m) (Le Bureau Export, 2018a, pp. 2–3). In the United Kingdom, successive *Measuring Music* reports tell a success story of considerable growth. A similar accounting of Sweden's export revenue also reveals consistent returns.

The contemporary evolution of export offices and schemes has also involved a shift from "subsidy" to "investment" discourses. This was not inevitable but based upon careful considerations of how funding returns economic benefits to

Year	Economic contribution of exports (£ billion)	Economic contribution of all music sectors (Gross Value Added) (£ billion)
2012	1.4	3.56
2013	2.26	3.86
2014	2.1	4.1
2015	2.2	4.1
2016	2.5	4.4
2017	2.6	4.5

Figure 6.5 UK music export revenue and economic GVA contribution of music industry. Source: Accumulation of *Measuring Music* report data: UK Music (2013, 2014a, 2015, 2016, 2017, 2018a).

Figure 6.6 Swedish export market revenue trend 2009–2017 (SEK billion). Source: Music Sweden, 2017.

both the state and industries. Of our seven nation case studies, all have maintained or increased funding.

In the case of Canada, federal government funding has increased significantly, with an increase in funding of $20m over two years to the Canada Music Fund from 2019:

> In a previous report, I asked if government dollars into music is subsidy or investment, and it turns out that it is an investment. There are more dollars returned back to government coffers on what the government leverages. So it's not a subsidy … and provides investments back into artists' careers.
>
> (Interview 33, 2017)

As with the United Kingdom, such shifts have to be viewed within wider changes in national intent. The Trudeau government's 2018 announcement of a CAN$125m Creative Export Strategy over five years revealed Canada's intentions in creative industries export growth, including increased funding to Music Canada as part of the programme's three "pillars": "Boost export funding in existing Canadian Heritage programs"; "Increase and strengthen the presence of Canadian creative industries abroad"; and "Create a new creative export funding program and build the relationships needed to make business deals" (Government of Canada, 2018). This has included a new programme, Creative Export Canada, designed to support larger scale and high-potential projects.

For the United Kingdom, coordinators of the Music Export Growth Scheme (MEGS) reflect international thinking in their assertion that MEGS is "not a cultural fund, we're not an arts fund, we are a business fund" (Tamms cited in Malt, 2017). A report for the Arts Council of England, *Supporting UK Musicians Abroad*

(Payne and Jeans, 2010), highlighted questions confronting most export agency/support structures: Whether to continue with international showcase events that may have reached "saturation point", the need to better inform potential grantees and participants about applications and markets and improved coordination between different government bodies (Payne and Jeanes 2010, pp. 1–9). Also, the tendency to measure "outputs rather than outcomes" reflected the need for a "a simple quantitative and qualitative evaluation framework" in evaluating activities (ibid., p. 9).

Domestic infrastructure

We have discussed the broader economic and cultural goals, and particular programmes situated within national schemes and offices. Returning to the Freedman (2008) distinctions between policy as a set of goals and intentions discussed in Chapter 1, the roles of *regulation* (operational instruments and agencies) and *governance* (institutions and instruments shaping industry systems) remain important. All of our interviewees stressed the importance of domestic infrastructure in ensuring export success.

This includes ensuring basic models of cultural funding are maintained; the Scandinavian case studies are often highlighted here as examples of growing domestic support structures in alignment with export strategies. For example, Arts Council Norway's Cultural Fund averaged 6–10% of the Council's total funding from the 1960s to the 1990s; with a significant restructure to incorporate a greater number of music programmes, the Cultural Fund averaged 22% of the Arts Council's funding from 2000 (Hyland and Stavrum, 2018, p. 74). In similar ways, the Canadian industries' efforts to retain state local touring, recording and developmental funds are regarded as a primary reason for ongoing export successes.

Live music structures and regulations are a useful example of linkages between local, national and international activities. Real concern was shared by interviewees across all nations about the cyclical nature of the health of local music venues and national circuits. This has been echoed in national research and policy – in Britain, the UK Music Trust was established in 2014 to protect venues amidst a considerable loss of venues in London. In France, SACEM has warned of threats to festivals, and new noise laws threatening Paris nightclubs (Chrisafis, 2017). In Canada, the *Mastering of a Music City* report (Music Canada/IFPI, 2015) has been successful as a strategy and policy handbook for "music cities" to maintain and strengthen venues. While several nations have adopted or are examining the Australian "Agent of Change" laws that provide some protections for existing venues, these are not uniformly available or practised across all Australian States. The Live Music Office has been effective in achieving some level of uniformity across Australian States in relation to licensing, noise and building laws, especially difficult across eight jurisdictions. Different combinations of urban gentrification, accelerating development of scarce central business district land and rising costs of existing stock are common across cities:

> In Toronto, there have been rising real estate costs and losses of venues. There's no single cause, but include rising real estate prices when [venue managers] don't own their properties, so they're suddenly faced with exorbitant rents, or their properties are put up for sale to a higher bidder … I insist on calling it "sound ordnances", not noise … It's a myriad of problems and issues which we share with cities like San Francisco and Austin, and we share so that we see what's working elsewhere.
>
> (Interview 33, 2017)

Another "glocal" (Robertson, 2018, pp. 25–44) issue of particular concern among net importer case nations is the local/global role of digital aggregators in presenting content to different territories. In contrast to prior analogue media eras, ideas of "the local" are becoming harder to define. In Australian contexts,

> I think being across what's happening in the digital space generally, music and that distribution world, understanding how that's going to work in the future in a global context is really important. At the moment there's a very small, finite number of curators who have got their hands on these playlists. Trying to filter, somehow, the world's repertoire of music, which is a ridiculously complicated thing to do. When you're trying to overlay on that some consideration around local contexts, Australian content, there's a bit of pushback when we're talking to digital services at the moment here, saying, don't you think there should be a benchmark? Let's not use the word "quota", because that might upset people, but let's use a benchmark for locally curated playlists. There's a degree of pushback. There's a feeling "we're the new kids and we don't want to be told what to do and what not to do; we want to be cool and free to do whatever". But I think, coming back to that cultural piece, there's an obligation. You're in this territory; we need to ensure that there's an opportunity for Australians to be heard.
>
> (Interview 22, 2017)

This has led to increasing debates about how companies such as Apple and Spotify can be "encouraged" to have more meaningful relationships with individual territories. Of our case nations, Canada has conducted the most extensive debate, with music and other creative industries calling on federal governments to regulate digital music platforms in similar ways to radio and television companies. The country's Broadcasting and Telecommunications Legislative Review Panel (BTLRP) completed its *Canada's Communications Future: Time to Act* report in January 2020. It noted the decline in the ability of media sectors to pay into Canadian content initiatives (BTLRP, 2020, p. 142) amidst the rise in international media platforms across entertainment and news content. Rather than imposing local content quotas upon digital curators/aggregators, the Panel "favour the imposition of spending obligations on audiovisual media curation companies … as a means of generating investment in Canadian content" (ibid., p. 146). Expressing the desire for "modernizing" regulatory frameworks, the report emphasised and argued for

"Discoverability requirements" for app platforms for Canadian content, with a recommendation for content providers to observe an "obligation to offer Canadian media content choices" (ibid., pp. 146, 143, 148). This would require providing the Canadian Radio-television and Telecommunications Commission with the authority to monitor and enforce "discoverability" requirements (ibid., p. 149). How such "obligations" are to be interpreted and enforced remains unclear. The debate is a reminder of the complexities in envisaging contemporary meanings of "the national" and attempts to enforce virtual borders.

For all the talk of collaboration, older barriers still remain within physical borders. The bureaucratic mechanisms for international touring are still difficult in some territories. In October 2018, United States Citizenship and Immigration Services announced an increase of the premium processing fee from USD$1,225 to USD$1,410 (AUD$1,940.68) for all petitions. In Australian contexts, Sounds Australia has argued for a reciprocal Music Exporters Provisional Visa that allows artists the opportunity to showcase and tour in each other's countries on up to three occasions before they need to apply for a working permit. The problem of obtaining artist visas was acknowledged in the Australian Parliament Inquiry into the Australian Music Industry, which recommended that "the Department of Foreign Affairs and Trade work with the United States of America to develop mutually beneficial visa arrangements that allow artists from both countries to more easily showcase and tour" (Australian Government, 2019, p. iv).

Conclusion

All our case study nations engage in the global showcase/trade fair circuits; despite continual questions about their ability to be useful for aspiring artists, they have retained their appeal as intense forums for networking, with the related potential for access to key gatekeepers. As "one-stop shops" for artists, labels and managers, they remain instantaneous benchmarks in evaluating new markets and strategies. In making sense of the different activities, governmental arrangements and support, we applied Craik's (2007) descriptors assessing the different roles of the state and industries within wider arts/cultural policy. As we have seen, there is considerable fluidity within the model in accounting for contemporary practices.

It is clear that net importer nations such as Finland, Canada and Australia have increasingly invested in export strategies, with an eye to popular music as one cultural form with the potential for global visibility and economic impact. The Swedish model—linked, concentrated efforts funding music education, songwriting, international performance and company expertise and encouraging hubs of industry concentrations/success—is being studied elsewhere. This in effect represents a mature Architect model, with some components of Elite Nurturing within the music industries. While an export scheme or office might be in evidence, it is an ensemble effort.

What is also striking is that net exporter nations such as the United Kingdom have retained a substantial collaborative export programme. This is partly about ensuring that UK acts are prominent, but it is also about better integrating music and associated cultural and trade sectors, with an acknowledgement that traditional mechanisms (showcase and touring support) are no longer enough. In place of a dedicated export office, the United Kingdom's structure remains a good example of a mix of industry, and government (trade) support with programmes for artists, managers and small music businesses.

Whatever the model adopted by our export case nations, it is clear that traditional funding models are changing, or at least being accompanied by new funding aims and directions. The older Patron model—where the state funded classical and art musics, with perhaps selective funding of commercial music activity—has been replaced by different forms of the Architect model that implies different roles for both industries and government. Collaboration is now at the heart of industry–state relationships, with national histories of governance often influencing the extent to which the state should be additionally involved. These "neo-patronage" models (Craik 2007, p. 20) herald new forms of national entrepreneurialism, striving to overcome different music sectors' instincts for division (and in some instances, distrust of government). For example, Music Export Finland, established in 2002 by 12 recording labels, was restructured in 2005 to incorporate other peak bodies and organisations; in 2012, the Finnish Music Information Centre merged with Music Export Finland to become Music Finland. It is also an acknowledgement by governments that properly staffed music export offices can accumulate considerable expert knowledge spanning a wide range of networks, industries and territorial sectors. In keeping with the entrepreneurial instinct, nations are increasingly highlighting innovation in funding criteria, attempting to reward businesses (and business models); as one Canadian report suggested, "the traditional risk/reward analysis is reversed, and the risk of not innovating as an applicant for public funding would be much higher than the risk of innovating" (Music Canada, 2013, p. 31).

Established music nations such as Canada, Sweden and the United Kingdom report favourable return on investment (ROI) trends for government support. The music industries in all of our case nations have largely won internal arguments about the economic promise of exports, in most cases able to argue that financial and other returns are in evidence beyond allocated export scheme funding, with other ancillary benefits across other music sectors. Yet for many of our interviewees working in net importer nations, the spectre of older cultural imperialism debates was certainly evident. For example, in Canadian contexts:

> We share this border with the world's biggest exporter of cultural product and so a certain degree of protectionism is really in our best interests, lest we be swallowed entirely, and that's been part of our national identity from the get-go, as a longstanding part of our social contract.
>
> (Interview 32, 2017)

While we have seen greater harnessing of government and industrial resources, several problems remain for all interested parties. Firstly, as discussed in Chapter 2, properly measuring the impact of export activities remains an inexact science.

Amidst the usual indicators of airplay, sales, concert attendances and royalties, export schemes also claim the importance of business meetings, Internet traffic and showcase performances as outcomes (with parallel increases in marketing/promotional support). The more crucial question of linking increased revenues or visibility to these activities is either loosely estimated or largely ignored. In relation, one interviewee believed that export offices should apply stricter criteria before funding support:

> I think it's really complicated, because if we move slightly away from export, we think about how we don't know where the artist is going to break … Because the digital has fudged the border of what your audience is, but I don't hear any big question mark of the export offices pulling usage data in from the artists and saying, where is your audience online? We want to know your Facebook stats, your Twitter stats, your Spotify, your YouTube, your Sound Cloud, we want all that data so we can check your footprint online. They seem to still do this thing, you've got that domestic success, you can go.
>
> (Interview 12, 2017)

In relation, the same interviewee argued for a shift from "push" (decisions about aspirational markets) to "pull" (data revealing emerging markets) strategies:

> [We need to see] almost genre-based strategies rather than territory-based strategies. And then once you define the genre and see where the success is, then you can easily identify geographical hubs that you can then do trade missions to. Which is completely different from saying to a bunch of indie labels, you're looking around for new solutions, new markets, new business models, we'll give you some cash to go to China because everyone knows China's going to be big. I don't know if that's a strategic use of money to support the artists, but I don't have a simple solution as to, they should be doing this. Because it's so diffuse how you measure the artist.
>
> (Interview 12, 2017)

Our investigation in part reinforces a recent study of European music export strategies that revealed a lack of coordination between domestic and international arms (and regionally) as significant factors in prohibiting growth for some nations (European Commission, 2019). Beyond the comparative advantages of already healthy domestic sectors, we may well see more targeted examples of "elite nurturing" by nations in instances where track records in industry growth and identity construction are most relevant.

Note

1 A 2016 survey of French artists found that 40% of performers receive less than €15,000 per year; for recording artists, the figure was 69% (ADAMI, 2016). French cultural workers share the problems of their international counterparts in that work is

represented by "more flexible jobs, more short-term contracts, more scattered remunerations" (Perrin, 2017, p. 28). Welfare support is available for artists: Through the *Intermittent du spectacle* programme, a capped unemployment benefit is available at average salary rates for musicians to continue full-time work as artists. This continues to be controversial; an agreement was reached in 2016 that "maintains the regime while introducing modifications (increasing financing from employers, for instance)"; and the government established a national fund to support "durable employment in the performing arts" (ibid., p. 29).

References

Ackerman, P. (1971). East meets West at MIDEM and deals made. *Billboard*, 6 February, p. 70.

ADAMI (2016). MIDEM 2016: artists' compensation figures. *Communique de Presse*, 3 June.

Australian Government (2019). *Report on the Inquiry into the Australian Music Industry*. House of Representatives Standing Committee on Communications and the Arts, March.

Bang, S.E. (2018). *MU:CON 2018: Laying the Foundations for the Next Step for Korean Music in the World*. KOCCA website, 18 October.

BPI (2018). Music Export Growth Scheme. British Phonographic Industry (BPI). Retrieved from https://www.bpi.co.uk/news-analysis/music-export-growth-scheme/

BPI (2019). *Music Export Growth Scheme*. https://www.bpi.co.uk/news-analysis/music-export-growth-scheme/

British Council. (2013a). *Influence and Attraction: Culture and the Race for Soft Power in the 21st Century*. London: British Council.

British Council. (2013b). *Culture Means Business*. London: British Council.

Broadcasting & Telecommunications Legislative Review Panel (2020). *Canada's Communications Future: Time to Act*. Ottawa: Innovation, Science and Economic Development Canada.

Caves, R. (2000). *Creative Industries: Contracts Between Art and Commerce*. Cambridge, MA: Harvard University Press.

Chrisafis, A. (2017). France's music scene under threat from new restrictions on noise. *The Guardian*, 24 October. https://www.theguardian.com/world/2017/oct/23/frances-music-scene-under-threat-from- new-restrictions-on-noise

Coalition française pour la diversité culturelle (2008). *Cultural Policies in France*. Paris: Coalition française pour la diversité culturelle.

Craik, J. (2007). *Re-Visioning Arts and Cultural Policy: Current Impasses and Future Directions*. Canberra: ANU E-Press, Australian National University.

European Commission (2019). *Music Moves Europe – A European Music Export Strategy, Final Report*. Brussels: Directorate-General for Education, Youth, Sport and Culture.

FACTOR (2019). *Support for Eligible Music Companies. FACTOR (Foundation Assisting Canadian Talent on Recordings)*. https://www.factor.ca/programs/support- eligible-music-companies/

Freedman, D. (2008). *The Politics of Media Policy*. Cambridge: Polity Press.

French Coalition for Cultural Diversity (2008). *Cultural Policies in France*. http://www.coalitionfrancaise.org/wp-content/uploads/2013/11/Cultural-policies-in-France.pdf

Government of Canada (2018). *Minister Joly Launches the New Creative Export Strategy for Creative Industries, Including a New Export Funding Program*. Canadian Heritage. https://www.newswire.ca/news-releases/minister-joly-launches-the-new-creative-export- strategy-for-creative-industries-including-a-new-export-funding-program-686573291.html.

Government Offices of Sweden (2012). *The Swedish Innovation Strategy*. Stockholm: Ministry for Foreign Affairs.

Government Offices of Sweden (2015). *Sweden's Export Strategy*. Stockholm: Ministry for Foreign Affairs.

Hann, M. (2019). 'We're not being given a viable future': how Brexit will hurt British music. *The Guardian*, 4 April. https://www.theguardian.com/music/2019/apr/03/brexit-effects-on-british-pop-classical-music

Harris, R., Hart, J. & Payne, J. (2016). *Going International: Supporting British Musicians and Music Organisations to Work Internationally*. London: British Council / The Hub.

Homan, S. (2016). A contemporary cultural policy for contemporary music? *Media International Australia* vol. 158, no. 1, pp. 37–47.

Hylland, O.M. & Stavrum, H. (2018). 50 years of aesthetic construction work: the music policy of Arts Council Norway 1965-2015. In O.M. Hylland & E. Bjurstrom (eds.), *Aesthetics and Politics: A Nordic Perspective on How Cultural Policy Negotiates the Agency of Music and Arts*. London: Palgrave Macmillan, pp. 67–94.

IFPI (2018). *Global Music Report 2018*. https://www.ifpi.org/downloads/GMR2018.pdf

Jang, G. & Paik, W.K. (2012). Korean wave as tool for Korea's new cultural diplomacy. *Advances in Applied Sociology* vol. 2, no. 3, pp. 196–202.

Kim, G. (2017). K-pop female idols: culture industry, neoliberal social policy, and governmentality in Korea. In V. Durrer, T. Miller & D. O'Brien (eds.) *The Routledge Handbook of Global Cultural Policy*. Abingdon: Routledge, pp. 520–537.

Kirk, M. (2016, 9 August). K-Pop makes the scene in Seoul. *Citylab*. https://www.citylab.com/solutions/2016/08/k-pop-gets-its-own-mecca-in-seoul/494966/.

KOCCA (2010). *Music Industry White Paper*. Seoul: Korean Creative Content Agency.

KOCCA (2013). *Music Industry White Paper*. Seoul: Korean Creative Content Agency.

KOCCA (2014). *Music Industry White Paper*. Seoul: Korean Creative Content Agency.

KOCCA (2015). *Music Industry White Paper*. Seoul: Korean Creative Content Agency.

KOCCA (2016). *Music Industry White Paper*. Seoul: Korean Creative Content Agency.

KOCCA (2018a). Introduction. Korean creative content agency website. https://www.kocca.kr/en/main.do

KOCCA (2018b). *Create new Wave*. http://eng.kocca.kr/img/foreign/file/DirectoryBook.pdf

Korean Culture and Information Service (2011). *K-Pop: A New Force in Pop Music*. Seoul: Ministry of Culture, Sports and Tourism.

Korean Culture and Information Service (2017). *A Great Journey with the People through Change and Innovation*. Seoul: Government of the Republic of North Korea.

KOTRA (2017). *Cultural Content Brochure*. Seoul: Korea Trade Investment Promotion Agency.

Laing, D. (2003). Cultural policy/regulation. In J. Shepherd, D. Horn, D. Laing, P. Oliver & P. Wicke (eds.) *Continuum Encyclopedia of Popular Music of the World, Vol. 1: Media, Industry and Society*. London: Continuum, pp. 198–200.

Laing, D. (2009). World music and the global music industry: flows, corporations and networks. *Collegium* vol. 6, pp. 14–33.

Le Bureau Export (2015). *Rapport D'activite 2014*. Paris: Le Bureau Export, January.

Le Bureau Export (2017). *French Music All over the World. Press Dossier*. Paris: Le Bureau Export.

Le Bureau Export (2018a). *Export in the French Music Industry: The 2017 Economic Report*. Paris: Le Bureau Export.

Le Bureau Export (2019). *Le Bureau Export Website*. https://www.lebureauexport.fr/

Lee, H-K. (2013). Cultural policy and the Korean Wave: from national culture to transnational consumerism. In Y. Kim (ed.) *The Korean Wave: Korean Media Go Global*. Abingdon: Routledge, pp. 185–198.

Littoz-Monnet, A. (2007). *European Union and Culture: Between Economic Regulation and European Cultural Policy*. Manchester University Press, 1–19.

Loosely, D. (2001). *Cultural Policy in France Since 1959: Arm's Length, or 'Up Close and Personal?'*. Copenhagen: Nordic Cultural Institute. http://fgimello.free.fr/documents/florida/cultural_policy_in_france.pdf

Maistre, R-O. (2017). *Bring Together Music: For a National Centre*. Paris: Mission report to Ministry of Culture, October.

Mäkelä, J. (2008). The state of rock: a history of Finland's cultural policy and music export. *Popular Music* vol. 27, no. 2, pp. 257–269.

Malt, A. (2017). CMU@TGE 2017: facilitating export – UK export initiatives. *CMU (Complete Music Update)*, 26 May. https://completemusicupdate.com/article/cmutge-2017-facilitating-export-uk-export-initiatives/

Marvasti, A. (1994). International trade in cultural goods: a cross-sectional analysis. *Journal of Cultural Economics* vol. 18, no. 2, pp. 135–148.

McLeay, C. (2006). Government regulation in the Australian popular music industry: the rhetoric of cultural protection, the reality of economic production. *GeoJournal* vol. 65, pp. 91–102.

Mendelssohn J. (2015). Arm's length? Forget it – it's back to the Menzies era for arts funding. *The Conversation*, 13 May. http://www.theconversation.com/arms-length-forget-it-its-back-to-the-menzies-era-for-arts-funding-41743

Messerlin, P. & Shin, W. (2013). The K-pop wave: an economic analysis. *SSRN Journal*, July, pp. 1–39.

Ministry of Culture (2018). *Culture: A Budget of Transformation*. Paris: Government of France.

Moon, S-I., Barnett, G.A. & Lim, Y.S. (2010). The structure of international music flows using network analysis. *New Media and Society* vol. 12, no. 3, pp. 379–399.

Music Canada (2013). *The Next Big Bang: A New Direction for Music in Canada*. Toronto: Music Canadian.

Music Sweden (2017). *The Music Industry In Numbers: Statistics for 2016*. https://static1.squarespace.com/static/584ecd35725e2509ff6e669e/t/5a37a0b60d92972a19a6ee0a/1513595108678/TheSwedishMusicINdustryInNumbers2016.pdf

MXD (2016). A Brief Overview of the Swedish Music Market, Music Export Denmark Resources. Available at: https://mxd.dk/vidensbank/a-brief-overview-of-the-swedish-music-market/ (Accessed: 13 December 2018).

Negus, K. (2015). *The South Korean Music Industry: A Literature Review*. CREATe working paper. London: Goldsmiths, University of London.

Nyssen, F. (2018). Françoise Nyssen, Minister of Culture, welcomes the Bureau export of music to celebrate the international influence of French music. *Press Release*, 7 February.

Oh, I. (2013). K-pop in Korea: how the pop music industry is changing a post-developmental society. *Cross-Currents: East Asian History and Culture Review E-Journal* vol. 9, pp. 105–124.

O'Kane, J. (2018). The other Stockholm syndrome. *The Globe and Mail*, 15 January. https://www.theglobeandmail.com/arts/music/how-stockholm-became-a-dominant-force-in-global-popmusic/article37541953/

Payne, J. & Jeanes, A. (2010). *Supporting UK Musicians Abroad: Executive Summary*. London: Arts Council of England.

Perrin, T. (2017). Country profile: France. *Compendium Cultural Policies and Trends in Europe*, 18th edition. Council of Europe. http://www.culturalpolicies.net

Robertson, R. (2018). Glocalization: time-space and homogeneity-heterogeneity. In H. Callan (ed.) *The International Encyclopedia of Anthropology*. London: Wiley-Blackwell, pp. 25–44.

Se-jeong, K. (2016). 'Seoul to establish K-pop complex'. *The Korea Times*, 14 July, http://www.koreatimes.co.kr/www/news/nation/2016/08/117_209426.html

Shin, S.I. and Kim, L. (2013). Organizing K-Pop: emergence and market making of large Korean entertainment houses, 1980–2010. *East Asia* vol. 30, pp. 255–272.

Shuker, R. (2008). 'We are the world': state music policy, globalization and national identity. In R. Shuker (ed.) *Understanding Popular Music Culture,* 3rd Edition. London: Routledge, pp. 205–224.

Soesmanto, T. (2018). K-popnomics: how Indonesia and other nations can learn from Korean pop music industry. *The Conversation*, 7 December. https://theconversation.com/k-popnomics-how-indonesia-and-other-nations-can-learn-from-korean-pop-music-industry-107229

St. Michel, P. (2017). PSY's 'Gangnam Style' changed pop music, whether you like it or not'. *Pitchfork*, 13 July. https://pitchfork.com/thepitch/psys-gangnam-style-changed-pop-music-whether-you-like-it-or-not/

Swedish Institute (2019). 8 reasons why Sweden rocks. *Sweden*, 23 April. https://sweden.se/culture-traditions/8-reasons-why-sweden-rocks/

Tous pour la musique (2015). *Les Enjeux de la Filiere Musicale A L'International – Livre Blanc*. Paris: Tous pour la musique. https://www.tplmusique.org/wp-content/uploads/TPLM-Livre-Blanc-Version-finale-08102015.pdf

UK Music (2013). *Measuring Music*. London: UK Music.

UK Music (2014a). *Measuring Music 2014 Report*. London: UK Music.

UK Music (2014b). *Measuring Music: Methodology*. London: UK Music. https://www.ukmusic.org/assets/general/UK_MUSIC_Methodology.pdf

UK Music (2015). *Measuring Music 2015 Report*. London: UK Music.

UK Music (2016). *Measuring Music 2016 Report*. London: UK Music.

UK Music (2017). *Measuring Music 2017 Report*. London: UK Music.

UK Music (2018a). *Measuring Music: 2018 Report*. London: UK Music.

UK Music (2018b). UK music warns Brexit could put fast-growing live music sector at risk. 26 November. https://www.ukmusic.org/news/uk-music-warns-brexit-could-put-fast-growing-live-music-sector-at-risk

UK Music (2018c). *Securing Our Talent Pipeline*. London: UK Music.

UK Trade and Investment (2014). *UK Creative Industries International Strategy: Driving Global Growth for the UK Creative Industries*. London: UKTI.

Um, H. (2014). *K-pop on the Global Platform: European Audience Reception and Contexts*. Seoul: Korean Foundation for International Cultural Exchange.

Wallis, R. & Malm, K. (1984). *Big Sounds from Small Peoples*. London: Constable.
Zhang, T. (2016). Korean wave boots economic growth. *Waltham Trade Policy Review*, 15 April. https://tradepolicy.wordpress.com/2016/04/15/korean-wave-boots-economic-growth/

7 Born global

Introduction

At the beginning of this book, we posed the following questions in relation to our investigations of contemporary export activity:

- What are the economic and cultural contributions of the music export sector?;
- What are the export strategies and practices of artists, managers and related industry workers?; and
- What are the entrepreneurial modes of national export activity, including national music export offices and schemes?

As stated in Chapter 1, these central questions initially derived from an Australian Research Council project, with particular emphasis upon Australian practices and contexts. The project team brought different disciplinary backgrounds to the work, primarily business studies, musicology, music technology, media and cultural studies approaches. It also comprised industry surveys; attendance by project researchers at key export events; and interviews with artists, industry workers and government departments across seven countries.

As we began the project, it was quickly made clear that national boundaries were in part illusory, where music exports in this century embody an interconnected series of gatekeepers, local and national structures and a range of different music industry stakeholders. While artists (and their output) are the focus, export activity is useful to study for the range of behind-the scenes players, partnerships and ambitions that broaden thinking about entrepreneurial work related to creativity. We also undertook this work at an interesting time. At the start of the project, national music industries were still attempting to claw back revenues lost from both the Global Financial Crisis downturn and earlier illegal downloading eras. At the end of the project, industries were confronting the enormous impacts of COVID-19, underlining that there is never a "normal" or "stable" period in the creative industries. Not unrelated, artists—and their labels and managers—will increasingly look to the state for assistance, and we have charted the rise in export assistance for aspiring musicians, where our national case studies were firmly (and increasingly) "promotional" (Cloonan, 2007).

In our conclusion, we return to the central concepts and changes raised in the previous chapters. While Australia is emphasised throughout, it is important to place music exports within the now considerable number of nations devoting resources. The sector also resonates with contemporary discussions of technological change, and how artists, companies and managers make sense of how much effort to expend, and the most appropriate markets to which to allocate time and resources. To begin, we reassess rhetorics of globalisation raised in the process of completing the project, and by extension, ideas of the "national" in relation to export activities and representations.

"Born global"?

In Chapter 1, we briefly discussed tendencies in government and industry reports to explicitly or implicitly invoke a "born global" approach to the creative industries that have consequences for how states and music industries organise production. Here we return to themes of globalisation across national, organisational and artist contexts. Our examination of music exports continues work that confirms (popular) music as one of the more visible economies of cultural trade. Similarly, older core–periphery models accounting for cultural imperialist dominance ("West vs. the Rest") are increasingly redundant as new centres of production appear (e.g. Tomlinson, 2007; Robertson, 1992) (evident in the success of C-pop, K-pop and J-pop, for example). They are also inevitably complicated by the particular structural conditions of trade, and various "home country" advantages related to domestic markets in specific creative industries. While musical performers and works from other countries are receiving recognition on the world stage, US-based performers and works still dominate world popular music markets and the US still remains the largest consumer market for popular music.

At the same time, "an overly romanticized version of the anti-homogenization thesis tends to be blind to the issue of unequal relations among countries within a certain regional media bloc" (Nam, 2013, p. 215). Our case study nations revealed differing levels of anxiety about their relationships to larger exporters: Canada to the US, or the Scandinavian countries in relation to their larger European counterparts, for example. How to deal with near neighbours who possess longer histories of music trade, reputational advantages within the foundational blocs of popular music genres and much larger "backroom" (domestic) infrastructures is still a concern for some. As discussed in Chapter 6, nations with smaller global footprints have realised economic and promotional gains through different combinations of state/industry effort suited to local conditions, often accompanied by substantial re-thinking about the best uses of resources. Ultimate ambitions to achieve cultural trade parity with larger nations may be beyond them, but for nations such as Finland, the music export has provided a means of struggle, particularly in ensuring the prominence of local content back home, and consequent battles related to remuneration in digital environments. This, perversely, sees nation-states promoting qualified versions of globalisation—senses of being part of an active, global network that enables financial and national identity returns—if it permits them to enter the game.

In some ways, the expansion of music export activities, coupled with an increasingly sophisticated circuit of trade and showcase events, offices and personnel, is one of the outcomes of classic late capitalism: The need for advanced creative economies to dispel fears of over-saturated local markets in favour of new international horizons. The export office/scheme/programme has evolved as one of the last acceptable, practical examples of government support that has seen steady increases (as more widely, cultural funding has been reduced between the pillars of the GFC and COVID-19). The heightened role of the music export is made more acute by the gradual disappearance of some of the key furniture of national protectionism (e.g. local content broadcasting quotas). However, predictions of the demise of "the national" in its ability to collectively harness policies and resources remain premature; efforts assembled in the name of the music export are a reminder of the power nations still possess, even with structures of cultural globalisation.

In their discussion of "nationing"—the various projects involved in the formation, maintenance and discourses of "nation"—Rowe, Turner and Waterton (2018, pp. 7–8) argue that contemporary states confront the paradox of "a partnership between the internationalist embrace of a global economy and a nationalist program of modernization and cultural development". The recent strengthening of export infrastructure in many countries has become part of "broader policy settings within which engagement with the global or the transnational has an explicitly higher priority than is applied to an earlier model of cultural nationalism" (ibid., p. 8). The interdependent networks evident in export settings have provided some spaces for fierce assertions of cultural nationalism and identity branding. And, in many cases, this has been about particular music industries successfully providing local inflections of global sounds; "imitation being followed by innovation across cultures" (Acheson, 2011, p. 223). It has been argued that the success of South Korea's complex integration of entertainment companies and state structures in producing K-pop is due to "wide tours, aggressive marketing, and cross-promotion" and the successful emulation of predominant US styles associated with dance and hip hop genres (Nam, 2013, p. 218). The recent success of Sounds Australia has witnessed not only the gradual increasing allocation of resources, but Australian artists' similar abilities to tap into international genres, ranging from wry indie guitar rock (Courtney Barnett) to nostalgic psychedelia (Tame Impala).

For artists, the complexity of the current environment can be daunting. Aside from the financial investment required for exporting, new skills are required in the digital landscape including technological savviness, literacy across platforms, being able to value-add and being entrepreneurial. As discussed in Chapter 3, the music manager/entrepreneur by necessity develops collaborative skills to access the many opportunities available to artists through team building, networks, fan development and partnerships.

Indeed, the "born global" term can be a double-edged sword. Greater accessibility can lead to an increase in the number of users. Spotify in 2019 reported that nearly 40,000 new tracks are uploaded daily (Music Business Worldwide, 2019). While digital accessibility via analytics to a multitude of demographics is possible, the demands of such require more human and financial resources. It takes a lot of time and energy to keep one's fans engaged. Getting access to curated playlists demands an assertive strategy in order to cut through the many millions of other artists who are also wanting to be heard when "choice is now the most defining feature of the global music industry – Artists have every imaginable route to their fans, from direct uploads to full service contracts" (Wenham cited in WINTEL, 2018, p. 7). However, these routes are not prescriptive or easily traversed.

Despite the often-stated claim that digital technologies will lead to a more level playing field, our research shows that the disparity between Epic (those with global audiences) and Emerging musicians—who are barely able to eke out a living—is still present in the "born global" world. Income distribution is highly skewed towards a small number of internationally recognised artists. Global revenue figures do not always reflect global audience figures. For example, our study showed that the audience for top Australian artists is distributed in a wide range of countries around the world; yet record sales/record sales remain concentrated in a relatively small number of countries (US, UK, major European markets). This suggests that recorded music is being listened to in many markets where it does not earn much money, or it might be that artists cannot recoup any money owing to the lack of strong legal institutions for the collection of royalties.

With streaming and tech platforms now operating as a powerhouse in the distribution of recorded music, we are still yet to see artists realise the full benefits. Copyright models and royalties are still catching up to this new digital "born global" environment. There is no international standard or monetisation framework to support a digitised music distribution model. Micro payments from online services are often not worth the time it costs to collect them. This leaves the majority of artists never seeing any substantial revenue.

> Musicians are struggling to balance their passion for music with the need to be knowledgeable and vigilant about the financial rewards for their talents. Of the $15 billion in global recorded music revenue for sound recordings reported by the IFPI for 2014, only a small portion of the money beyond the initial recording advances ultimately makes its way to artists as ongoing revenue.
>
> (Rethink Music, 2015)

To add to the current complexity facing artists, the "born global" phenomenon implies that the gatekeeper is no longer as powerful, when artists can make their work public through the uploading of files onto a platform. In 2020, Soundcloud alone had 25 million creators and over 200 million uploaded tracks (Leftronic, 2020). With such large numbers, being discovered without any promotion or careful marketing is virtually impossible. Chapter 4 discussed some of the theories of gatekeeping and their relevance to playlists and music industry events. Indeed, accessing highly visible curated playlists is no different to getting programmed on radio in earlier times (Royalty Exchange, 2017).

While the pull of the Internet through digital marketing strategies, tagging, sharing and number of likes is fundamental, artist representation in a "born global" world still requires old-fashioned "push" techniques to attain a deal and the necessity to be entrepreneurial. Gatekeeping is still present but has expanded to include influencers, curators and in some instances, cultural intermediaries such as nation export offices, whose role is to mediate, introduce and promote local content in international settings. It is no coincidence that the emergence of international industry events has been concurrent with the overwhelming complexity of the digitised industry. This ever-growing complexity as well as competitiveness of the music industry has meant that networking is still a crucial vehicle for success. While digital music seems to be replacing records, it does not appear to have replaced live music, still the major income stream for most artists, and where digital technologies seem to be complementary. However, the costs for touring can be exorbitant, which is why government support is crucial. Our research found that artists with support from both government and industry had the highest success rate in establishing deals for export. Successful music exporters across all career levels require support and assistance to realise their export strategies.

The music industry is reliant on innovations in technology. A more connected shift in music and technology industries sees new start-ups and businesses rapidly emerging. Wang (2020), writing in *Rolling Stone*, states that "Everyone flush with cash in the music industry is looking for the next Spotify". Wang reports that the "Tech Stars" music-focused start-up mentorship programme has ten music tech ideas that "it believes will be key to the industry's future" (ibid.):

> The chosen startups include a machine-learning fan analytics platform, an audio/visual content company focused on audience experience, a skills-training startup that teaches DJing without professional equipment, and a company making blockchain-enabled collectibles.

The constant changes with technology mean that music entrepreneurs must be on top of emerging ICT innovations. A growing music technology sector can be observed in many countries including the United Kingdom, France, Sweden and Finland. Innovative production tools, new forms of consumption and emerging interactive technologies offer new tools and opportunities to musicians, songwriters and music entrepreneurs, resulting in new collaborative engagements and immersive experiences. Music Finland estimated that music technology accounted for as much as 54% of Finland's music-related export revenue in 2017 (Music Finland, 2019).

The upheavals and innovations brought about by digitisation, the imperative to engage with an internationally focused industry, income disparities between Epic and Emerging artists and the rise of export offices bring into question whether "born global" success is a *fait accompli* for all artists wishing to export. Where datafication can optimistically be seen as a great equaliser, enabling increased market penetration and exposure, more resources and investment are needed to cut through a highly competitive and fluctuating environment. The datafication of music underpins streaming companies' use of music as content to support their platform. In avoiding the problem of miniscule royalty pay-outs, Spotify's CEO Daniel Ek believes artists need to be continually creating content.

> The artists today that are making it realize that it's about creating a continuous engagement with their fans … It is about putting the work in, about the storytelling around the album, and about keeping a continuous dialogue with your fans.
>
> (Ek cited in Schatz, 2020)

Apart from ignoring the problem of miniscule royalty payments from streaming, Ek's quote reinforces the shift from the creation of content from an aesthetic, social and cultural perspective to that of a sweatshop culture: Cheap labour, low wages, long hours and continual production. This is exacerbated by datafication, with its ability to call for artists to be always "on" in supporting an international presence.

The various policy models discussed in Chapter 6 show a more concerted effort by countries to export. While there are different support mechanisms for artists (grants, workshops, information sessions and awards), clear benchmarks and pathways are needed at various stages of an artist's career trajectory. Some countries seem to do this more successfully than others, such as Korea's promotion/assembly of its K-pop artists (discussed later in this chapter). Australia also has a good advantage with the Australian Broadcasting Corporation's Triple J Unearthed programme and its radio stations which have helped launch many artists' careers (Triple J Unearthed, 2020). Being "export ready" now requires more strategically aimed infrastructures from creation and production to promotion and dissemination. Industry and government support based on an artist's career path can be provided once specific deliverables are met that reflect that career path. The "deliverables" can be based on, for example, information acquired from digital analytics, recognition of achievement, recognition or number of fans, all of which can help identify an artist's career stage and the support needed for future investment.

National models and perspectives

The case study nations considered in Chapters 5 and 6 (Australia, France, the United Kingdom, Canada, Sweden, Finland, Norway, South Korea) have, in the main, continued organisational strategies evident since the 1970s: Pouring mixtures of state and industry funds into an office that delivers a crucial role in facilitation, with the understanding that modes of collaboration between state and industry are effective in emphasising knowledge transfer and the sharing of practices. However, significant differences now exist in comparison to export schemes and programmes from the last century.

As discussed in Chapter 6, older "Architect" national models (assistance in the name of broader social welfare and cultural nationalism, driven by ministries of arts or culture) remain, often, tied to notions of "excellence" and international "standards" (the "Patron" model). Yet these are increasingly providing the foundation for more complex structures comprising "Elite Nurturer" characteristics, with targeted development funds (from both the state and industry) selecting and rewarding "elite" knowledge and track records. Canada has recently invested in wider arts development for international exposure and visibility through a series of Patron/Architect strategies through "Arts Abroad" funding. FACTOR and Canada Music Fund activities (part of wider Creative Export Strategy funding) have also provided increased and direct support for recording companies, artists and managers with demonstrable momentum in international territories. Finland's "Fast Track" funding programme is another example of scaling support to those deemed to possess the most potential.

All our case study nations possess a patchwork of regional, sectoral, industrial and government support that includes direct funding, embassy/consular assistance, workshop facilitation and a range of support roles. The United Kingdom's structure is a good example of the ways in which different industrial (PRS, UK Music), national government (UKTI, British Council, Arts Council England) and regional government (Beyond Borders, Welsh, Scottish and Northern Ireland and development fund initiatives) components can produce a national ensemble working interdependently for common causes. All our case study nations had achieved a maturity of collaboration, in some instances putting aside decades of in-fighting and suspicion regarding the allocation of funding and other resources. While exact inputs and economic outcomes might be at times hard to discern, it is striking that all of the nations examined claim to have achieved the base outcome desired by the state: A return on investment. In turn, all of our case study nations have maintained or (in most cases) increased their share of state funding. Cynics might question some of the metrics used which vary considerably with countries choosing different ways to define the music industry and different ways to measure economic impact. This was certainly not inevitable, yet the shift in presentations to governments from "subsidy" to "investment" arguments has been deliberate and reflects an increasing emphasis on economic output and impact as opposed to cultural output and impact. For example, in the United Kingdom, coordinators of the Music Export Growth Scheme (MEGS) reflect international thinking in their assertion that MEGS is "not a cultural fund, we're not an arts fund, we are a business fund" (Tamms cited in Malt, 2017).

If questions about placements and flows of central funding structures in our case study nations have been largely settled, other roles of the state are not. All those interviewed with export scheme/office roles called on their governments to play larger Facilitator roles in removing regulatory obstacles (especially sorting the complexities of touring visa provisions) and engaging more forcefully in perennial debates (for example, consideration of tax relief and copyright structures). The collaboration witnessed at showcase and trade events—environments amenable to "friendly competition"—exists in wilful ignorance of longstanding issues that invoke national structures and defences. For example, how a song is tracked across regional industries, audiences and what might be loosely termed "accounting mechanisms" remains subject to many national differences and organisational perspectives.

Pathways to international success are also changing. The fabled instance of "instantaneous" success—an artist's song breaking a territory, followed by a hurried assortment of touring, promotional and showcase experiences to leverage the initial interest—can still occur (evident in the number of grants designed to provide "quick turnaround" funding). The increasing assemblage of state/industry actors, responsibilities and activities, however, also attests to the desire for structural reform that enables the assembly line to produce a greater ratio of hits. There is now more likelihood that an artist will interact with some aspects of their national export structure, and be more aware of industry expectations of being "export ready" in ways that now discount the "instant success". Despite claims that creative outputs can be carefully manufactured (in the original sense of the word) and tailored to individual international markets (e.g. Lash and Zhao, 2016), pathways to "success" remain frustratingly opaque at times. Through its "Star Development Process", South Korea's model is one that promises direct benefits from a methodical approach. Yet even this direct alignment of careful planning, promotion and production designed for repeated international success has revealed uneven results in different periods, notwithstanding media appetites for an "export miracle" narrative. What is clear is that successful export nations exhibit strong domestic infrastructures: Solid local components are required not just for the experiential leap from national to international, but in ensuring that there is a continuum of training for artists, labels and managers where more concentrated periods of career development are required. More work is needed on the extent to which emphases on broader *cultural participation* provide direct industrial benefits.

Beyond the range of actors and gatekeepers noted in Chapter 4, in many respects the contemporary export office/scheme performs the role of a cultural intermediary at a broad national level. Increasing resources are allocated to providing knowledge and access to the primary figures and networks (and affiliated promotional, media and industry sectors) to "break through" across performance and media contexts. In this Bourdieusian sense, an export office brokers different fields across a range of industry sectors, exchanging and dispensing expertise across many layers. Most national structures reflect the realisation that the organisation of knowledge and practices at the interface of national and international can short-circuit pathways embarked upon by the lone manager or artist. Indeed, their roles in ensuring a national discourse of "export readiness" ("have you talked to the export office?") have proved to be influential. Such power, however, remains contingent upon the continuation of healthy trends of ROI and industrial growth, and exploitation of the series of interpersonal relationships and knowledge evident within global showcase circuits, both heavily threatened by COVID-19 effects upon the music industries.

Policy implications

What is evident from our research is that the "born global" concept is a great deal more complicated than some have argued, at least in the music industry. The changes in the global economy, culture and technology are complex and raise many conundrums for global music industry participants and policymakers. For example, while increased use of social media and advances in communication technologies have reduced the costs of entry into global music markets, they have paradoxically reduced the returns to the average artist and increased the importance of live music tours which are of most benefit to Epic performers. This is leading to an increased disparity between "superstars" and the rest and raises questions about equity between economic earnings of performers and government policy to develop the industry. What should be government policy for supporting artists? Focus on a small number of "winners" (as in other fields, such as athletics), which might increase incomes and recognition for the country; or provide support more widely, even for people who are unlikely to make it? While the latter would provide support to needy (and all) artists, the results might well be mixed in terms of overall export incomes.

As global Internet technology has made it easier for artists to reach a wider global audience, economic returns are still largely concentrated in traditional developed markets, leading to increasing divergence between cultural and economic objectives. For example, economic objectives might favour targeting major markets and ignoring less profitable ones. If the objective is to promote national culture and build a national brand, then this might favour a strategy to spread music (and state assistance) as widely as possible, even in markets that are not providing financial returns. The increasing dominance of a few global corporations in music streaming, many of whom are associated with global media corporations, also raises questions about the control of media. Like other media industries such as newspapers, television and film (Compaine and Gomery, 2000), the increasing threat of monopolies raises questions about the need for national or international government regulation in the global music industry.

Coda: Exports and COVID-19

This book has been completed as the effects of a global pandemic become obvious to the creative industries, and within the live performance/music sector in particular. A range of governments, industry bodies and companies have provided significant support in attempting to lessen the individual and collective effects related to the reductions in business activity. Spotify and Live Nation are examples of larger companies with global footprints providing initial and matched donations to supporting artists and live performance crews (CMU Daily, 2020a; Malt, 2020a). Similarly, Apple Music created a $50 million advance fund for "indie" labels and distributors, with one-off advances, "recoupable out of future royalties … available to labels and distributors that earn over $10,000 in quarterly revenue from the

Apple streaming service and which have a direct relationship with the company" (CMU Daily, 2020b).

National responses were (mostly) substantial in recognising the impacts of COVID-19 upon the creative industries. In Sweden, the Cultural Council has provided SEK 370 million, and the Artists' Committee has distributed SEK 70 million to artists (including musicians) (Export Music Sweden, 2020). In Australia, the first three months of venue closures and social isolation were estimated to produce a reduction of $100m in revenue, with 65,000 job opportunities lost (I Lost My Gig Australia, 2020a). Beyond ensuring that artists and related workers have access to temporary welfare payments, industry bodies also called for tax relief for venues (APRA AMCOS, 2020) and a funding package of $750m to support businesses, principally those in the live music sector (I Lost My Gig, 2020b). In Germany, a Berlin initiative, United We Stream, raised over €700,000 in March 2020 for artists and nightclub workers (Barber, 2020). The German government also announced a €750 billion stimulus package, including €50 billion for the cultural, creative and media sector and freelancers, small businesses and artists; applicants are eligible for up to €15,000 in direct subsidies over a period of three months (BYP Group, 2020).

In France, the National Music Centre provided an emergency fund for the entertainment industry of €11.5 million to assist small and medium enterprises in particular, with grants capped at €11,500, and incentives to pay artists compensation for cancelled shows (BYP Group, 2020). For Norway, the Arts Council established a NOK300 million scheme for the cultural industries to be managed by the Cultural Council, with measures targeting freelancers, self-employed people and cultural organisations. In addition, NOK30 million from the Norwegian Cultural Fund has been provided to encourage production and dissemination, especially of digital works (ibid.). In Korea, specific support for artists has included an "Emergency Livelihood Stabilization Loan for Artists", a "Creative Reserve Fund Support Project" and a "COVID-19 Special Loan for Artists" (BYP Group, 2020). The Seoul Foundation for Arts and Culture allocated an additional budget of ₩4.5 billion in order to provide emergency support for artists, companies, art educators and planners (ibid.). In the United Kingdom, calls were made for an injection of £1m as an emergency fund to prevent venue closures (Music Venue Trust, 2020a), with this achieved through donations from recording labels, digital platforms, booking agencies and the Mayor of London (Music Venue Trust, 2020b).

While many countries singled out live venues as especially worthy of immediate support, the festivals sector is a good example of the multiple challenges confronting the music industries. The Association of Independent Festivals (AIF) in the United Kingdom has warned that at least 90% of UK festivals will not proceed in 2020, with promoters facing refunds of up to £800 million, and most of that sum not covered by insurance (Malt, 2020b). According to AIF CEO Paul Reed:

> [It] is not a temporary shutdown of business, it is an entire year of income and trade wiped out. If support is not offered throughout the autumn, then the sector will face widespread job losses that will seriously inhibit its ability

> to deliver events in 2021 … There is no safety net for independent festivals, many of which have fallen between the cracks of current government support measures such as loans and grants … For example, 0% of AIF members have been able to successfully access the Coronavirus Business Interruption Loans Scheme … UK festivals are not only an intrinsic, defining part of British culture but also an economic powerhouse that generates hundreds of millions for the economy – we urge government to recognise them as such.
>
> (cited in Malt, 2020b)

In early July 2020, the Johnson UK Government announced a €1.57b package for cultural organisations, including combinations of loans, grants, capital investment and other funding (Brown, 2020). At the time of writing, it was unclear about the extent of assistance to the mix of live performance organisations and venues within a package designed to cover the performing arts, heritage and other related organisations. The pandemic has reinforced the notion of artists as sole traders and SMEs, challenging some of the broader discourses of "the artist" in public and governmental circles. This has provoked wider public discussions of value of the creative industries, and the role of the music sector as distraction/entertainment (e.g. Langley and Coutts, 2020).

Beyond the immediate concerns of national live music sectors in crisis, the effects of COVID-19 may be more lasting in other export activities. Firstly, all export schemes and offices have investigated the means to shift traditional activities (such as song-writing camps, business meetings) online, doing their best to shift promotions online. This includes the shuttering of the global showcase circuit, with online performances a poor substitute for the hustle of the usual physical gatherings. Secondly, the decimation of national budgets wrought by the virus raises questions about the extent and willingness of states to continue traditional export funding (even as the role of domestic ecosystems of recording, live performance, retail and publishing has been brought into sharper focus). Thirdly, the effects of COVID-19 might enforce some of the earlier calls for a reduced exports bureaucracy, with less paperwork and digital programmes increasingly supplementing physical presences.

Indeed, the many after-shocks of COVID-19, as they continue to be felt in 2021 and beyond, could provoke at least a reduction in "born global" discourses. As national governments look to greater control of their borders (for populist economic reasons as much as health concerns), nations will inevitably fall back on domestic infrastructures. Similarly, artists, managers and labels will be confronted with the problems of 20th-century export arrangements, including longer lead-in times, greater border bureaucracies, travel restrictions and an inability to bring immediacy to export arrangements. These will be interesting developments in a music sector that has grown to be an intriguing mixture of industries, states and artistic ambitions.

References

Acheson, K. (2011). Globalization. In R. Towse (ed.) *Handbook of Cultural Economics*. Cheltenham: Edward Elgar, pp. 220–228.

APRA AMCOS (2020). Music and hospitality sectors call for urgent support. *APRA AMCOS Website*. 13 March. https://apraamcos.com.au/news/2020/march/music-and-hospitality-sectors-call-for-urgent-support/

Barber, J. (2020). Germany: Berlin's United we stream has nearly raised 1m for nightclubs and artists during pandemic. *Nighttime.org*, 24 March. https://www.nighttime.org/news-we-get-it-berlins-nightlife-is-legendary/

Brown, M. (2020). Boris Johnson pledges £1.5bn lifeline to keep UK's arts sector afloat. *The Guardian*, 6 July. https://www.theguardian.com/world/2020/jul/05/boris-johnson-uk-lifeline-arts-heritage-sector-afloat

BYP Group (2020). *Government Responses to the Impact of COVID-19 on the Arts and Creative Industries*. https://www.bypgroup.com/blog/2020/3/21/government-arts-responses-to-covid-19?fbclid=IwAR2UyFZax-Om7Ejhlj92cdf115Jf75wYWUOElK0oAMWQDiMdu9cP5CRN7Do

Cloonan, M. (2007). *Popular Music and the State in the UK: Culture, Trade or Industry?* London: Routledge.

CMU (2020a). Live nation launches COVID-19 relief fund for live industry practitioners. *CMU Daily*, 1 April. https://completemusicupdate.com/article/live-nation-launches-covid-19-relief-fund-for-live-industry-practitioners/

CMU (2020b). Apple music sets up fund to advance monies to COVID-19 hit labels. *CMU Daily*, 8 April. https://completemusicupdate.com/article/apple-music-sets-up-fund-to-advance-monies-to-covid-19-hit-labels/

Compaine, B.M. & Gomery, D. (2000). *Who Owns the Media? Competition and Concentration in the Mass Media Industry*. Abingdon: Routledge.

Export Music Sweden (2020). Covid-19, crisis support: the culture council allocates SEK 370 million and the artists' committee distributes SEK 70 million. *Export Music Sweden*. https://exms.org/covid-19-krisstod-kulturradet-fordelar-370-miljoner-kr-och-konstnarsnamnden-fordelar-70-miljoner-kr/

I Lost My Gig (2020a). An industry in crisis: $100 million and counting. *Australian Festivals Association and the Australian Music Industry Network*, 17 March. https://ilostmygig.net.au/latest-news/f/an-industry-in-crisis-100m-counting

I Lost My Gig (2020b). Immediate government action required to save Australia's live performance industry. *Australian Festivals Association and the Australian Music Industry Network*, 20 March. https://ilostmygig.net.au/latest-news/f/music-industry-calls-for-750m-relief-package

Langley, M. & Coutts, L. (2020). *Why Do We Turn to Music in Times of Crisis?* World Economic Forum. 30 March. https://www.weforum.org/agenda/2020/03/coronavirus-music-covid-19-community/

Lash, M. & Zhao, K. (2016). Early predictions of movie success: the who, what, and when of profitability. *Journal of Management Information Systems* vol. 33, no. 3, pp. 874–903.

Leftronic (2020). *15+ SoundCloud Statistics That Will AMAZE You in May 2020. Leftronic Website*. 14 October. https://leftronic.com/soundcloud-statistics/#:~:text=In%20total%2C%20SoundCloud%20has%20more,SoundCloud%20creators%20share%20their%20music

Malt, A. (2017). CMU@TGE 2017: Facilitating export – UK export initiatives. *CMU (Complete Music Update)*. 26 May. Retrieved from https://completemusicupdate.com/article/cmutge- 2017-facilitating-export-uk-export-initiatives/

Malt, A. (2020a). Spotify, PRS and help musicians launch financial support initiatives for music-makers struggling amid COVID-19 outbreak. *CMU Daily*, 28 March. https://

completemusicupdate.com/article/spotify-prs-and-help-musicians-launch-financial-support-initiatives-for-musicians-struggling-amid-covid-19-outbreak/

Malt, A. (2020b). As many as 92% of independent festivals could go out of business this summer without government action, says AIF. *CMU Daily*, 13 May. https://completemusicupdate.com/article/as-many-as-92-of-independent-festivals-could-go-out-of-business-this-summer-without-government-action-says-aif/

Music Business Worldwide. (2019). Nearly 40,000 tracks are now being added to spotify every single day. *Music Business Worldwide*, 29 April. https://www.musicbusinessworldwide.com/nearly-40000-tracks-are-now-being-added-to-spotify-every-single-day/

Music Finland (2019). Growth in music exports reflects the industry's changing revenue models. 6 September. https://musicfinland.com/en/news/growth-in-music-exports-reflects-the-industrys-changing-revenue-models

Music Venue Trust (2020a). Grassroots music venues in crisis – music venue trust call to action. *Music Venue Trust*, 30 March. http://musicvenuetrust.com/2020/03/grassroots-music-venues-in-crisis-music-venue-trust-call-to-action/

Music Venue Trust (2020b). Crisis fund passes £1million mark. Music venue trust. 4 May. http://musicvenuetrust.com/2020/05/crisis-fund-passes-1million-mark/

Nam, S. (2013). The cultural political economy of the Korean Wave in East Asia: implications for cultural globalization theories. *Asian Perspective* vol. 37, no. 2, pp. 209–231.

Rethink Music (2015). Fair music: transparency and payment flows in the music industry. *Rethink Music*, 14 July. http://www.rethink-music.com/research/fair-music-transparency-and-payment-flows-in-the-music-industry

Robertson, R. (1992). *Globalization*. London: SAGE.

Rowe, D., Turner, G. & Waterton, E. (2018). *Making Culture: Commercialisation, Transnationalism, and the State of 'Nationing' in Contemporary Australia*. Abingdon: Routledge.

Royalty Exchange (2017). Playlists are the new radio. *Royalty Exchange Website*, 6 February. https://www.royaltyexchange.com/blog/playlists-are-the-new-radio

Scatz, L. (2020). Spotify CEO to artists: "You Can't Record Music once Every Three to Four Years and Think That's Going to Be Enough". *Consequence of Sound Website*, 2 August. https://consequenceofsound.net/2020/08/spotify-daniel-ek-artist-recording-comments/?utm_expid=.I2OkZS06Riahk3U0vrA5rQ.0&utm_referrer=

Tomlinson, J. (2007). Globalization and cultural analysis. In D. Held & A. McGrew (eds.) *Globalization Theory: Approaches and Controversies*. Cambridge: Polity Press, pp. 148–170.

Triple J Unearthed (2020). ABC website. https://www.triplejunearthed.com/

Wang, A.X. (2020). Meet the tech world's 10 newest bets on the future of music. *Rolling Stone*, 5 February. https://www.rollingstone.com/pro/news/techstars-music-startup-accelerator-2020-946426/

WINTEL (2018). *Worldwide Independent Market Report*. http://winformusic.org/files/WINTEL%202018/WINTEL%202018.pdf

Appendix 1: Interview list

Interview no.	*Job title*	*Year*
1.	Australian Epic artist manager	2018
2.	Australian Emerging artist manager	2018
3.	Australian Emerging artist manager	2018
4.	Australian Breakthrough artist manager	2017
5.	Australian Emerging artist manager	2018
6.	Australian Epic artist manager	2019
7.	Australian Emerging artist agent	2018
8.	Australian Breakthrough artist manager	2018
9.	Australian Established artist manager	2017
10.	Australian Established artist manager	2018
11.	Australian Epic artist manager	2019
12.	United Kingdom artist management body administrator	2017
13.	Australian Established artist manager	2018
14.	Australian Established artist manager	2018
15.	United States SXSW representative	2016
16.	Australian export administrator	2018
17.	Australian export administrator	2009
18.	Australian management advocacy organisation administrator	2018
19.	Brazilian export administrator	2016
20.	Australian export administrator	2018
21.	Australian national funding body administrator	2018
22.	Australian copyright body administrator	2018
23.	United Kingdom export administrator	2016
24.	United Kingdom export administrator	2017
25.	United Kingdom arts administrator	2017
26.	French export administrator	2017
27.	French government cultural administrator	2017
28.	South Korean export administrator	2016
29.	Canadian exports administrator	2017
30.	Swedish copyright body administrator	2017
31.	Swedish export administrator	2017
32.	Canadian national funding body administrator	2017
33.	Canadian music organisation administrator	2017
34.	Australian Emerging artist	2018

Appendix 2: Australian music industry exports survey

You are invited to participate in the research project identified as "The economic and cultural value of Australian music exports" which is being conducted by Professors Richard Vella and Stephen Chen from the University of Newcastle and Associate Professor Shane Homan from Monash University. This project has been funded by The Australian Research Council: LP150100709.

Why is the research being done?

The research investigates the nature and characteristics of Australian music exports within the context of globalisation and digitisation. It will identify and analyse how globalisation and digitisation are affecting the contexts and processes involved in the creation of a music export's cultural value and economic value. The purpose of the research is to map:

The nature and assess the economic and cultural contribution of the Australian music export industry;
The role of the different participants in the Australian music industry value chain.

Who can participate in the research?

You are invited to participate because your name has been provided by the Australia Council for the Arts or Sounds Australia as someone who is involved with the production or distribution of Australian music. You do not need to have export experience. We are also interested in responses from people who have not exported in order to understand why some people do not export. Please note that you are ineligible to participate if you are not involved with any part of the Australian music industry either nationally or internationally.

What would you be asked to do?

If you agree to participate, you will be asked to complete an online survey which asks about:

Services you provide;
Your employment status;

The number of your employees;
Your earnings and expenses from music activities in Australia and overseas;
Any financial support you have received for your musical activities;
Your attendance at international showcase events;
Your education;
Any awards you have received for your musical activities;
Your music and your audience (if you are an artist).

What choice do you have?

Participation in this research is entirely your choice. Only those people who give their informed consent will be included in the project. Whether or not you decide to participate, your decision will not disadvantage you. If you do decide to participate, you may withdraw from the project at any time prior to publication of the research.

How much time will it take?

The survey should take about 20–30 minutes to complete, depending on how many jobs/roles you have. You may also need to spend some time collecting the necessary information prior to completing the survey.

What are the risks and benefits of participating?

The survey findings will help policy makers in setting policies and funding for exporting in the Australian music industry as well as improve understanding of the process of exporting Australian music. As a token of our appreciation, you will receive a 20% discount voucher to use in Levi's stores in Australia.

Your name will also be entered in a prize draw for:

Levi's® Retail Voucher to the value of $1,000 (redeemable at any Levi's® main-line retail store nationally);
2 × domestic return flights Eastern Seaboard (Brisbane, Sydney, Melbourne, Adelaide);
2 nights' accommodation at any TFE Hotel, https://www.tfehotels.com/;
2 badges to BIGSOUND 2017 Conference;
Terms and conditions apply (link to terms and conditions).

You will be asked for your name and email. This information is only used to make sure no answers are counted twice and to contact you in the event you win the prize draw for participating in the survey. Your personal information will never be shared with any third party. The survey responses will be aggregated and you will not be identified in any publications so there are no anticipated risks to you personally associated with participating in this research. However, if you have any concerns, you may withdraw from the project at any time prior to publication of the research.

How will your privacy be protected?

The collected data will be stored securely (on a password-protected computer/in a locked filing cabinet) in the Chief Investigator's office. Data will be retained for a minimum of five years as per University of Newcastle requirements.

How will the information collected be used?

The collected data may be presented in academic publications or conferences. Non-identifiable data may be also be shared with other parties to encourage scientific scrutiny and to contribute to further research and public knowledge, or as required by law. You can access a summary of the results of the research by visiting our website at http://www.newcastle.edu.au/research-and- innovation/centre/education-arts/cecar/about-us.

What do you need to do to participate?

Please read this Information Statement and be sure you understand its contents before you consent to participate. If there is anything you do not understand, or you have questions, please contact the researcher. If you would like to participate, please click the button below to continue to the survey.

Further information

If you would like further information please contact:

> Professor Stephen Chen, Professor of International Business, Newcastle Business School, University of Newcastle, Callaghan NSW 2308, Australia, T: +61(0) 2 49216680, Email: stephen.chen@newcastle.edu.au.
>
> Or
> Tracy Redhead, Senior Research Assistant, School of Creative Arts, Faculty of Education & Arts, Email: Tracy.Redhead@newcastle.edu.au.

Complaints about this research

This project has been approved by the University's Human Research Ethics Committee, Approval No. H-2016-0070.

Should you have concerns about your rights as a participant in this research, or you have a complaint about the manner in which the research is conducted, it may be given to the researcher, or, if an independent person is preferred, to the Human Research Ethics Officer, Research Office, The Chancellery, The University of Newcastle, University Drive, Callaghan NSW 2308, Australia, telephone (02) 49216333, email Human-Ethics@newcastle.edu.au.

Question block 1

Please enter your name below. This information is only used to make sure no answers are counted twice. Your personal information will never be shared with any third party.

Please enter your email address. This information is only used to make sure no answers are counted twice. Your personal information will never be shared with any third party.

Q1 What is your age group?
<16 (1)
16–20 (2)
21–30 (3)
31–40 (4)
41–50 (5)
51–60 (6)
61–70 (7)
>70 (8)
Prefer not to say (9)

Q2 What sex are you?
Male (1)
Female (2)
Transgender (3)
Prefer not to say (4)

Q3 Which state do you live in?
ACT (1)
NSW (2)
VIC (3)
QLD (4)
SA (5)
NT (6)
TAS (7)
WA (8)
Overseas (9)

Q4 What is the highest level of education you have completed?
High school certificate (1)
TAFE diploma (2)
Bachelor degree (3)
Master degree (4)
PhD or equivalent (5)

Q5 How many years of music education have you received from the following? Please enter 0 if none.
TAFE (1)
University (2)
Private (3)
Other (4)

Q6 Have you received any financial support from the following? If yes, please enter amount.

	Before 2000 (1)	*2001–2005 (2)*	*2006–2010 (3)*	*2011–2015 (4)*	*2016 (5)*
Australia Council for the Arts (1)					
Federal Arts Funding (2)					
APRA-AMCOS (3)					
State government (4)					
Local government (5)					
Other grant (6)					
Family and friends (7)					
Personal loan (8)					

Q7 How many international showcase events have you attended? (Enter 0 if none.)

Q8 Did you earn any income in the tax year 2015–2016 in any of the following jobs/roles? Tick all applicable boxes.
Musician (1)
Manager (2)
Record label (3)
Music publisher (4)
Music producer (5)
Music production services (6)
Music promoter/booking agent (7)
Other music-related job/role (8)
Non–music related job/role (9)

Question block 2 musician

Q9 How many years have you been working professionally as a musician, songwriter, DJ or composer?

Q10 What best describes your work as a musician/performer/composer/songwriter/DJ?
Full-time (1)
Part-time (2)
Casual (3)
Contractor (4)
Other (5)

Q11 How much did you earn as a musician/performer/composer/songwriter/DJ in the tax year 2015–2016 before tax?

Q12 What percentage of the above income came from the following (should add to 100%)?

______ Royalties (1)
______ Digital recordings (2)
______ Live performances (3)
______ Sponsorships and brand endorsements (4)
______ Merchandising (5)
______ Synchronisation (6)
______ Physical recordings (7)
______ Session fees (8)
______ Other (9)

Q13 How much did you spend in the tax year 2015–2016 as a musician, performer, composer, songwriter or DJ?

Q14 What percentages of the above expenses were on the following items?

______ Wages and salaries (not including yourself) (1)
______ Travel (2)
______ Promotion and marketing (3)
______ Recording (4)
______ Other (5)

Q15 How many people did you employ in the tax year in 2015–2016?

Full-time (1)
Part-time (2)

Q16 Please list any services that you have provided/received as a musician, performer, composer, songwriter or DJ without financial payment.

Q17 Did you earn any income or incur any expenses as a musician, performer, composer, songwriter or DJ outside of Australia in the tax year 2015–2016?

Yes (1)
No (2)
If no is selected, then skip to Q24.

Q18 How much income did you earn outside of Australia as a musician, performer, composer, songwriter or DJ in the tax year 2015–2016 before tax (in AUD)?

Q19 What percentage of the above income outside of Australia came from the following sources (should add to 100%)?

______ Royalties (1)
______ Digital recordings (2)
______ Live performances (3)
______ Sponsorship and brand endorsements (4)
______ Merchandising (5)
______ Synchronisation (6)
______ Physical recordings (7)
______ Session fees (8)
______ Other (9)

Q20 What are the top three countries from which you earned the above income outside of Australia?
Top-earning foreign country (1)
Second highest earning foreign country (2)
Third highest earning foreign country (3)

Q21 How much did you spend outside of Australia as a musician, performer, composer, songwriter or DJ in the tax year 2015–2016 (in AUD)?

Q22 What percentages of the above expenses were on the following items?
______ Wages and salaries (other than yourself) (1)
______ Travel (2)
______ Promotion and marketing (3)
______ Recording (4)
______ Other (5)

Q23 How many people did you employ outside of Australia in the tax year 2015–2016?
Full-time (1)
Part-time (2)

Q24 Please list any awards you have won for your music (e.g. ARIA) with dates (multiple entries possible).

Q25 How many weeks in the last year have your songs been in the top foreign charts (e.g. Billboard 200)? (Please specify chart and times.) (Multiple entries possible.)

Q26 How many times in the last year has your music been played on the following online streaming services?
YouTube views (1)
Spotify streams (2)
Apple music streams (3)
Pandora spins (4)
Other streaming (5)

Q27 Which best describes your music (select one only)?
Alternative (1)
Blues (2)
Classical (3)
Country (4)
Electronic dance (5)
Folk/roots (6)
Hip hop (7)
Jazz (8)
Metal (9)
Pop (10)
RnB (11)
Rock (12)
Soul (13)
World (14)
Other (15)

Question block 3 music manager

Q28 How many years have you been working as a music manager?

Q29 What best describes the time you work as a music manager?
Full-time (1)
Part-time (2)
Casual (3)
Contractor (4)
Other (5)

Q30 How much did you earn as a music manager in the tax year 2015–2016 before tax?

Q31 How much did you spend in the tax year 2015–2016 in your music management business?

Q32 What percentages of the above expenses were on the following items?
______ Wages and salaries of staff (other than yourself) (1)
______ Travel (2)
______ Other (3)

Q33 How many people did you employ in your music management business in the tax year 2015–2016? Please enter 0 if none.
Full-time (1)
Part-time (2)

Q34 Please list services you have provided/received as a music manager without financial payment.

Q35 Did you earn any income or incur expenses in your music management business outside of Australia in the tax year 2015–2016?
Yes (1)
No (2)
If no is selected, then skip to Q41.

Q36 How much income did you earn outside of Australia in your music management business in the tax year 2015–2016 before tax (in AUD)?

Q37 What are the top three countries from which you earned the above income outside of Australia?
Top-earning foreign country (1)
Second highest earning foreign country (2)
Third highest earning foreign country (3)

Q38 How much did you spend in total outside of Australia in your music management business in the tax year 2015–2016 (in AUD)?

Q39 What percentages of the above expenses outside Australia were on the following items?
______ Wages and salaries of staff (1)
______ Travel (2)
______ Other (3)

Q40 How many people did you employ outside of Australia in the tax year 2015–2016?
Full-time (1)
Part-time (2)

Q41 How many music acts do you manage?

Q42 What type of acts do you manage?
Artists (1)
Songwriters (2)
Producers (3)
Musicians (4)
Other (5)

Q43 Which best describes the music of the artists you manage?
Alternative (1)
Blues (2)
Classical (3)
Country (4)
Electronic dance (5)
Folk/roots (6)
Hip hop (7)
Jazz (8)
Metal (9)
Pop (10)
RnB (11)
Soul (12)
World (13)
Other (14)

Question block 4 record label

Q44 How many years has your record label been operating?

Q45 How much did you earn from your record label in the tax year 2015–2016 before tax?

Q46 What percentages of your record label income came from the following sources?
______ Physical formats (1)
______ Online and mobile downloads (2)
______ Subscriptions (3)
______ Public performance and broadcast (4)
______ Synchronisation (5)
______ Digital exploitation of audio-visual content (6)
______ Merchandising (7)
______ Other (8)

Q47 How much did you spend in total in the tax year 2015–2016 in your record label business?

Q48 What percentages of the above expenses were for the following items?
______ Wages and salaries of staff (other than yourself) (1)
______ Travel (2)
______ Other goods and services (3)

Q49 How many people did you employ in your record label business in the tax year 2015–2016? Please enter 0 if none.
Full-time (1)
Part-time (2)

Q50 Please list services you have provided/received as a record label without financial payment.

Q51 Do you have international co-label partnerships? If yes, please list.

Q52 Did you earn any income or incur any expenses in your record label business outside of Australia in the tax year 2015–2016?
Yes (1)
No (2)
If no is selected, then skip to end of block.

Q53 How much income did you earn outside of Australia in your record label business in the tax year 2015–2016 before tax (in AUD)?

Q54 What are the top three countries from which you earned the above income outside of Australia?
Top-earning foreign country (1)
Second highest earning foreign country (2)
Third highest earning foreign country (3)

Q55 What percentages of the above income outside of Australia came from the following sources?
______ Physical formats (1)
______ Online and mobile downloads (2)
______ Subscriptions (3)
______ Public performance and broadcast (4)
______ Synchronisation (5)
______ Digital exploitation of audio-visual content (6)
______ Merchandising (7)
______ Other (8)

Q56 How much did you spend in total outside of Australia in your record label business in the tax year 2015–2016?

Q57 What percentages of the above expenses outside of Australia were on the following items?
______ Wages and salaries of staff (other than yourself) (1)
______ Travel (2)
______ Other (3)

Q58 How many people did you employ outside of Australia in the tax year 2015–2016?
Full-time (1)
Part-time (2)

Question block 5 music publishing

Q59 How many years has your music publishing business been in operation?

Q60 How much did you earn from music publishing in the tax year 2015–2016 before tax?

Q61 What percentages of your income as a music publisher came from the following?

______ Royalties and rights (1)
______ Mechanical royalties (2)
______ Direct licensing (3)
______ Other (4)

Q62 How much did you spend in the tax year 2015–2016 in your music publishing business?

Q63 What percentages of the above expenses were on the following items?

______ Wages and salaries of staff (other than yourself) (1)
______ Travel (2)
______ Other (3)

Q64 Please list services you have provided/received as a music publisher without financial payment.

Q65 How many people did you employ in your music publishing business in the tax year 2015–2016? Please enter 0 if none.

Full-time (1)
Part-time (2)

Q66 Did you earn any income or incur any expenses in your music publishing business outside of Australia in the tax year 2015–2016?

Yes (1)
No (2)
If no is selected, then skip to end of block.

Q67 How much income did you earn outside of Australia from your music publishing business in the tax year 2015–2016 before tax (in AUD)?

Q68 What are the top three countries from which you earned the above income outside of Australia?

Top-earning foreign country (1)
Second highest earning foreign country (2)
Third highest earning foreign country (3)

Q69 What percentages of the above income came from the following sources outside of Australia?

______ Royalties and rights payments from APRA, music publishers and labels (1)
______ Mechanical royalties (2)
______ Direct licensing (3)
______ Other source (4)

Q70 How much did you spend in total outside of Australia in your music publishing business in the tax year 2015–2016 (in AUD)?

Q71 What percentages of the above expenses outside of Australia were on the following items?

______ Wages and salaries of staff (other than yourself) (1)
______ Travel (2)
______ Other (3)

Q72 How many people did you employ outside of Australia in your music publishing business in the tax year 2015–2016?

Full-time (1)
Part-time (2)

Question block 6 music producer

Q73 How many years have you worked as a music producer?

Q74 How much time do you work as a music producer?

Full-time (1)
Part-time (2)
Casual (3)
Contractor (4)
Other (5)

Q75 How much did you earn from your activities as a music producer in the tax year 2015–2016 before tax?

Q76 What percentages of your income as a music producer came from the following sources?

______ Payments from artists/musicians (1)
______ Payments from record companies (2)
______ Royalties and rights payments (3)
______ Royalties as eligible studio produce (4)
______ Renting out your studio (5)
______ Soundtrack/jingle work (6)
______ Voiceover work (7)

Q77 How much did you spend in the tax year 2015–2016 as a music producer?

Q78 What percentages of your expenses were on the following items?

______ Wages and salaries of staff (other than yourself) (1)
______ Travel (2)
______ Other (3)

Question block 7 music production

Q79 How many people did you employ in your music production business in 2015–2016? Please enter 0 if none.

Full-time (1)
Part-time (2)

Q80 Please list services you have provided/received as a music producer without financial payment.

Q81 Did you earn any income or incur any expenses as a music producer outside of Australia in the tax year 2015–2016?
Yes (1)
No (2)
If no is selected, then skip to end of block.

Q82 How much income did you earn outside of Australia in your music production business in the tax year 2015–2016 before tax (in AUD)?

Q83 What are the top three countries from which you earned the above income outside of Australia?
Top-earning foreign country (1)
Second highest earning foreign country (2)
Third highest earning foreign country (3)

Q84 What percentages of the above income outside of Australia came from the following sources?
______ Payments from artists/musicians for services as a music producer (1)
______ Payments from record companies for services as a music producer (2)
______ Royalties and rights payments (3)
______ Royalties as eligible studio producer/performer (4)
______ Renting out your studio (5)
______ Soundtrack/jingle work (6)
______ Voiceover work (7)
______ Other (8)

Q85 How much did you spend in total outside of Australia in your music production business in the tax year 2015–2016 (in AUD)?

Q86 What percentages of the above expenses were for the following items?
______ Wages and salaries of staff (other than yourself) (1)
______ Travel (2)
______ Other (3)

Q87 How many people did you employ outside of Australia in your music production business in the tax year 2015–2016?
Full-time (1)
Part-time (2)

Q88 How many years has your music production services business been operating?

Q89 How much time do you work in music production services?
Full-time (1)
Part-time (2)
Casual (3)
Contractor (4)
Other (5)

Q90 How much did you earn from your activities in music production services in the tax year 2015–2016 before tax?

Q91 What percentages of the above income came from the following sources?

______ Payments from artists/musicians for music production services (1)
______ Payments from record companies (2)
______ Payments from venues and/or festivals (3)
______ Renting out your studio (4)
______ Renting out equipment (5)
______ Repair and equipment maintenance (6)
______ Other (7)

Q92 How much did you spend in total in the tax year 2015–2016 in your music production services business?

Q93 What percentages of the above expenses were on the following items?

______ Wages and salaries of staff (other than yourself) (1)
______ Travel (2)
______ Other (3)

Q94 How many people did you employ in your music production business in 2015–2016? Please enter 0 if none.

Full-time (1)
Part-time (2)

Q95 Please list services you have provided/received in your music production services business without financial payment.

Q96 Did you earn any income or incur any expenses outside of Australia in your music production services business in the tax year 2015–2016?

Yes (1)
No (2)
If no is selected, then skip to end of block.

Q97 How much income outside of Australia did you earn in your music production services business in the tax year 2015–2016 before tax (in AUD)?

Q98 What are the top three countries from which you earned the above income outside of Australia?

Top-earning foreign country (1)
Second highest earning foreign country (2)
Third highest earning foreign country (3)

Q99 What percentages of the above income outside of Australia came from the following sources?

______ Payments from artists/musicians (1)
______ Payments from record companies (2)
______ Payments from venues and/or festivals (3)
______ Renting out your studio (4)
______ Repair and equipment maintenance (5)
______ Other (6)

Q100 How much did you spend in total outside of Australia in your music production services business in the tax year 2015–2016?

Q101 What percentages of the above expenses outside of Australia were on the following items?

______ Wages and salaries (1)
______ Travel (2)
______ Other (3)

Q102 How many people did you employ outside of Australia in your music production services business in the tax year 2015–2016?

Full-time (1)
Part-time (2)

Question block 8 music promoter/booking agent

Q103 How many years have you been working as a music promoter/booking agent?

Q104 How much time do you work as a music promoter/booking agent?

Full-time (1)
Part-time (2)
Casual (3)
Contractor (4)
Other (5)

Q105 How much did you earn from your activities as a music promoter/booking agent in the tax year 2015–2016 before tax?

Q106 What percentages of the above income came from the following sources?

______ Ticket sales (1)
______ Sponsorship (2)
______ Other (3)

Q107 How much did you spend on your activities as a music promoter/booking agent in the tax year 2015–2016 before tax?

Q108 What percentages of the above expenses were on the following items?

______ Wages and salaries of staff (other than yourself) (1)
______ Travel (2)
______ Other (3)

Q109 Please list services you have provided/received as a music promoter without financial payment.

Q110 How many people did you employ in your music promotion/booking agency business in 2015–2016? Please enter 0 if none.

Full-time (1)
Part-time (2)

Q111 Did you earn any income or incur any expenses as a music promoter/booking agent outside of Australia in the tax year 2015–2016?

Yes (1)
No (2)
If no is selected, then skip to end of block

Q112 How much income did you earn outside of Australia from your music promotion/booking agency business in the tax year 2015–2016 before tax (in AUD)?

Q113 What are the top three countries from which you earned the above income outside of Australia?
Top-earning foreign country (1)
Second highest earning foreign country (2)
Third highest earning foreign country (3)

Q114 What percentages of the above income came from the following sources outside of Australia?
______ Ticket sales (1)
______ Sponsorship fees (2)
______ Other (3)

Q115 How much did you spend in total outside of Australia in your music promotion/booking agency business in the tax year 2015–2016 before tax (in AUD)?

Q116 What percentages of the above expenses outside of Australia were on the following items?
______ Wages and salaries of staff (other than yourself) (1)
______ Travel (2)
______ Other (3)

Q117 How many people did you employ outside of Australia in your music promotion/booking agency business in the tax year 2015–2016?
Full-time (1)
Part-time (2)

Question block 9 other music-related job

Q118 What is your other music-related job or role?

Q119 How many years have you been working in this job or role?

Q120 How much did you earn from your activities in this job/role in the tax year 2015–2016 before tax?

Q121 How much did you spend in this job/role in the tax year 2015–2016?

Q122 How many people did you employ in this job/role in 2015–2016? Please enter 0 if none.
Full-time (1)
Part-time (2)

Q123 Please list services you have provided/received in this role without financial payment.

Q124 Did you earn any income or incur any expenses outside of Australia from this job/role in the tax year 2015–2016?
Yes (1)
No (2)
If no is selected, then skip to end of block.

Q125 How much income outside of Australia did you earn from this other job/role in the tax year 2015–2016 before tax (in AUD)?

Q126 What are the top three countries from which you earned this income outside of Australia?
Top-earning foreign country (1)
Second highest earning foreign country (2)
Third highest earning foreign country (3)

Q127 How much did you spend in this job/role outside of Australia in the tax year 2015–2016 (in AUD)?

Q128 How many people did you employ outside of Australia in this job/role in the tax year 2015–2016?
Full-time (1)
Part-time (2)

Question block 10 Non–music related employment

Q129 How much did you earn from non–music related employment in the tax year 2015–2016 before tax?

End of survey

Q130 That's the end of the survey! Are you interested in entering the prize draw?
Yes (1)
No (2)

Appendix 3: Music export snapshots

Derived from the Export Strategies survey conducted in 2018 (see the Methodology section in Chapter 1), we collated data which provided some insight into individual activities and revenues, based upon one artist and one artist manager snapshot. They support themes discussed elsewhere in the book, particularly the Australian contexts related to strategies, funding, advantages and challenges, and the role of Sounds Australia.

Artist snapshot

The participant self-nominated as an artist, who also had established an "indie" label and publishing companies, representing one artist at an established international level, and eight domestic artists in the genres of pop and "indie". The artist had attended four international music market events, with five to ten years of export experience, and considered themselves "very knowledgeable" in relation to exports and had established international contacts.

The artist reported their activities as 70% domestic and 30% international in terms of time/effort. Figure A.1 lists the artist's investments and revenue related to exports; revenue totalled $5.24 million for the nine-year period. Revenue of $1,000,000 was reported from securing a major recording/licensing deal within a 12-month period after an investment of $3,000.

As with the majority of experienced exporters, the artist employed publicists, streaming and tastemakers as tools to export. However, they did not use playlists and digital analytics. Having a local partner in place before showcasing at an international market event was "important". The artist's advance planning was shorter than average; we can speculate that the artist received opportunities that required a quick turnaround (that could in turn explain a listing of shorter than average time on a return on investments). For example, when engaging in a major and independent recording/licencing deal, the artist saw a return within 6–12 months.

The artist reported an immediate return from touring or support slot activities, publishing and synchronisation opportunities, brand partnership/sponsorship, product endorsement and international TV and radio appearances.

The artist employed four staff and had received substantial investment from the music industry, including a $400,000 investment from a record label and

Export activity	Investment	Revenue
International physical or digital sale and distribution of recorded music	$3,000	$1,000,000
International streaming (free or paid)	$3,000	$1,000,000
Engaged in a major recording /licensing deal	$3,000	$1,000,000
Engaged in an independent recording/licensing deal	$3,000	$100,000
International festival	$10,000	$500,000
International tour or support slot	$10,000	$20,000
International showcase events	$5,000	NA
International music market event	$5,000	NA
Engaged in a publishing or sub-publishing deal	$3,000	$1,000,000
International management/co-management	$3,000	NA
International TV/film synchronisation placement	$0	$400,000
International video gaming synchronisation placement	$0	$20,000
Engaged international publicist	$0	NA
International TV and radio promotion / appearances	$10,000	NA
Engaged an international record producer	$10,000	NA
International press / media coverage	$3,000	NA
Brand partnership/ sponsorship / product endorsement	$0	$200,000
Re-negotiated existing partnerships	$0	$0
Conducted business meetings	$3,000	NA
Total	$74,000	$5,240,000

Figure A.1 Artist snapshot: Investment and revenue.

publisher, and $10,000 from a financial institution. The artist's family invested $50,000 and were acknowledged as being "very important". The artist received a further $35,000 in government funding (a $30,000 Australia Council grant and $5,000 from State or Territory government funding). Survey participants were also questioned about obstacles to export activities. For this artist, restrictive visa regulations were a significant barrier, as well as travel costs, financing, access to funding and the types of funding available.

The artist acknowledged Sounds Australia's role as "very important" in their past export strategies, introducing them to networks which enabled attendance at showcase opportunities (resulting in engaging an international record producer

Under 3 months	3-6 months before	6 months to 1 year
International TV/film synchronisation placement	International streaming (free or paid)	International physical or digital sale and distribution of recorded music
International video gaming synchronisation placement	International tour or support Slot	Engaged in a major recording /licensing deal
International press / media coverage	International showcase events	Engaged in an independent recording/licensing Deal
Brand partnership/ sponsorship / product endorsement	Engaged international publicist	International festival
	International TV and radio promotion / appearances	Engaged in a publishing or sub-publishing deal
	Engaged an international record producer	International music market event
	Re-negotiated existing partnerships	International management/co-management
	Conducted business meetings	

Figure A.2 Artist snapshot: Export activities and advance planning.

and publicist, and perhaps influencing the later success of the major recording deal/licencing opportunity listed earlier).

Established artist manager snapshot

This survey participant provided data over the past nine years, identifying their role as an artist manager who also ran an independent label and was an independent publisher. The manager reported utilising two employees and represents seven artists/bands across hip hop, pop, alternative and "indie" genres. Characterised by the methods discussed in Chapter 3, the manager was responsible for two Emerging artists, four Breakthrough artists, four Established artists and one Epic artist.

It is unclear if all seven artists/bands are managed, published and released through the business. However, the manager had established international networks and self-identified as "extremely knowledgeable" about exports, working in the domestic and international markets for 15–20 years and attended over 15 international market events.

Immediate Return	within 3 months	within 3-6 months	within 12 months
International tour or support slot	International streaming (free or paid)	Engaged in a publishing or sub-publishing deal	Engaged in a major recording /licensing deal
International TV/Film Synchronisation Placement	International festival	Engaged an international record producer	Engaged in an independent recording/licensing deal
International video gaming synchronisation placement	International showcase events		International management/co-management
International TV and radio promotion / appearances	International music market event		
Brand partnership/ sponsorship / product endorsement	Engaged international publicist		
Re-negotiated existing partnerships	International press / media coverage		
Conducted business meetings			

Figure A.3 Artist snapshot: Time and return on activities.

Given their artists' higher domestic profile, activities were listed as 50% domestic and 50% international. Domestic success was considered "important" but not very important in developing a successful export strategy. Averages and estimates were provided that revealed revenue of over $AU10m over the past nine years with an approximate investment of $AU6,330,000. Over the past nine years, the manager had undertaken all the export activities listed in the survey (as shown in Figure A.2) except for international management/co-management. This could be an indication that they represent their artists internationally. An estimate of their activities, financial investment and revenue is provided in Figure A.4.

A $20,000 grant was received by the Australia Council for the Arts and $40,000 from other government funding. The manager had borrowed or received financial support from family ($10,000) and a publisher ($20,000) to assist with export costs. Family/peer support was listed as "important" in realising export strategies.

As with other survey participants, the manager used similar tools to other "knowledgeable" exporters, including playlists, tastemakers and digital analytics (see Figure A.3). These were "very important" in affirming the need for "having a local partner in place before showcasing at an international market event".

Export activity	Investment	Revenue
International physical or digital sale and distribution of recorded music	$400,000	$3,000,000
International streaming (free or paid)	$100,000	$300,000
Engaged in a major recording /licensing deal	$200,000	$1,500,000
Engaged in an independent recording/licensing deal	$150,000	$2,000,000
International festival	$200,000	$200,000
International tour or support slot	$2,000,000	$500,000
International showcase events	$200,000	NA
International music market event	$200,000	NA
Engaged in a publishing or sub-publishing deal	$60,000	$2,000,000
International TV/film synchronisation placement	$50,000	$150,000
International video gaming synchronisation placement	$50,000	$50,000
Engaged international publicist	$300,000	NA
International TV and radio promotion / appearances	$150,000	NA
Engaged an international record producer	$1,500,000	NA
International press / media coverage	$250,000	NA
Brand partnership/ sponsorship / product endorsement	$40,000	$200,000
Re-negotiated existing partnerships	$80,000	$500,000
Conducted business meetings	$400,000	NA
Total	$6,330,000	$10,400,000

Figure A.4 Artist manager snapshot: Investment and revenue.

Figure A.5 shows the longest planning time was for international music market events. This exemplifies the importance of building networks in planning for export activities, and the importance of attending international market events. Research and partnerships take time to develop. Showcase events are also planned up to two years in advance.

The manager listed major and independent recording/licensing deals as taking the longest to see an expected return.

In terms of barriers, the manager listed quicker response times for grant applications, immigration issues, more ground support in foreign countries and the relocation of band/artist to a new market as "very important". They did not

3 years	1 - 2 years	6 months to 1 year	3-6 months before	Under 3 months
International music market event	International physical or digital sale and distribution of recorded music	International festival	International TV/film synchronisation placement	Brand partnership/ sponsorship / product endorsement
	International streaming (free or paid)	International tour or support slot	International video gaming synchronisation placement	Conducted business meetings
	Engaged in a major recording/licensing deal	Engaged international publicist	Engaged an international record producer	
	Engaged in an independent recording/licensing deal	International TV and radio promotion / appearances	Re-negotiated existing partnerships	
	International showcase events	International press / media coverage		
	Engaged in a publishing or sub-publishing deal			

Figure A.5 Artist manager snapshot: Export activities and advance planning.

nominate competition of international acts, access to education and information, resources or completing an Export Market and Development Grant (EMDG) application as barriers to their export activities. The EMDG scheme is a government initiative providing financial assistance to small and medium export-ready businesses. Exporters are reimbursed up to 50% of eligible promotion expenses to a maximum of $150,000 (Austrade, 2019). However, significant barriers were financing, travel time and costs in following up opportunities.

The manager listed Sounds Australia as "very important" in their export strategies and believed that for Australian musicians to successfully realise profitable export careers, more financial support for Sounds Australia was "very important". Introductions by a team member of Sounds Australia were listed as being the main reason certain opportunities arose and could be linked to subsequent successful export activities. These included international showcase events, international festivals and publishing or a sub-publishing deal. These introductions resulted in very successful outcomes, including $2 million profit via sub/publishing, and

Immediate Return	1 - 2 years	2 -5 years	5 - 10 years
International festival	International TV and radio promotion / appearances	International physical or digital sale and distribution of recorded music	Engaged in a major recording licensing deal
International music market event	Engaged an international record producer	International streaming (free or paid)	Engaged in an independent recording/licensing deal
International TV/Film synchronisation placement	International press / media coverage	International tour or support slot	
International video gaming synchronisation placement	Re-negotiated existing partnerships	International showcase events	
Brand partnership/ sponsorship / product endorsement	Conducted business meetings	Engaged in a publishing or sub-publishing deal	
		Engaged international publicist	

Figure A.6 Artist manager snapshot: Export activities time to see expected return.

$200,000 profit from an international festival. One international showcase event was listed as being very successful, even though it resulted in a financial loss that was planned as a future investment into opportunities and/or profile building.

Reference

Austrade (2019). *Export Market Development Grants (EMDG)*. Retrieved from: https://www.austrade.gov.au/Australian/Export/Export-Grants

Glossary

A2IM	The American Association of Independent Music
AAM	Association of Artist Managers
ABC	Australian Broadcasting Corporation
AIM	Association of Independent Music
AIR	Australian Independent Record Labels Association
AMCOS	Australasian Mechanical Copyright Owners Society
AMIN	Australian Music Industry Network
AMPAL	The Australasian Music Publishers Association
APRA	Australasian Performing Right Association
ARC	Australian Research Council
ARIA	Australian Record Industry Association
B2B	Business to business
B2C	Business to consumer
BBC	British Broadcasting Corporation
BPI	British Phonographic Industry
CMJ	College Media Journal Music Marathon (New York, United States trade fair)—no longer operating
CMW	Canadian Music Week
DFAT	Department of Foreign Affairs and Trade
EMDG	Export Market and Development Grant
EMI	Electric and Music Industries
FACTOR	Foundation Assisting Canadian Talent on Recordings
FIPP	Fédération Internationale de la Presse Périodique
ICT	Information and communications technology
IFPI	International Federation of the Phonographic Industry
Midem	Marché International du Disque et de l'Edition Musicale (Cannes, France music trade fair)
NEIS	New Enterprise Incentive Scheme
NOMEX	Nordic Music Export Programme
PPCA	Phonographic Performance Company of Australia Limited
PRS	Performing Right Society

SACEM	Society of Authors, Composers and Publishers of Music
SXSW	South by Southwest (Austin, United States music trade fair)
TME	Tencent Music Entertainment
UKTI	United Kingdom Trade and Investment
UoN	University of Newcastle, Australia

Index

**Page numbers in *italics* reference figures.

For Product Safety Concerns and Information please contact our EU representative GPSR@taylorandfrancis.com
Taylor & Francis Verlag GmbH, Kaufingerstraße 24, 80331 München, Germany

www.ingramcontent.com/pod-product-compliance
Lightning Source LLC
LaVergne TN
LVHW021126300926
849160LV00010B/884
* 9 7 8 0 3 6 7 7 4 4 6 3 2 *